ELECTRONIC RESOURCE MANAGEMENT IN LIBRARIES
Trends, Issues and Challenges

ELECTRONIC RESOURCE MANAGEMENT IN LIBRARIES
Trends, Issues and Challenges

Editors
Bhojaraju Gunjal
Dibya Kishor Pradhan
Dhanwantari Prakash Tripathi
Vinod Kumar Mishra
Puspita Mishra
Kshirod Das

Ess Ess Publications
New Delhi

ELECTRONIC RESOURCE MANAGEMENT IN LIBRARIES
Trends, Issues and Challenges

ISBN: 978-81-7000-807-1

First Published 2016

Published by:
Ess Ess Publications
4831/24, Ansari Road,
Darya Ganj,
New Delhi-110 002.
INDIA
Phones: 23260807, 41563444
Fax: 41563334
E-mail: info@essessreference.com
www.essessreference.com

Cover Design by *Patch Creative Unit*

Printed and bound in India at Salasar Imaging Systems.

Contents

ABSTRACTS

Preface

Electronic Resources are important components of the collection building process of the library. E-resources refer to those materials accessed through computer or mobile device either remotely or locally. Some of the frequently used e-resources in the libraries are e-journals, e-books, e-database such as full text, citation and abstracting, reference, images, audio-video materials, etc. The other examples of e-resources include but not limited to website, online database, e-journals, e-books, whether free or fee-based resources. Libraries are always committed to preserve its e-resources to ensure permanent access to its collections along with other formats for its users to support research and academic activities of an institute.

In this age of rapidly changing technologies, it is essential for all library professionals to keep abreast of the latest developments, emerging trends & techniques in the area of Electronic Resource Management (ERM) in libraries. Certain issues and challenges faced in these areas need to be taken care of with proper solutions.

This book intend to present 26 Full papers and 22 Abstracts pertaining to the themes such as Electronic Resource Management in Libraries (ERM), its associated Issues & Challenges, Emerging Trends & Techniques in ERM. Search and Discovery techniques and Scholarly communications. It aims to help all library and information professionals about the emerging trends and technologies in Electronic Resource Management (ERM) arena. It helps in understanding the various issues and challenges faced by the library professionals and attempt to provide the probable solutions to adopt in their workplaces.

The theme of the book covers various perspectives of ERM. The authors have contributed the papers based on their experiences. I hope this book will be one of the key resources in ERM field for library practitioners, researchers and academicians.

— Editors

Acknowledgements

We would like to express our deep gratitude to all the contributors for their time and efforts for the preparation of the papers. We gratefully acknowledge the help and support of our colleagues and staff in completing this work. We are indebted to Prof. Sunil Kumar Sarangi (FNAE), Director. National Institute of Technology. Rourkela for his support and encouragement. We would like to thank all our family members for the support, encouragement and inspiration they showed. Finally, we thank Ess Ess Publications, New Delhi for kind support during the preparation of this book.

Bhojaraju Gunjal
Dibya Kishor Pradhan
Dhanwantari Prakash Tripathi
Vinod Kumar Mishra
Puspita Mishra
Kshirod Das

Acknowledgements

Electronic Resource Acquisition and Implementation

1

Collection Development of E-Resources : A Case Study of National Library of India

Partha Sarathi Das
Assistant Library & Information Officer
National Library of India, Kolkata -700027
Smitanjali Panda
Library & Information Assistant
National Library of India, Kolkata-700027

ABSTRACT

This paper explains the background concept of collection development and electronic resources, advantages and limitations of e-resources. A brief history of National Library is narrated along with its objectives. The paper describes briefly the need and background of the collection development of electronic resources in National Library. All the electronic resources which could be accessed at the Library are presented in a tabular form. It is also discussed the workflow followed during the acquisition of e-resources and suggested a checklist for the librarians. It also discusses the common problems generally faced and future plans.

Keywords : Collection Development, E-resources, National Library

1. INTRODUCTION

"Electronic resources" refer to those materials that require computer access, whether through a personal computer, mainframe, or handheld mobile device. They may either be accessed remotely via the Internet or locally. Some of the most frequently encountered types are:

- E-journals
- E-books
- Full-text (aggregated) databases
- Indexing and abstracting databases
- Reference databases (biographies, dictionaries, directories, encyclopaedias, etc.)
- Numeric and statistical databases
- E-images
- E-audio/visual resources

2. CHARACTERISTICS OF E-RESOURCES

(i) Accessibility : E-resources are accessible across geographical boundaries, 24 x 7 and simultaneously to a number of users

(ii) Space management : Electronic resources has no physical existence, therefore virtually no space is occupied except for the equipment & storage media.

(iii) Multiplicity : Electronic resources can be multiplied without any limit.

(iv) Seamless integration : Integration of multiple resources can be done through hyper linking of texts and multimedia to a number of offline and online data sources leading to a seamless integration. Such integration is impossible in print media.

(v) Economical : Comparatively economical, can conserve the energy of the users in finding information. It is estimated that when total processing and space costs are taken into account, electronic collections may result in some overall reduction in library costs (Montgomery and King, 2002)

(vi) Time lag : Publication in digital format reduces the time lag of publication and delivery in print media

(vii) Portability : Information content can be stored and carried in any portable storage medium.

(viii) Search ability : Improved search logic, federated search techniques increase the browse ability of electronic resources far beyond any print resources. Precision value is much higher in digital resources than print media.

(ix) Convenience : Most important factor for popularity of e-resources is convenience which users prefer at the cost of authority of information which is not certain and authentic as compared to printed peer reviewed papers and published books by eminent authors and publishers.

There are some limitations of e-resources also which are as follows:

(i) Technology dependent : E-resources are technology-driven and are becoming complex day by day. The longevity of digital data depends on periodic hardware refreshment and software emulation.

(ii) Information handling skill : The handling of e-resources need IT literacy and special skill to locate, search, evaluate and use information.

(iii) Impact of information-seeking behaviour : Users are becoming habituated in getting information only through e-resources which are easily available and accessible to them. Thus, they are deprived of consulting such resources which are not accessible to them but are more important. In this context, Pankake (1991) has rightly commented that "we see that the types of materials scholars use correspond poorly with the types of material most readily accessible by computer". This has impacted the information-seeking behaviour of users. Users have become more impatient and cannot wait for long to find information.

3. BACKGROUND OF NATIONAL LIBRARY OF INDIA

The genesis of the National Library of India can be traced back to the establishment of the Calcutta Public Library in 1835. The Imperial library was established in the year 1891 by amalgamating a number of secretariat and record room libraries. The Calcutta Public Library and the Imperial Library were merged together and declared open for public on 30th of January 1903. The Imperial Library was renamed, through an enactment of Parliament as The National Library in the year 1948 and was shifted to its present location at Belvedere Estate. The National Library inherited a rich and valuable collection in the shape of the collections of the Home Department, East India College, Fort William and the Library of the East India Board in London. Copies of each publication published in Bengal province was deposited in Calcutta Public Library under Press Registration of Books Act, 1867 (Kesavan, 1961).

4. NEED FOR HYBRID LIBRARY ENVIRONMENT IN THE NATIONAL LIBRARY

The National Library being a Depository Library also acts as a permanent repository of India's publication output, as such India's largest public library offer both reading and lending services to larger sections of the society. As there is a service element besides its normal activities, the National Library is also bound to change into hybrid nature in order to make its collection development more comprehensive and dynamic. This may be enumerated as follows:-

(i) Advancements in digital technology and increasing application of this technology in libraries have brought in a revolutionary paradigm shift in all types of libraries; National Library is not an exception. The shift has been shown in the following table (Sabarathnam, 1995)

From	*To*
Custodian of Books	Service-oriented information providers
One medium	Multiple media
Own collection	Library without walls
In good time	Just in time
In-sourcing	Outsourcing
Local reach	Global reach
User goes to library	Library goes to user

(ii) With the advent of newer media of documents, the term "collection development" is being replaced as "Information Resource Base Development" (IRBD) since the collection serve as information resource base (Chatterjee, 2002/03) and what is needed is development of "a potent and balanced collection to meet the changing needs and demands of the target audience for the present and the future" (Choudhury,1993). The acquisition policy of the National Library seeks to integrate traditional print resources with electronic resources to provide seamless access to information resources which support blended learning. E-migration is an important step towards growing an e-resource collection. In fact, National Library is the first public library in India to start procuring e-resources.

(iii) As a public library, the National Library supports a heterogeneous user groups that ranges from students, scholars, researchers, teachers, professionals who uses these e-resources as their supplementary resource base in addition to their print resources.

(iv) These e-resources encourages self-learning especially to those students who are continuing their studies through Open Universities, where there is no such library facilities.

5. E-RESOURCES: THE BEGINNING

The National Library, in its systematic up gradation of ICT, introduced online resources for its users in April 2010. Apart from that, the necessity was also felt due to pressure from different corners to modernize and upgrading the services and products of library to cope with the need of the time. Therefore, infrastructure was utilized and online journals and electronic books were introduced in a phase wise manner. Online journals of reputable publishers such as Oxford University Press, Cambridge University Press, Taylor & Francis Group, Sage Publication, American Chemical Society, and aggregators' products such as Project Muse and Hein Online were acquired first. These were followed by journals of Emerald Group, Springer, and IndianJournals.com. E-reference of Cambridge University Press was introduced and later references of Oxford University Press, ProQuest were added to the collection. Currently, the library possesses about 6500 online journals and 2.7 million full-text dissertation and thesis, an archive of 125,000 e-books (Early English Books Online), e-books(World e-book Library) along with other online references. E-books entered the library in March 2012. The National Library of India is the first public library in the country to introduce e-books. E-books of OUP, CUP, Taylor & Francis, Springer and Wiley have been purchased and at present the library has about 4300 titles in its possession.

6. E-BOOKS

In accordance with the decision of the second meeting of the Advisory Board of the National Library held on 3rd April, 2010, The Director General, National Library has constituted a Committee, known as the Advisory Committee for Book Selection & Ordering to advice the Library on selection and acquisition policy for procurement of foreign books. The Committee presently has eight members with the Director General as the

Chairperson, along with five academicians in different fields of Humanities & Science with two Library officers of the National Library.

The Advisory Committee for Book Selection and Ordering on its meeting on 5th January, 2012 advised the National Library to introduce e-books in the year 2011-2012 for its users. The Library presently acquired e-books from OUP, CUP, Taylor & Francis, Springer, Wiley-Blackwell. There is no platform fee as the Library already using the OUP, CUP & Taylor & Francis products. The access is unlimited and the products are one-time purchase on perpetual access mode. The subject-wise breakup of individual publishers is given below:

6.1. Cambridge University Press

Sl.No.	*Subjects*	*No. of E-books*
1	Drama, Theatre, Music	221
2	Humanities, Film Media, Classical studies	354
3	Mathematics	264
4	Physics	108
5	Social Sciences	168
	Total	1115

6.2. Oxford University Press

Sl. No.	*Subjects*	*No. of E-books*
1	Classical Studies	159
2	History	239
3	Linguistics	125
4	Literature	203
5	Philosophy	452
6	Social Work	92
7	Political Science	196
8	Early English Book Online (English titles printed between 1475-1700 in England, Scotland, Wales etc. are available)	1,25,000
	Total	1,26,466

6.3. Project Muse

Sl. No.	*Subjects*	*No. of E-books*
1	Area & Ethnic Studies	2466
2	Art & Architecture	222
3	Creative writing	897
4	Education	519
5	Film, Theatre & Performing Arts	595
6	History	4080
7	Language & Linguistics	347
8	Library Science & Publishing	32
9.	Literature	1631
10.	Medicine & Health	475
11.	Music	215
12.	Philosophy	760
13	Religion	1101
14	Science, Technology & Mathematics	689
15	Social Sciences	4372
16	Studies by time period	387
17	Women's studies, Gender , and Sexuality	801
	Total	19, 589

6.4. Springer

Sl. No.	*Subjects*	*No. of E-books*
1.	Lecture Notes on Computer Science(LNCS)	550

6.5. Taylor & Francis

Sl. No.	*Subjects*	*No. of E-books*
1	Asian Studies	100
2	Economics	100
3	English Language& Linguistics	100
4	Education	100
5	Geography	100
6	History	100

7	Media & Communication	100
8.	Philosophy	100
9	Religion	100
10	Social work & Development	100
11	Sports & Tourism	100
	Total	1100

6.6. Wiley Blackwell

Sl. No.	*Subjects*	*No. of E-books*
1	Business, Economics, Finance & Accounting	2
2	Chemistry	131
3	Computer Science & Information Technology	35
4	Earth & Environment	25
5	Mathematics & Statistics	25
6	Psychology	46
	Total	264

7. E-JOURNAL BOUQUET

The Advisory Committee for Book Selection and Ordering in its meeting on January 2012 recommended bringing out a directory of online resources in order to provide easy access to readers. Following the recommendation, the job was undertaken on a priority basis. After careful thought a scheme was worked out. The main section of the directory contains the list of titles in alphabetical order with URLs, subjects and providers. However, the prefixed articles of the titles have been ignored in alphabetical order. Other section includes subject index to make the main section accessible by the users through linking the respective serial numbers of titles. It is the constant endeavour of the library to increase its readership by providing simple and smooth access to its resources. In this direction, the first initiative was taken with a massive online campaign to popularize the resources of the library among the faculties of different academic institutions. The directory is already uploaded in the web portal of National Library (www.national library.gov.in) and will also be available hard form to the users. It is believed that the directory will be immensely helpful to the users and save their precious time. The e-journals bouquet includes the following:

7.1. Cambridge University Press

Sl.No.	*Subjects*	*No. of E-Journals*
1	African Studies	7
2	Agriculture	18
3	Aquatic Science	4
4	Architecture	1
5	Australasian Studies	2
6	Biomedical Sciences	25
7	Classical Studies	11
8	Cultural Studies	9
9	Ecology and Conservation	19
10	Education	4
11	Environmental Studies	12
12	General Interest	4
13	History and Philosophy of Science	5
14	Latin American Studies	3
15	Literary Studies	2
16	Mathematics	29
17	Medicine	20
18	American Studies	9
19	Animal Science	17
20	Archaeology and Anthropology	15
21	Asian Studies	10
22	Biology	5
23	Business and Management	5
24	Computer Science	16
25	Earth and Atmospheric Science	13

26	Economics	19
27	Engineering	13
28	European Studies	11
29	History	46
30	Language and Linguistics	21
31	Law	29
32	Materials Research	5
33	Medical Policy	10
34	Medieval Studies	5
	Total	398

7.2. Oxford University Press

Sl. No.	*Subjects*	*No. of E-journals*
1	Economics	29
2	Humanities	69
3	Law	44
4	Life Sciences	51
5	Mathematics and Physical Science	44
6	Medicine	81
7	Social Sciences	61
	Total	379

7.3. Hein Online

Sl.No.	*Subjects*	*No. of E-journals*
1	Law Journal Library	———
2	English Reports, Full Reprint(1220-1867)	———
	Total	

7.4. Indian Journals.Com

Sl.No.	Subjects	No. of E-journals
1	Agriculture	73
2	Applied Science & Technology	47
3	Biology	25
4	Business/Economics/Management	54
5	Dental Science	10
6	Earth Science	4
7	Education	2
8	Engineering Mechanics/Materials	16
9	Environment	21
10	Humanities	6
11	Library & Information Science	8
12	Medical Science	36
13	Physics	3
14	Social Science	29
15	Veterinary/Animal Sciences	25
	Total	359

7.5. J-Stor

Full access to about 3606 journals across 54 subjects.

7.6. Project Muse

Sl.No.	Subjects	No. of E-journals
1	Area & Ethnic Studies	142
2	Art & Architecture	9
3	Creative writing	16
4	Education	24
5	Film, Theatre & Performing Arts	34
6	History	71
7	Language & Linguistics	15
8	Library Science & Publishing	5

9.	Literature	160
10.	Medicine & Health	18
11.	Music	14
12.	Philosophy	23
13	Religion	28
14	Science, Technology & Mathematics	11
15	Social Sciences	122
16	Studies by time period	45
17	Women's studies, Gender , and Sexuality	22
	Total	759

7.7. Sage Journals

Sl.No.	*Subjects*	*No. of E-journals*
1	Health Sciences	344
2	Life & Biomedical Sciences	32
3	Materials Science & Engineering	78
4	Social Sciences & Humanities	809
	Total	1263

8. REFERENCE E-COLLECTION BOUQUET AND SUBJECT COVERAGE

The reference e-collection of National Library includes the following:

Sl No.	*Title*	*Subject Coverage*
1	Cambridge University Press	This collection deals with the following: • The Cambridge Companions to Literature and Classics (263) • The Cambridge Companions to Philosophy, Religion and Culture (166) • The Cambridge Companions to Music (57) • Shakespeare Survey (64)

2	Oxford English Dictionary	Provides users with information on semantic evolution of words
3	Oxford Bibliographies Online	Biblical Studies • Buddhism • Classics • Communication • Criminology • Hinduism • International Relations • Islamic Studies • Medieval Studies • Philosophy • Public Health • Social Work
4	Pro-Quest Dissertation and Thesis Full Text	2.7 million full-text dissertation from the year 1861- till date is available

9. RECENT ACQUISITIONS (TILL 2015)

The following e-resources are added to the collection of National Library

Taylor & Francis

9.1 South Asian Archive: http://www.southasiaarchive.com/

Informatics Publishing Pvt. Ltd.

9.2 J-Gate Plus: http://jgateplus.com/search/

9.3 i-Scholars: http://i-scholar.in/

9.4 World e-Books: http://Community.WorldLibrary.org/?AffiliateKey=WPLNatLibAAcRes

Proquest

9.5 Bowker's Books in Print: http://www.booksinprint.com/

9.6 Library Information Science Abstract (LISA): http:/

/www.proquest.com/products-services/lisa-set-c.html

9.7 Literature Online (LION): http://literature.proquest.com/marketing/index.jsp

9.8 Historical Newspaper Collections: http://www.proquest.com/products-services/pq-hist-news.html

9.9 Ulrichsweb: Global Serials Directory: http://ulrichsweb.serialssolutions.com/login

10. WORKFLOW FOLLOWED IN ACQUISITION OF E-RESOURCES IN NATIONAL LIBRARY OF INDIA

1. Proposals received from publishers/aggregators after initial negotiation
2. Meticulous scrutiny of the merit of the product and assessing the suitability
3. Sorted proposals placed before the Advisory Committee for Book Selection & Ordering
4. After approval from the Advisory Committee for Book Selection & Ordering, these proposals are placed before the Committee for the Subscription/Purchase of Online Resources for final price negotiation
5. On final approval of the Committee for the Subscription/Purchase of Online Resources, the order for the activating the access of the e-resource across the static IP range is issued
6. On activation of access, each and every titles of e-books are checked for their access as per the order and databases are checked for access as per negotiation
7. MARC records supplied by the publisher are integrated with the ILMS database through Z39.0 protocol. Bar code is generated for each e-book
8. License agreements are signed between the publisher and National Library

11. CHECKLIST FOR E-RESOURCES

Characteristics	*Sub Characteristics*	*Remarks*
Collection Development		
Content	Organizational goals	Type of library & users
	Complementing or adding existing collection	Volumes of print references may be replaced with e-versions or fill the gap areas
	Quality	Per-reviewed, reputable publisher
	User Demand	May be accessed through questionnaires
	Generate an acceptable level of use.	It depends on value addition, availability of back issues
	Currency	Frequency of updates
	Value for money	Extra facilities over print equivalents
	Accuracy and completeness	It needs to compare with the print equivalents
	Duplication	Duplicate checking with the e-titles should be done meticulously
	Content consistency	It needs to check the chapter wise checking of e-books/ journals
Technical feasibility	Access	Static IP based, Remote
	Authentication,	IP filtering or login password
	Hardware and software compatibility	
	Storage and maintenance	Remote hosting, local hosting
	Compatibility	Browser, Content format etc.
	Platform	Must be platform independent

Vendor support	User training and support.	It is needed for user education
	Trials and product demonstrations	To understand and verify claims
	Technical support and system notification process	It helps to render user service effectively
	Statistical reporting	Cost-effectiveness and justification of investment
	Customization	To make more user-friendly
	Provision of bibliographic data	MARC records.
	Data security and archiving policies	Consideration needs to be given to the options available from the vendor for customization and branding of the product. This is often helpful in giving products used within the library a similar look and feel.
Supply	Pricing models	Selective/ Big deal
	Access options	Single user, multiple users
	Archiving and post termination rights	
	Maintenance fees	Needs Negotiation
	Cancellation rights	
Collection Management		
Licensing	Governing laws.	
	Liability for unauthorized use	
	Definition of authorized users	
	Definition of authorized sites	

	Fair Dealing (or "Fair Use") Provision	
	Termination.	
	Refunds	
	Period of agreement	
	Compliance with the governing laws of the library's or consortium's legal jurisdiction (province, state, country)	
	Terms of payment	
	Grace period	
Functionality and reliability	Search and retrieval functionality	Truncation, browsing, search history, transliteration.
	Exporting and downloading	printing, e-mail, downloading to a machine, and downloading to an electronic device.
	Sorting and ranking abilities for database results	author, title,date, relevancy, facets, etc
	Interface	system intuitiveness, navigation, help and tutorials
	Integration	
	Reliability and availability	response times, 24/7 access

12. NEGOTIATION

Successful negotiation is required before finalizing license agreements. (Harris, 2000) opines that flexibility in negotiations is vital; one must know what he/she is willing to give up in order securing what is determined to obtain. Librarians should also know the interests and needs of the "other side"-the people and company they are negotiating with. During negotiations, one must listen carefully and actively, making sure everything is clear understood. Never assume anything, Harris writes. During negotiations one should be assertive, but not aggressive.

Scanning a number of original License agreements from various publishers/ aggregators of E-resources, the author tries to summarise the various rights & restrictions given to libraries:

Rights & Restrictions	*Details*
Permitted	Educational, scholarly research, personal non-commercial use
	Access, display search, browse, view the subscribed products, print, make electronic copies, reproduce, store, preservation, refreshing, migration
	Download and print up to 10 pages of a book per session; download work to a maximum 5 handheld devices for the personal use; make printed copies of one chapter or up to 20% of the pages from the total collection, whichever is greater for personal use, during any four-week period; copy & paste one chapter of each title in the collection in question, or up to 5% of the pages from the total collection, whichever is the greater, for personal use only during any 4-week period
	Print and deliver book chapters from the subscribed products to fulfil the requests as part of the practice known as Interlibrary Loan for non-commercial libraries located within the same country
	Access to new start-up journals that is included at no additional cost
	Adding MARC records to group catalogues or bibliographic utilities for reference needs

	Incorporate links to the subscribed products on the subscriber's intranet and internet websites, provided that the appearance of such links and/or statements accompanying such links will be changes as reasonably requested by the licensor
Permitted with permission from the publisher	Publicly use the name, trademark, or logo of the licensor in any publicity, promotion, news release, website posting, announcement, client list, marketing materials or other disclosure
	Collection may be used in Course Packs, Electronic Reserve Collection
	Recompiling, publication, or republication of the data or any portion thereof, in any form or medium whatsoever
Prohibited	Automated searching/downloading by use of scripted searches, robots, spiders, crawlers, algorithms or devices to continually and automatically search, scrape, extract, deep link, index or disrupt the working of subscribed product
	Substantially or systematically download, reproduce, retain or redistribute
	Abridge, modify, translate or create any derivative work based on the subscribed products except to the extent necessary to make them perceptible on a computer screen
	Remove, obscure or alter the authors' names or the Publisher's copyright notices or other means of identification or disclaimers as they appear in the in the licensed materials, including complete issues for any purpose and distribute any

part of the licensed material on any electronic network

Commercially exploit the collections or the MARC records or portions including without limitation, sale, exchange, barter, transfer, assign, distribute or public display

Transfer, assign or sublicense any rights or obligations

Reverse engineer, decompile, disassemble or otherwise alter software

Allowing other library to download, update or otherwise use the records in their own catalogue

---

13. PROBLEMS GENERALLY FACED WITH THE E-RESOURCES IN AND AFTER ACQUISITION

1. Sometimes, publishers intentionally or mistakenly provide access to inappropriate titles of e-books. Therefore, meticulous duplicate checking of each and every selected title is absolute necessary.
2. Sometimes, the publishers upgrade the hosting platform, therefore the librarians need to aware of such changes and intimate the users of the anticipated changes of access.

14. PROPOSED/DESIRED FUTURE PLANS REGARDING E-RESOURCES

14.1. Integration of MARC records with VIRTUA

The MARC records of the e-books are added in the Virtua ILMS so that these are equally searchable in OPAC.

14.2. Integration of Chamos Discovery

In the second phase of the ICT up gradation of National Library the Virtua ILMS will be upgraded to the latest version and Chamos Discovery module will be integrated to enable the users with federated search within the OPAC among the available e-resources and digitized materials in the National Library Digital Library.

Chamos Discovery fully integrates the discovery process within the OPAC and gives users the types of self-service capabilities they have come to expect through the web, by placing the library and its unique offerings at the forefront, with all library functions directly available for the users. Through an accessible, familiar web environment, vtls-Chamos Discovery presents the user with powerful search capabilities as well as facets to allow browsing and narrowing of results. Users are guided with "did you mean" functionality to suggest alternative searches as well as the ability to do sophisticated, complex searching. Graphical icons allow instant recognition of material formats, while the integration of content enrichment data from Google Books, Syndetic, and NoveList gives user instant access to book jackets, reviews, audio clips, recommendations, and more and with eBook integration with both OverDrive and 3M™ Cloud Library, and federated search functionality for the electronic databases, vtls-Chamo Discovery provides access beyond the library's physical collection.

14.3. Integration of EZ Proxy Software

National Library will integrate access and authentication software viz, Ezproxy software to deliver secure Web access to e-content simply and effectively. EZproxy facilitates a single sign-on to e-content using existing library-issued credentials, such as a library card number and PIN or username and password. EZproxy removes barriers for remote information seekers. This allows users to gain secure, remote access to the library's online licensed content without having to manage additional passwords and authorizations.EZproxy will allow the library's users to connect to e-content through a single sign-on and without any proxy configuration on the user's client. The software dynamically alters the database vendor's URLs to reflect the EZproxy server, directing users to return to the Library's server as they click on links for licensed content. The vendors will identify the request as coming from an authorized IP address and automatically provides seamless access.

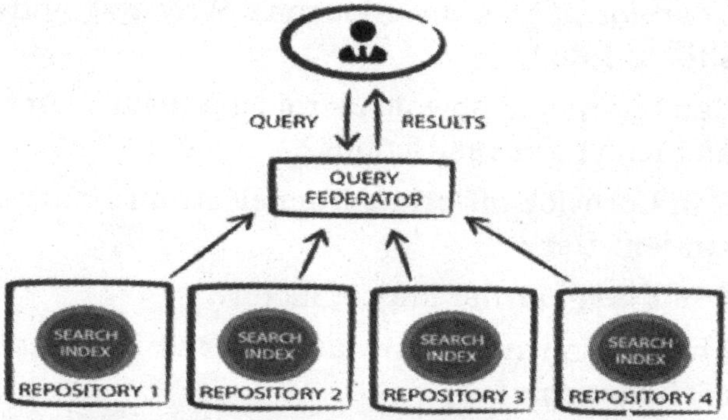

Fig. 1. Intigration of EZ Proxy Software

14.4. Helping Assistance to E-resources: Documentation of FAQ's for E-resources

The following FAQs may be documented for assistance with the common uses of E-resources

E-Resources FAQs

- How can I find a specific resource quickly?
- What resources are available in my subject area?
- Why are many e-resources restricted to National Library users only?
- How can I access a resource off site?
- I can't access a resource despite being on a National Library PC
- How do I access resources on my laptop?
- How can I find the full text for a specific citation?
- Where can I perform a literature search for my subject area?
- Where can I get training materials for a particular resource?

- Where can I search for e-book titles?

E-Journals FAQs

- What is an e-journal?
- Can I access e-journals from off-site?
- I cannot access an e-journal. Why not and what should I do?
- Can I print and download from e-journals? Are there any copyright restrictions?
- Can I provide off-prints from electronic journals for student use?
- What is a journal impact factor?
- I have a journal abbreviation. What is the full title of the journal?

14.5. Creation of new Assistant Library & Information Officer for managing E-resources

With the ever-increasing collection of E-resources like e-books, e-journals, databases etc, there is an urgent need for creation of a post of Assistant Librarian for management of E-resources with the following nature of duties:

1. To negotiate complex license agreements, and pricing with vendors of electronic resources.
2. To serve as the Libraries' internal coordinator regarding the use, creation and dissemination of copyrighted works and to provides direction regarding copyright, licensing, and permissions. To recommend best practices, for example, with documentation and training on compliance issues.
3. To communicate with vendors and maintain good working relationships regarding electronic resource technical issues.
4. To provide technology support to users for electronic resources.

5. To update and maintain electronic resource holdings in Electronic Resource Management System
6. To update and maintain: link resolver, license records, electronic resource acquisitions data for electronic resources in Electronic Resource Management System and search and/or other federated search tools for electronic resources.
7. To take responsibility for cataloging and improving MARC records for electronic resources
8. To provide feedback about electronic infrastructure compatibility.
9. To recommend and facilitate improvements to existing tools and workflows
10. To gather usage statistics and other assessment data for electronic resources.
11. To develop and maintains Library Web pages and online resource portals for electronic resources, including database description, links, text, and other information as appropriate to ensure access for users.
12. To develop and maintain services to permit users to read eBooks and use other electronic resources offline.
13. To oversee editing of MARC records and/or other metadata schema
14. To work collaboratively with other library Divisions
15. To develop and maintain services for archiving and/ or ensuring perpetual access to electronic resources.
16. To brand and customize electronic resources provided by vendors with appropriate links, logos, and other symbols of National Library.
17. To arrange and oversee trials and demonstrations of electronic resources.
18. To manage the budget for electronic resources and

advise the Director General regarding spending for electronic resources.

19. To coordinate payment processing for electronic resources with the Library's Administration
20. To identify and track changes in the law, technology, business models, organizational structures and user culture relevant to electronic resources.
21. To identifies free/open electronic resources for possible inclusion in National Library information services.

14.6. Targeted Communication to Stakeholders

Communication of various news related to electronic resources to different readers, students, teachers researchers, policy makers and others may be channelized in the following ways:

- Announcements through RSS feed, Social Networking sites like Blog, Facebook, Twitter etc. Press Releases, articles in Newspapers, reviews in scholarly journals mass communication media like Radio, etc.
- Flat Screen Television Displays
- Use of promotional materials like Door Hangers, Coasters/Beer Mats, Book Marks, Handouts, Brochures
- Regular User orientation programs by the publishers to make the users aware of their special characteristics of their products.

15. CONCLUSION

National Library of India is in the process of transforming its resources and services suitable for the modern Knowledge Society. An E-resource Centre with about seventy think line clients and a network printer will be opened soon to give opportunity to more number of users at a time. Besides, the City Hub, proposed to set up at the heart of Kolkata will another state-of-the art library for access of the entire electronic resources owned and created by the Library.

Acknowledgement : The authors are grateful to Dr. P.Y.Rajendra Kumar, Director-General, National Library of India for providing the facilities, encouragement and support.

REFERENCES

1. Chatterjee, A. (2002). Development of information resource base in academic libraries/ : process and policy. *Librarian*, 9-10, 69–80.
2. Choudhury, B. (1993). Need for collection development programme/ : some parameters. In *Proceedings of the All India Library Conference of IASLIC.* Ranchi: IASLIC.
3. Harris, L. (2000). Licensing, Copyright Law, Technology and Education. *Copyright & New Media Law Newsletter, 4*(2). Retrieved from http://www.copyrightslaw.com
4. Kesavan, B. S. (1961).India's National Library.Calcutta: National Library.
5. Kumar, S., & Singh, M. (2011). Design and file formats of E-books in electronic learning. In *Knowledge Management in Digital Era.* New Delhi: Westville Publishing House.
6. Montgomery, C., & King, D. (2002). Comparing library & user related costs of print and electronic journal collections: a first step towards comprehensive analysis. *D-Lib Magazine, 8*(10).
7. Retrieved from http://www.dlib.org/dlib/october02/montgomery/10montgomery.html
8. National Knowledge Commission. (n.d.). National Knowledge Commission. Retrieved December 30, 2014, from http://knowledgecommission.gov.in
9. Sabarathnam, D. (1995). Transforming libraries to support change and growth. In *Networking and the future of libraries.* London: Library Association. Retrieved from http://www.loc.gov/acq/conser
10. Thanuskodi, S. (2011). Usage of electronic resources at Dr. T.P.M. Library, Madurai University/ : a case study. *DESIDOC Journal of Library and Information Technology, 30*(6), 437–445.

2

Acquisition and Collection Development Policy for Electronic Resources : Issues and Challenges

Puspita Mishra
Assistant Librarian
National Institute of Technology, Rourkela

ABSTRACT

Electronic resources are very much broader term that includes different documents which are instant accessible with an electronic device within a fraction of time. These resources are of importance to faculties and students for research and teaching purpose. The libraries are focused on taking an authority part in teaming up with scholastic departments in giving electronic resources to help the research and study. This document provides the life cycle of the e-resources with a guideline to the policy document for selection and evaluation of electronic resources in all respects.

Keywords : E-Resources, Licensing of E- Resources, Life cycle of E-Resources, Collection development, Evaluation.

1. INTRODUCTION

Today in national scenario, the library funds are decreasing, while the cost of the electronic resources has continued to increase as the availability of e-journals has increased exponentially. Practically, all associate investigated science, technology and medicine journals are presently accessible electronically. As per Ulrich's Periodicals Catalogue," in excess of 80 percent of today's dynamic, peer-reviewed journals are currently accessible electronically alongside some open source Journals". As the electronic resources are growing exponentially day by day, the librarians are facing challenges because they are involving in the selection /acquisition of the endless variations of the packages offered by the different publishers, aggregators and the subscription agencies where there is huge monetary involvement. There is no such tool to deal with the complications of e-resource management. As librarians are pushed to manage some control over their e-accumulations, they end up lost in an issue of spreadsheets and email messages, and in charge of managing a mixed bag of autonomous frameworks and databases that are not consolidated with one another.Librarians depend on their memory alone to arrange frameworks, for example, the securing module of their incorporated library framework, their alphabetic arrangements of e-journals and databases, their meta search device, and their nearby connection server. Notwithstanding the beginning effort of setting up data in different spots and the potential absence of consistency between frameworks, significant duplication of work is liable to emerge.

2. TYPES OF ELECTRONIC RESOURCES

Electronic resources define to"those materials that require an electronic device to be accessed, whether through a personal computer, mainframe, or handheld mobile device" (Sharon Johnson, 2012). We can easily access them intangible. These are more useful due to inherent capabilities for searching, accessing, acquiring, storing and maintaining the information in very smooth and cheaper way. Some of the useful resources in this category are:

- E-books
- E-journals
- Full-text (aggregated) databases
- Indexing and abstracting databases
- Reference databases (biographies, dictionaries, directories, encyclopedias, etc.)
- Numeric and statistical databases
- E-images
- E-audio/visual resources

3. THE LIFE CYCLE OF AN E-RESOURCE

Being the Library professionals, we may compare the tricky and complex life cycle with human beings. Like human beings, E-resources are originated, and at different times they also die or are re-born under a different name or in a different shape; they form families, and the families may combine with other families, divide by part; agreements between families are signed and can be later discarded; and so on.

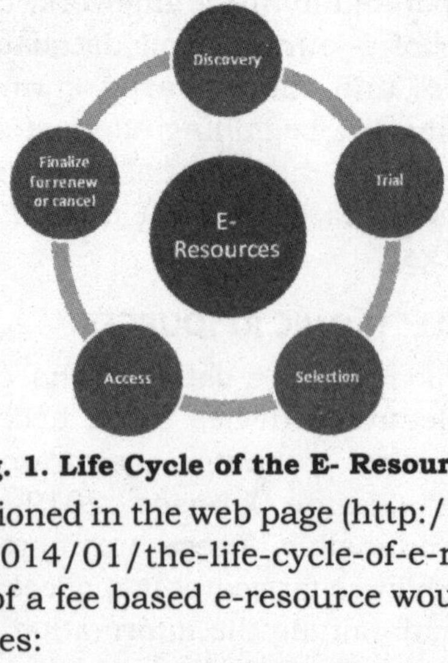

Fig. 1. Life Cycle of the E- Resources

As mentioned in the web page (http://edu-helpline.blogspot.in/2014/01/the-life-cycle-of-e-resource.html) the life cycle of a fee based e-resource would include the following stages:

1. Discovery : At the library, the information about the new e-resources reach from many sources like Faculties request, subject experts, catalogues from vendors and much more. The librarian then starts investigating about the particular e-resource and collect different Information like the bibliographic details of that e- resource, the exposure period covering, the packages that include this e-resources, and the interface or interfaces through which such packages are accessible, the access compatibility etc.

2. Trial : A trial empowers the librarian to put forward the new resources for some or all user groups – who may incorporate supporters and curators alike – and afterward have a choice on their feedback. Along with the trial practice, the librarian enacts the e-asset in the wanted areas of the library environment, informs the important audience, and gets feedback as input. Librarians give careful consideration to particular issues when testing an e-asset like specialized base needed by the client interface. At the point when the trial is finished, the librarian ought to have the capacity to support the decision of interface for the establishment in general and in addition to its different divisions.

3. Selection : Once the trial is over, the librarian collects the feedback from the group users for which the retail access is enabled. If there is a positive response, then the librarian may proceed with the purchase procedure to acquire the same.

4. Acquisition : If it is decided for further processing and subscription of the resource acquisition process is to be followed. An extra level of point of interest is needed, for example, data about the license and the accessibility of the asset to different population of users. Likewise, when a library is obtaining e-journals as a major aspect of a bundle from an e-resource aggregator, for example, EBSCO, the curator needs to know which journals are covered by the bundle and for what time frame; in a perfect world, the administrator would have the alternative to pay one not whole for the whole bundle or to pay independently for each one title. Here is the time to play keenly to discover every upsides and downsides created by the aggregators. An alternate issue is the manner by which to handle the dispersion of an instalment between the licensor of the bundle and one or more interface providers.

5. Access : Once a library has acquired an e-resource, the librarians want to ensure that it is decently utilized. It is first and foremost responsibility of the library to take proper initiative so that the defined user community should access the resources effortlessly. The list of the resources can be available to users either by an A-Z list or from the OPAC from a meta search tool overall make it user friendly to extract more benefit from the resources. Issues such as access by specific user groups or by remote users (for instance, proxy setup) also additionally need to be tackled. After the initial configuration of access, which might have been taken care of, at least partially, at the trial stage, librarians must familiar to solve the problems like temporary unavailability of the resource, and changes in the provider's address or the manner of access. The insights of the uses ought to be kept up legitimately to showcase the utility of the same asset.

6. Finalize for renew or cancel : An e-resource membership enrollment is typically generous for a characterized time period, usually in the majority of the cases the calendar year is emulated. Just before the period closes, the librarian should either renew the subscription or scratch off it. Dissimilar to the case at the determination stage, this choice is focused around measurable information, for example, the genuine use of the e-resource while it was accessible, the dependability of the interface, and the responsiveness of the supplier. Whatever the conclusion of the choice – renew or retraction – the framework needs to help it. Moreover, considerably after a membership has been crossed out, the library may have interminable get to or documenting rights to the information, an alternate region that administrators must manage on a continuous premise. Numerous e-resources today are acquired through consortia, which have impressive acquiring force. In a consortium based environment, the strategies included in securing, access, and choice making is substantially more complex

4. COLLECTION DEVELOPMENT POLICY FOR E- RESOURCES

Obviously accumulation advancement in collection development criteria, for example, subject, the target user applies to the determination of most e-resources, the administration of the electronic arrangement is more complex and, all things considered, it is great practice to create a supplementary policy which addresses particular configuration related issues. Such a strategy ought to be utilized as a part of conjunction with the more customary gathering improvement approach.

The approach ought to give the right way to support selectors or obtaining custodians in securing the library's desires and inclination in connection to:

Technical feasibility : When we are going to adapt the electronic resources, we should aware of all kinds of technical aspect of the usability of that .The resource should be very much familiar with the existing hardware and software of the library so that the library has the ability to successfully keep up access to assets on a progressing and financially savvy premise. Policy ought to be framed, including the accompanying focuses:

- Availability, e.g., Remote access/ remains solitary access
- Authentication, e.g., IP base or login watchword
- Hardware and programming similarity and capacity

- Storage and support, e.g., remote facilitating/ neighborhood facilitating
- Platforms which facilitate access to e-resources

Functionality and reliability : The e-resource interface should be easy to understand, simple to explore and instinctive. User-friendly resources regularly incorporate such components as online tutorials, introductory screens, navigation aids and context-sensitive help and personalization options such as subscribing to feeds/e-mail alerts, keep search history etc.

They may include (Sharon Johnson, 2012):

- Search and retrieval strategy, e.g. -More advance facility
- Exporting and downloading (by requiring portion not systematic)
- Interface, e.g., System intuitiveness, navigation, help and tutorials
- Integration
- Reliability and availability, e.g., Response times, 24/ 7 access

Vendor support : Thought needs to be given to how well working and solid an e-resource vendor is and to the scope of specialized and user helpsservice they find themselves able to provide. It is valuable to focus the scope of vendor support services accessible, including:

- User orientation and training support
- Trial access and product demonstrations
- Technical backing and framework notice process
- Statistical reports
- Customization
- Provision of bibliographic data, e.g., MARC records
- Data security and archiving policies

Supply : It is critical to consider the scope of the procurement/evaluating models accessible and figure out which one best address the needs of the library as far as get to, user's requirements, archival rights, and value for money of the institution.

It includes the following points

- Purchase model, e.g., Purchase/ subscribes
- Pricing models, e.g., Select / package
- Access options, i.e. Single user/multiple users/all users
- Archiving and post termination rights
- Maintenance fees
- Cancellation rights

Licensing : Unlike print publications, e-resources are not purchased outright and normally oblige a permit, consent/License to be set up. Before buy, the license must be checked in and arranged to educate and backing the evaluation process, and to guarantee that it reflects the selector's desire. It is desirable over acquire, where conceivable, a standard model license agreement that depicts the privileges of the library in an easy-to-understand and explicit language.

The licensing agreement includes the following points as:

- Standard license format
- Rules and the governing body
- Accountability for illegal use
- Definition of authorized users
- Definition of authorized sites
- "Fair Use" Provision
- Termination
- Refunds
- Period of agreement

- Observance with the governing laws of the library's or consortium's legal authority (province, state, country)
- Language of the license

The policy ought to likewise give direction to help selectors on arrangement inclination when confronted with the decision of substance accessible in both print and electronic formats. Contemplations identifying with organization inclination, including choices on de-duplication (i.e. Where titles are as of now gained in numerous organizations), may incorporate, however is not restricted to, the accompanying:

Currency : e-resources with print equivalents should not fall behind their print partners.

Esteem for money : The e-resources ought to give sufficient included value over the print proportional or other simple designs (e.g., expanded usefulness, expanded availability.

Exactness and culmination : The e-resource ought to reflect the indistinguishable or expanded substance as contrasted and the print identical.

Duplication : duplication of e-resources with equivalent simple arrangements may be considered if the electronic publication is not documented and maintenance is normal; if the expense of duplication is negligible, and various organizations best address the needs of distinctive clients as far as access and convenience.

At last the strategy ought to additionally give clear direction on cycles of survey and de-selection policies for e-resources, where extra criteria related particularly to configuration, Such as, obsolescence, platform reliability, etc.

5. CONCLUSION

Innovative advancement of technology has immensely affected on the exercises of libraries, creating a significant ideal model of transformation which challenges librarian and the profession. However, when it comes regarding the matter of gathering e-resources or upkeep of a hybrid collection various related difficulties go to the forefront. These incorporate the expense and financing justification for selecting e- resources, recognizing the utilization level also. Arrangement of compelling gathering criteria on approach which will direct the determination and securing choice with a specific end goal to accomplish an offset in between the print and electronic media focused around the utilization.

REFERENCES

1. Library and Information Science blog: The life cycle of an e-resource. (n.d.). Retrieved January 25, 2015, from http://edu-helpline.blogspot.in/2014/01/the-life-cycle-of-e-resource.html
2. Johnson, B. S., Evensen, G., Gelfand, J., Sipe, L., Zilper, N., Fronty, J. &Schmolling, R. (2012). Key Issues for E-Resource Collection Development/ : A Guide for Libraries.
3. Kiondo, E. (2004). Around the World to: The University of Dar es Salaam Library: Collection Development in the Electronic Information Environment. *Library Hi Tech News, 21*(6), 19–24. doi:10.1108/07419050410554861
4. Sadeh, T., &Ellingsen, M. (2005). Electronic resource management systems: the need and the realization. *New Library World, 106*(5/6), 208–218. doi:10.1108/03074800510595823
5. Xu, F. (2010). Implementation of an electronic resource assessment system in an academic library. *Program: Electronic Library and Information Systems, 44* (4), 374–392. doi:10.1108/00330331011083257

3

Management of Electronic Resources in Engineering College Libraries

K. Somasekhara Rao
Dept. of Library and Information Science
Andhra University, Visakhapatnam

N. Venkata Rao
Librarian, Anil Neerukonda Institute of
Technology & Sciences, Visakhapatnam.

ABSTRACT

The electronic resources are increasing continuously in libraries, particularly in engineering college libraries. It is necessary for professionals to understand the issues of management relating to electronic resources. About 26 aspects of managing electronic resources are listed and the information collected from selected engineering college libraries and presented.

1. INTRODUCTION

The development of information technology and the dissemination of Web environments have a dramatic effect on the user behaviors in information usage. The library user requests swifter and more convenient usage of information beyond the time and space barriers, which changes the library atmosphere. The workflows from acquisitions to user services and the life cycle of electronic resources is quite different from that of print resources since it is characterized by access without holding the physical objects. Also, the functional responsibilities for managing electronic resources are often distributed over departments such as serials, acquisitions, and library systems. As licensing electronic resources has greatly increased in recent years, libraries have struggled to control this information in paper files, integrated library systems, separate databases stored on local computers or network. Under these circumstances, the need to get a better handle on these resources has grown.

2. GUIDING PRINCIPLES

The Electronic resource management system should offer an integrated environment that supports both management and access, without maintaining duplicate systems. The system should offer a capacity for global updating and flexible addition of fields. It should offer the ability to hide fields and records from public view and have a single point of maintenance for each data element. It should support interoperation and dynamic data sharing with existing OPACs, Web portals, library-management systems, and link resolution services. It should offer users consistent information, regardless of the path they take in seeking it. Finally, the ERMS should, over time, support the ability to store, access, search, and generate reports of the information that it contains.

3. FUNCTIONAL REQUIREMENTS

3.1. Bibliographic Management Requirements

In many libraries, both traditional and auxiliary bibliographic data may be distributed among a variety of systems, including the library-management system, a federated searching portal, and a link resolution service. Nevertheless, to the extent possible, each unique data element should have to be maintained only once. Updates in one system should be automatically reflected in corresponding systems, either through the dynamic sharing of data or, where redundant storage cannot be eliminated, by propagation to other systems. Loading of data from external systems should also be supported. Specifically, it should be possible to: Provide a single point of maintenance for bibliographic and auxiliary descriptive data that can be exchanged or shared between the OPAC, portal lists, federated search tools, local resolution services, and other bibliographic systems and services; and Import subscription-management data from external providers using standard software and developing protocols, lists of titles, ISSNs, and uniform resource identifiers (URIs) delivered in Excel or delimited format changes to titles and dates of coverage in aggregated databases communicated via any XML-based or standards-based data transfer protocol, such as ONIX for serial holdings updates supplied by a publisher or subscription agent to facilitate electronic check-in.

3.2. Access-Management Requirements

All libraries rely on authentication and access-management systems that are external to the systems and tools. These external systems may be as straight forward as reliance on the remote-authorization mechanism of an online provider (via IP addresses or user names and passwords) or as complex as a locally developed access-management service that assigns persistent identifiers to resources, passes connection requests to a system that validates users according to a local authentication scheme (e.g., Kerberos), and routes valid users through a proxy server. Institutions with complex local environments can be expected to have customized systems and tools with which to perform these functions, and the ERM system must interoperate with them. The ERMS should accommodate both simple and complex environments with a disparate range of needs.

To accomplish this, the following generalized requirements are necessary:

- Management of basic access-related information, such as URIs, user IDs and passwords, and lists of institutional IP addresses; Support for the creation of persistent URIs and for additional data elements required to support complex local access management services, such as proxy servers;
- A set of export functions by which an ERMS can communicate its information to a local system or service. Specifically, it should be possible to: Store and maintain access URIs and make these actionable for end users, according to local requirements: store vendor-supplied primary and secondary URIs (e.g., for mirror sites) used for access to the resource support the creation, storage, and updating of persistent URIs and/or integration with external systems for managing persistent identifiers support authentication and access systems (such as proxy servers or statistics generating scripts), allowing for URIs to be constructed on the fly on the basis of stored data elements generate notifications and/or exports of URI information to appropriate linked or external systems according to local requirements (e.g., notification or export to cataloging and information technology departments or systems) provide seamless functional integration with external systems that record this information (e.g., through a shared pointer);
- Integrate proxy server/access management with other functionality provide a means for seamless integration of proxy server access for all or selected users and all or selected resources;

Store lists of IP addresses used to register access to specific resources and provide automated e-mail notification to online providers when IP addresses are update, support the creation and maintenance of multiple lists of IP addresses that can be associated or disassociated with one or more licensed locations and linked to one or more bibliographic entities for a given resource or online provider, indicate whether IP addresses are/were registered online and record the registration URI send automated e-mail notifications to vendors and providers when IP addresses are updated and record the date on which notifications are sent. Include the ability to record an acknowledgment date. This implies the ability to designate a vendor or provider contact address for IP address-notification purposes; Store one or more user IDs and passwords and provide the ability to generate secure screen displays of this information for authorized users and staff, with associated text or for JavaScript auto submission; and Implement access restrictions, record authorized user categories and authorized sites, including the ability to associate specific actions with those elements, such as; generating staff and user displays implementing access controls exporting information to a local access-management system (technical system in use at your institution such as an authentication system and/or proxy server (see also Resource Administrative and Management Functions).

4. STAFF REQUIREMENTS

4.1. Staff Interface

An ERM system requires a staff interface that enables library staff to efficiently carry out the work described in the sections that follow. The interface should be organized into views that are optimized for particular areas of staff activity or interest, such as resource acquisition, troubleshooting, license administration, or administration and statistics. Details of appropriate interface design are not addressed in these requirements; these are left to the art and discretion of system developers. Through this interface, staff should be able to Search, browse, and retrieve records by attributes unique to e-resources, such as license, vendor, interface, record status, licensed site, consortium, and library selector or other local contact individual. View the full range of information appropriate to the staff member's security profile and functional role. To the extent possible, link to other relevant information stored in library management systems, portals, or related systems and view records that are hidden from the public.

4.2. Methodology

In order to elicit the needed information for the present study, it is decided to employ the most popular survey method. In view of the objectives of the present study, it is meaningful to elicit the needed information from the Librarians concerned of the selected engineering college libraries in Andhra Pradesh.

In the present study, for the selection of the engineering college libraries, the following criteria have been followed:

- The college must be an NBA accredited private engineering college
- At least 4 courses should have received accreditation

For the purpose of the present study, following the criteria for selection, only those colleges which were accredited by NBA need to be selected with the assumption that best practices in selection, acquisition and management of electronic resources can be identified from the libraries of such accredited colleges.

Out of the 711 Engineering Colleges in Andhra Pradesh, at the time of the present study, there were only 61 private engineering colleges (8.6 percent) that were accredited by NBA. The distribution of these NBA accredited colleges is 29 in Telangana Region, 7 in Rayalaseema region and 25 in Coastal Andhra region. Accordingly, a sample of 30 college libraries has been selected and the contact details of the 61 engineering college libraries are obtained to facilitate data collection plan.

5. MANAGEMENT OF E-RESOURCES

Once the selection and acquisition of E-Resources the next major step is their management. It is necessary to observe and follow certain management aspects to provide electronic information resources harmoniously to users. The aspects like renewal of annual maintenance contract, content verification, content access, updating E-Resources, achieving etc., are to be taken care of in libraries for managing E-Resources.

5.1. Procedures for Management of e-resources

In all 26 different procedures that are followed in the management of e-resources have been listed. Responses of the 30 librarians regarding the procedures they follow are shown in the following table.

Table 1. Different procedures followed / Observed in the Management of E-resources

Criteria / Aspect	*Followed*		*Not Followed*	
	No	*%*	*No*	*%*
1. Verification of Access - Content	29	96.7	1	3.3
2. Verification of Access - No of users	30	100.0	0	0.0
3. Verification of Access - Access method	30	100.0	0	0.0
4. Organizational chart	12	40.0	18	60.0
5. Periodical reviewing	19	63.3	11	36.7
6. Enquiries and user feedback - Content not covered	25	83.3	5	16.7
7. Enquiries and user feedback - Down loading	22	73.3	8	26.7
8. Monitoring speed of Information Download Facility	26	86.7	4	13.3
9. Monitoring Information storage Facility	24	80.0	6	20.0

10.	Print facility to all documents/ part?	23	76.7	7	23.3
11.	Data Records of Electronic Resources	12	40.0	18	60.0
12.	Shelving of e-resources - Accessioning	20	66.7	10	33.3
13.	Shelving of e-resources - Classification	11	36.7	19	63.3
14.	Shelving of e-resources - Cataloguing	12	40.0	18	60.0
15.	Updating of new electronic resources in OPAC	14	46.7	16	53.3
16.	Information literacy program - Presentations by publishers	19	63.3	11	36.7
17.	Information literacy program - Announcements by library	26	86.7	4	13.3
18.	Staff training	24	80.0	6	20.0
19.	Database administration	19	63.3	11	36.7
20.	Communication with vendors	27	90.0	3	10.0
21.	Tracking of Utilization statistics	28	93.3	2	6.7
22.	License Tracking	29	96.7	1	3.3
23.	Conservation & Preservation	15	50.0	15	50.0
24.	Overdue alerts to management	26	86.7	4	13.3
25.	Archiving	18	60.0	12	40.0
26.	AMC Tracking	25	83.3	5	16.7

Multiple Responses

It is noticed that verification of access through number of users and method of access is considered in all the 30 libraries while verification of access by content is observed in 29 libraries. Tracking of utilization statistics is done in 28 libraries and license tracking is reported by 29 libraries. In 27 libraries, communication with vendors is taken into account. Aspects like monitoring speed of information download facility, overdue alerts to management and announcement of literacy programmes by libraries are considered in 26 libraries. Enquiries and user feedback on content not covered as well as AMC tracking are reported by 25 of the 30 libraries.

In 24 libraries, aspects like monitoring information storage facility and staff trainings are considered. Print facility of all or part of documents is looked into in 23 libraries while in 22 libraries, enquiries and user feedback through down loading is considered. Twenty libraries are considering shelving of e-resources after accessioning.

Periodical reviewing, presentation of information literacy programme by the publishers, database administration, are followed in 19 of the 30 libraries. Archiving is considered in 18 libraries while conservation and preservation is considered in 15 libraries. Updating in OPAC is reported in 14 libraries and in 12 libraries, organizational chart, data records of e-resources and shelving of e-resources after cataloguing are reported. Shelving of e-resources after classification is done in 11 libraries.

It is necessary to mention that the aspects considered for management of electronic resources be followed in all libraries. Some of the librarians have expressed their ignorance on aspects like organizational chat, shelving E-Resources, Classification, Cataloguing, conservation and preservation etc., these aspects are very much necessary for management of E-Resources. Therefore it is necessary to train these librarians on these aspects by encouraging them to attend short term and long term programs conducted by various professional bodies and institutions.

The number of aspects for management of e-resources followed in the 30 libraries is shown in the following table.

Table 2. Number of Listed Procedures followed by the libraries

Procedures listed in Table	libraries Following No	%
All 26	4	13.3
25	1	3.3
24	4	13.3
23	1	3.3
22	1	3.3
21	1	3.3
20	2	6.7
19	3	10.0
18	2	6.7
16	2	6.7
15	2	6.7
13	1	3.3
12	3	10.0
11	1	3.3
10	1	3.3
9	1	3.3

All the 26 listed aspects are taken into account in 4 libraries and 25 aspects are considered in one library. In 9 libraries 20 to 24 aspects are taken into account and another 9 libraries are considering 15 – 19 aspects and the remaining 7 libraries are using 9 to 13 of the listed aspects. It is understood from the table, 7 out of 30 libraries are following 13 or less aspect listed for management of E-Resources. These libraries should also considered to follow all are many aspects for management of E-Resources.

The number and aspects considered for management of e-resources by the libraries individually is shown in the following table.

6. DE-SELECTION OR WEEDING

It is a fact that the collections in the library, beet print or electronic source would get outdated or damaged in course of time. Just like for books that should be a weeding out mechanism for electronic resources. In case of E-Resources the out datedness of E-Resources is significant; the reason for this situation is changing appearing in information and communication technology from time to time. Therefore De-Selection of E-Resources in engineering college libraries is an administrative activity and followed.

Information on whether there is any de-selection policy and whether they are following guidelines for de-selection is shown in the given table.

Table 3. Different measures observed/followed for de-selection or Weeding of E-resources

S. No	*Criteria / Aspect*	*Followed*		*Not Followed*	
		No	*%*	*No*	*%*
A	Having any De-Selection (weeding) policy	7	23.3	23	76.7
B	Whether following the guidelines for De-Selection:				
1	Non circulated materials since no of years	8	26.7	22	73.3
2	Materials not compatible with existing hardware or software	7	23.3	23	76.7
3	Outdated or inaccurate materials	14	46.7	16	53.3
4	Duplication of materials	8	26.7	22	73.3
5	Materials damaged beyond repair	20	66.7	10	33.3
	Multiple Responses				

It is observed that only 7 out of the total 30 libraries have some policy for de-selection or weeding of e-resources. The remaining 23 libraries are not having any such policy.

Coming to the consideration of guidelines for de-selection or weeding, there are 5 items listed. Twenty libraries are taking into account 'material damaged beyond repair' for weeding. Fourteen libraries are following 'outdated or inaccurate material' for weeding out. In 8 libraries each, aspects like 'non-circulated material since number of years' and 'duplication of material' are considered for weeding. 'Materials not compatible with existing hardware or software' is taken into account in 7 libraries.

It obvious from the table, most of libraries are following the criteria fro De-selection of E-Resources i.e., materials damaged beyond repair. It is noticed that most of librarians have limited knowledge on De-Selection of E-Resources. Since the E-Resources are expensive and the content can be assessed by the subject experts, it is necessary to have an established policy for De-Selection of E-Resources.

Table 4. Number of Listed Procedures followed by the libraries

Procedures listed in Table- under Item B	*libraries Following No*	*%*
All 5	3	10.0
4	3	10.0
3	5	16.7
2	4	13.3
1	7	23.3
0	8	26.7

It is seen that all the 5 listed guidelines are followed for weeding in 3 libraries, while 4 aspects are considered in 3 libraries, 3 in 5 libraries, 2 in 4 libraries.

Among the remaining 15 libraries, 7 libraries are following only one aspect and in 8 libraries none of the 5 listed guidelines are followed for weeding out E-Resources. It is known fact that any resource be it a print or electronic, at a point of time these would be outdated or got damaged. In such case their existence in the library is questionable. Therefore the libraries that are not following any criteria for De-Selection should go for the aspects that are practicable in their libraries to De-Select the E-Resources.

Table 5. Procedures Followed in Management of E-resources by College Library

College	*S.No of Procedure Listed in Table- under Item B*				
	1	*2*	*3*	*4*	*5*
BVCE	Y	Y	Y	Y	Y
VRSE	Y	Y	Y	Y	Y
CMRK	Y	Y	Y	Y	Y
JPNC		Y	Y	Y	Y
BIET	Y		Y	Y	Y
CRRE	Y		Y	Y	Y
ANIL		Y	Y		Y
VISW		Y	Y		Y
GMRI		Y	Y		Y
AITK			Y	Y	Y
CEVP	Y		Y	Y	
PRAG			Y		Y
VIVP	Y				Y
CVSR			Y		Y
MVRG	Y		Y		
GRRR					Y
GVPE					Y
PPSV					Y
BCOP					Y
MRTN					Y
GIER					Y
GNTW					Y
ADIT					
GDCL					
JAYA					

ADTP

ASRK

GOKB

PREM

VTMV

It is necessary to weed out electronic resources for various reasons in libraries. An attempt has been made to elicit information from the selected engineering college libraries on De-Selection in consideration of following aspects – Having any De-Selection (weeding) policy, whether following the guidelines for De-Selection, Non circulated materials since no of years, Materials not compatible with existing hardware or software, Outdated or inaccurate materials, Duplication of materials and Materials damaged beyond repair. It obvious from the table, most of the aspects listed for De-Selected are not being followed in selected engineering college libraries. Very few libraries have weeding policy and the guidelines listed for De-Selection are also followed rarely. It is necessary to weed out E-resources based on policy or following said guidelines, otherwise the E-Collection would be unmanageable at a point of time.

7. CONCLUSION

About 26 procedures are identified in managing e-resources in libraries and most of the libraries giving highest priority for verification of access – content-wise and by users wise. And shelving of e-resources is not been followed in most of the libraries. It is necessary to give importance to this aspect in managing electronic resources. However aspects like information literacy, communication with vendors and utilization statistics are satisfactory in studied libraries. It is necessary to follow almost all the aspects listed above, so as to manage the electronic resources successfully, to provide uninterrupted access to information available in electronic resources.

REFERENCES

1. Holly, Yu (2008). *Electronic Resource Management in Libraries: Research and Practice*, New York: IGI Global.
2. Kallinikou D., et.al (2009). Intellectual property issues for digital libraries in the internet networked publish sphere. 8th International Conference of Computer Ethics: Philosophical Enquiry, Inseit, 241-269.
3. Somasekhara Rao K. &Venkata Rao N. (2012). Electronic Resources Development Policy for Engineering College Libraries. *Collection Development in Digital Environment*, 173-179.

4

Effective Information Literacy Program in VIIT Library for Better Utilization of Library Resources

Swati Jamkar
Librarian, VIIT
Hindurao S. Waydande
Deputy Librarian & Liaison Officer for (IITB, IITG, IITI)
Central Library, IIT Bombay, Powai, Mumbai 76

ABSTRACT

In this paper awareness programs run by VIIT Library to increase utilization of subscribed e-resources is discussed. Though it is supposed as Libraries are core facilities in Academic Institutes, sometimes they are sidetracked. So Libraries must emphasize themselves to establish themselves. It is always felt that a lot more money is spent on Library Resources and services and output of Library i.e. utilization of Library resources and services is not up to the mark. Library should come forward to resolve these issues by handling various activities. All these activities are discussed here.

1. INTRODUCTION

Engineering colleges subscribe e-resources to meet requirement of UG/ PG Students, Research Pursuers as well as faculty members; even they subscribe it as their

Apex body has made it mandatory to such colleges. All these resources are huge collection of current information but it is observed that they are not utilized by users fully. There are number of reasons behind this not utilization of e-resources, one and most important reason is, users are not aware of the resources and information available to them. Second reason is utilization of exam oriented reading material and third one is attitude towards Library. These three reasons work together hand in hand. If attitude of users towards Library is changed by increasing awareness of Library resources and services, utilization of such resources will be increased. Generally it is assumed that Engineering faculty and students do not get time to visit Library and search the information due to their busy schedule. So Library needs to come forward and communicate these resources and services openly.

This paper will discuss these issues in detail:

Increasing awareness about Library resources is a continuous process that will enhance the utilization of Library resources as well as visibility of Library. Libraries should go beyond their yearly Orientation programs for this purpose. Librarians learn information literacy theoretically but it is high time to teach our users information literacy skills. If we increase communication with our users that will help them to get more resources and will save their time; this also will help Libraries in Marketing Library Services.

2. HOW LIBRARIANS SHOULD PLAN THEIR INFORMATION LITERACY PROGRAM

- Organize the Collection
- Indexing
- Plan class wise awareness program OR call it literacy training
- Make users aware about resources and how to use them to meet their requirements.

- Give some activity based on this
- Get feedback
- As per the received feedback from users make changes accordingly.

In VIIT Library OPAC is made available throughout the campus. All Library collection is organized, indexed. Group wise awareness programs are planned. Groups such as newly joined staff, department wise staff and students, Class wise students are formed for awareness program. Marketing persons from e-resource publishers called for awareness program to deliver their presentation for various subscribed e-resources. All these activities helped to increase the utilization of e-resources as well as of total collection.

Utilization of subscribed e-resources is tabulated below. All these resources are subscribed from different years so there utilization data is also vary accordingly.

Table 1. Request for Full text Articles from All subscribed Resources

E-resources	*2010*	*2011*	*2012*	*2013*	*2014*
IEEE	7014	8201	7922	8490	10209
Science Direct	2101	1739	4055	4709	5555
ASME				28	107
ASCE			1621	319	1212
ASTM DL			01	17	06
Access Engineering			53	52	165

It is seen from above table that gradual increase in utilization of all e-resources since their subscription in VIIT. It is decreased somewhere especially utilization of ASCE is reduced drastically in 2013. Library tried to fill up the gap and increase the utilization by discussing the issue in Library Committee Meetings and HOD Meetings. Faculty members were asked to give Library oriented assignments to all classes as a result of discussion in meetings. When students come to Library to complete assignments, they are guided by Library staff to find various resources. Sometimes students have been told to download paper on particular topic and submit to their faculty. Meanwhile they have been motivated by Library through Information literacy programs where they have been told about resources useful to them and utilization of them to meet requirement of their curriculum. These activities help to make users aware of all resources subscribed by Library. Simultaneously department wise usage data is regularly presented to Management that helped to motive faculty and students of each department. Results of all these activities can be viewed in this table where increase in utilization is visible. Especially if we observe utilization of IEEE database we can see how it will became the necessity of users and nowadays faculty and users of Electronic and Telecommunication give first preference to this database.

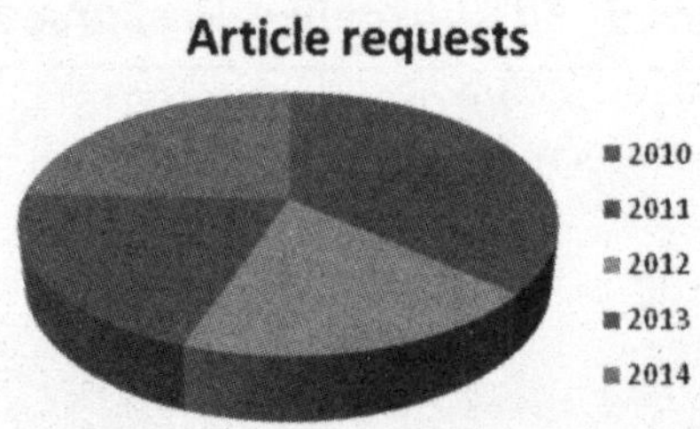

Fig. 1. Utilisation of IEEE

Same case happens with Science Direct database because it covers most of the programs run by our Institute, so this also got popular with the help of awareness program and result is as below;

Utilization of ASCE

As I told above Utilisation of ASCE is decreased in year 2013, but it is recovered up to some level by communicating with users and we are following same activity to increase other resources.

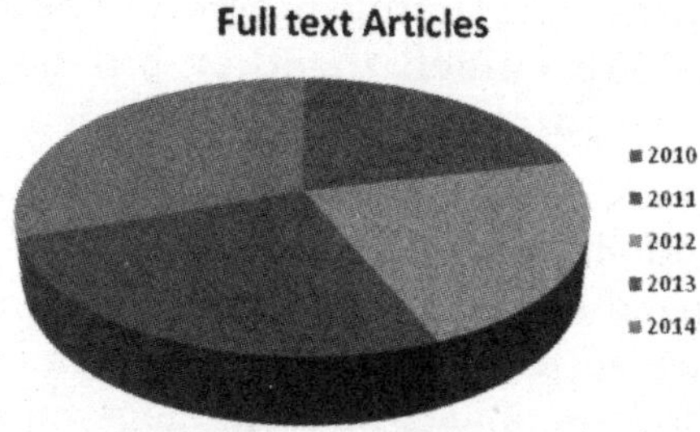

Fig. 2. Utilization of Science Direct

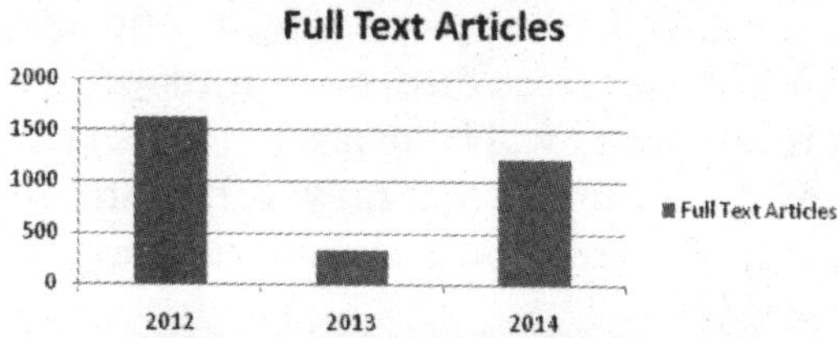

Fig. 3. Utilisation of ASCE

All e-resources are made easily accessible throughout the campus by linking their URL to online catalogue. Library also helps to Faculty members and research pursuers by providing online services. They ask their query through mail or demand full text which is send through mail. As per the users' request information is being searched for them through subscribed e-resources or other than these resources.

Every year at least 600 students get admission in VIIT. Library plan Orientation program to them. It is difficult to orient them simultaneously so they are divided into batches and oriented at different time and day. All this activity is done in coordination with First Year Engineering department. The program shows grand success on counter through increased issue/ returned data.

Sometimes person from publisher of e-resources come to the Library for user training program and solves query of faculty members. Webinar is also scheduled in coordination with renowned publisher, through this faculty got guidance about 'Publishing in Scientific

Journals'. In some training programs faculty from all departments are guided together but some training programs are separately scheduled for departments.

Increasing awareness is not A onetime activity; library has to follow it continuously because libraries are dynamic. Speed of revolution of libraries is highest at this moment so awareness activity has a lot more importance in this phase. In technology more and more information is generated and appears in digital form. Users get confused while accessing it and they may go away from information due to confusion. Awareness programs from library will be of great help to their learning process. At beginning user may reluctant to respond positively but after realization of its usability they will be responsive.

3. PLANS FOR RECENT FUTURE

It is planned that each class from each program will have subject oriented user training. They will be guided to find information to meet their syllabus need. Here Reading material is indexed with Class and subject. So class is added in access point under key word. When students use 'Class' as access point, they will get complete list of reading material required for the particular class. Reading material as per the syllabus is collectively available to them. This searching facility is available through OPAC. OPAC can be used as one point search facility to all resources. Even URLs of all subscribed resources are linked to OPAC students can view online information for their subject syllabus. They will be guided further to search information needed to complete syllabus by using subscribed and non-subscribed online information.

4. CONCLUSION

Engineering college Libraries are developed for the sake of students and Faculty members but are they really taking benefits of this development. Library must play crucial role to fill up this gap by increasing communication with users at different level. It must try to change the attitude of users towards Library. This will help not only users but Library also.

REFERENCES

1. Bopp, R. E. & Smith, L. C. (Eds.) (2001). Reference and Information Services. (3rd ed.). California: Libraries Unlimited.
2. Bridges, K. (Ed.). (2003). Expectations of Librarians in the 21st Century. London. Praeger Publishers.
3. Gorman, M. (Ed.). Technical Services Today and Tomorrow. (2nd) California: Libraries Unlimited
4. Ingersoll, P. (2004). Managing Information Technology. London. California: Libraries Unlimited
5. Ralhan, P. (2009). Advancement in Library and Information Science. (1st ed.). Jaipur: Oxford Book Co.
6. Shuman, Bruce A. (2001). Issues for Libraries and Information Science in the Internet Age. California: Libraries Unlimited.
7. Troll, Dennis A. How and Why Libraries are Changing?
8. Kumar, Sudhir (2012). Management of e-resources and Library 2.0: Issues and challenges for LIS Professionals. *Indian Journal of Information Science and Applications*, 2(1).
9. Schnell, E. (2006). Librarian 2.0 requires new skills. Retrieved on January 15, 2015 *http://ericschnell.blogspot.com/2006/03/libraria-20-requires-newskills.html*
10. Singh, R. & Sharma, R. (n.d.). Relevance of Library & Information Resources Centre in Pharmaceutical Research Development in context of New Digital era. Retrieved on January 10, 2015 *http://www.academicjournals.org/ijlis*
11. Beckman, M.(1983). Library Buildings in the network Environment. *Journal of Academic Librarianship.* 9(5).

5

E-Resources and Its Types

Satyabrata Garanayak
Santosh Kumar Bharati
MLIS Student, DLIS, B. B. Ambedkar University,
Lucknow, UP, India

ABSTRACT

Advanced Information Technology and Computer Applications during the past few decades have tremendous changes in the way of information gathered, stored, organized, accessed, retrieved and consumed. The traditional image of library is changed to digital due to the development of E- resources so old concept of acquiring information is replaced by new concept of accessing information online. This paper overview the different types of E- Resources commonly used by user.

Keywords : E- Book, E- Journal, E- Clipping, E- Databases, CD/ DVD-ROM

1. INTRODUCTION

E- Resources are nothing but the electronic versions of printed collection of resources that can be viewed online via computers, mobiles, or any other communication systems connected to the Internet. It may be online (Internet connectivity) and Offline (CD/ DVD- ROM). The user community is becoming more familiar with the new medium of resources because it gives latest and up-to date information in their respective fields.

In traditional library users have to spend more times to search a small piece of information but in the advanced library we can find and access that particular information within a single click. So it saves time, avoids duplication and smoothen services of library effectively.

2. TYPES OF E- RESOURCES

There are different types of e-resources are there. Here we discuss some of the e-resources such as e-book, e-journal, e-clipping, e-report, e-content page, e-newsletter, e-reference, e-databases, e-thesis and dissertation, CD / DVD-ROM.

2.1. E- Book

An E- Book (Electronic Book) is an electronic or digital equivalent of a printed book accessible via the web. E- Book is either read on personal computers, laptops, PDA's (Personal Digital Assistants), palmtops, CD- ROM, or any dedicated hardware handheld device known as 'E- Book Device' or 'E- Book Reader'. These can be free or may require payment. The portability, comfort, easy to read, note making and changeable font size are advantages of e-books. Figure 1 is an example of E-Book.

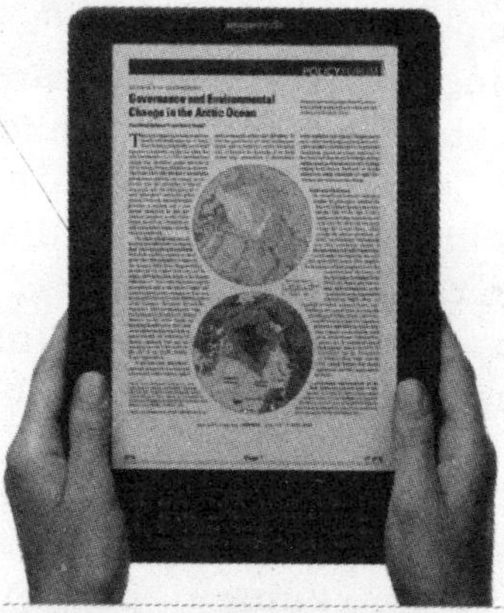

Fig. 1. e-Book Reader

Source : ***http://30daystox.com/ebook-sales/***

Fig. 2. e-Journal /

Source : *http://www.zeweb.org/index.php?post/2008/01/08/Un-nouveau-media-en-Picardie-%3A-le-e-journal*

2.2. E-Journals

E-Journals (electronic journals) are serial publication can be accessed via electronic transmission using computer, or any other communication technologies media etc. It is also known as online journals, e-periodicals, e- zincs, virtual journals, paperless journals, scholarly e- journals, networked journals and CD- ROM journals etc. Some electronic journals are online journals only; some are online versions of printed journals, and some consist of the online equivalent of a printed journal. One of the most important benefits is that multiple users at a one location can access the same article at the same time. Some e- journals are free and others are subscription basis. Figure 2 is an example of E- Journal.

2.3. E-Clippings

Clipping is the cutting-out of articles from a newspaper or magazines. E-Clippings are the retrospective search and comprehensive analysis of printed news items accessible via internet. It facilitates the users to retrieve news clips for future reference. It contains important news clips (Research and development, Science and technologies, sports, important invention, persons and animal etc.). The news items are archived into server and users have the option to view them by specific date, duration or news sources. News clippings are updated on a daily, weekly, monthly or quarterly basis. Figure 3 is an example of E- clipping.

Fig. 3. Press clipping

Source : http://active-insights.com/Press-Clippings/

4. E-REPORTS

Reports may refer to specific periods, events, occurrences or subject and may be communicated or presented in oral or written form. These can be represented in graphic, tabular, pie chart etc. These reports are scanned and converted to searchable PDF documents. Then these are classified according to subject categories and achieved in a server; detailed entry is made in a database for facilitating search. Figure 4 is an example of E- Report.

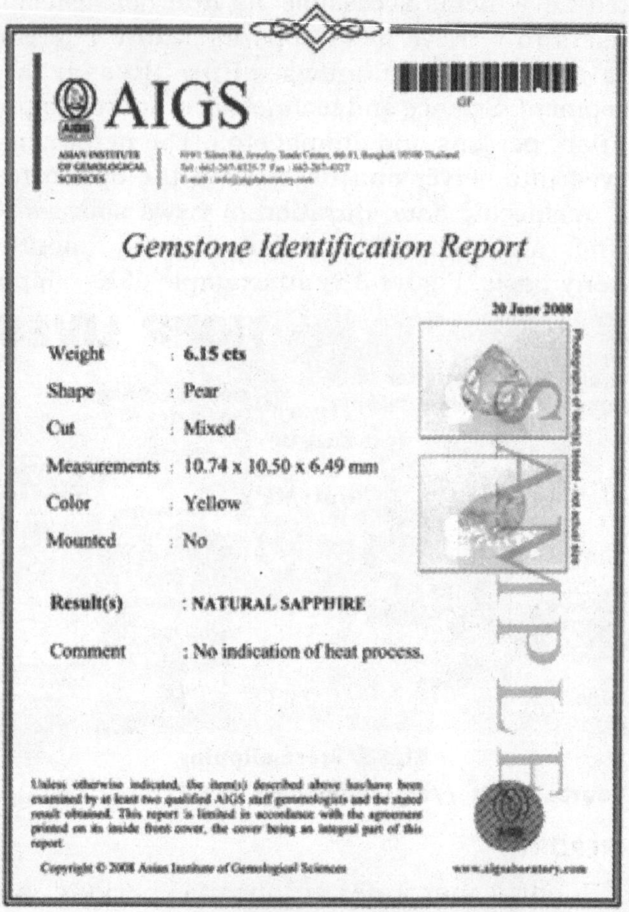

AIGS

ASIAN INSTITUTE OF GEMOLOGICAL SCIENCES

Gemstone Identification Report

20 June 2008

Weight	: **6.15 cts**
Shape	: Pear
Cut	: Mixed
Measurements	: 10.74 x 10.50 x 6.49 mm
Color	: Yellow
Mounted	: No
Result(s)	: **NATURAL SAPPHIRE**
Comment	: No indication of heat process.

SAMPLE

Unless otherwise indicated, the item(s) described above has/have been examined by at least two qualified AIGS staff gemmologists and the stated result obtained. This report is limited in accordance with the agreement printed on its inside front cover, the cover being an integral part of this report.

Copyright © 2008 Asian Institute of Gemological Sciences www.aigslaboratory.com

Fig. 4. AIGS Lab report

Source : http://www.glitteringstones.com/AIGS-lab-report.htm

5. E-CONTENT PAGE

E-Content page is the digital content such as text and images of books, journals, periodicals, conference proceedings designed for display on web pages. It provides desktop access to the digitized content. It helps the users to searching and browsing content pages on web. The textual information on content page can be processed using OCR method in order to provide full search option on content pages of documents. There are many file formats to represent E- content page such as PDF, JPEG, GIF, TIF etc. Figure 5 is an example of E- Content page.

CONTENTS

MAKING SANTA LOOK STINGY, JANUARY 2011

Fig. 5. FHM Content page

Source: https://www.behance.net/gallery/3565375/FHM-contents-pages

Fig. 6. e-Newsletter

Source: http://www.waveinternet.com/Item/Marketing-eNewsletter

6. E-NEWSLETTER

Electronic magazine (e-zine) is another name of E-newsletter. If text only, the e- zine is an 'E- Newsletter' and if published on website, it is a 'Webzine'. It is disseminated to users via email on web. E- Zine requires users to sign in as a member whether it is free or subscription basis. It is mostly used in Business Sectors, Research organization, Government Sectors. Figure 6 is an example of E- Newsletter.

7. E-REFERENCE

Reference sources are meant for casual consultation. These are encyclopedias, dictionaries, geographical sources, biographical sources, year- books/ almanacs, directories and handbooks. All the reference sources which are provided in electronic form called e-reference. It is very useful to refer the relevant matter. It saves time of users to search the required document and satisfy the 4th law of library science 'save the time of users'. It searches the alternative of the given matter. Figure 7 is an example of E-Reference.

Fig. 7. Image of e-encyclopedia

Source : http://www.amazon.in/Oxford-Encyclopedia-British-Literature-reference/dp/0195169212

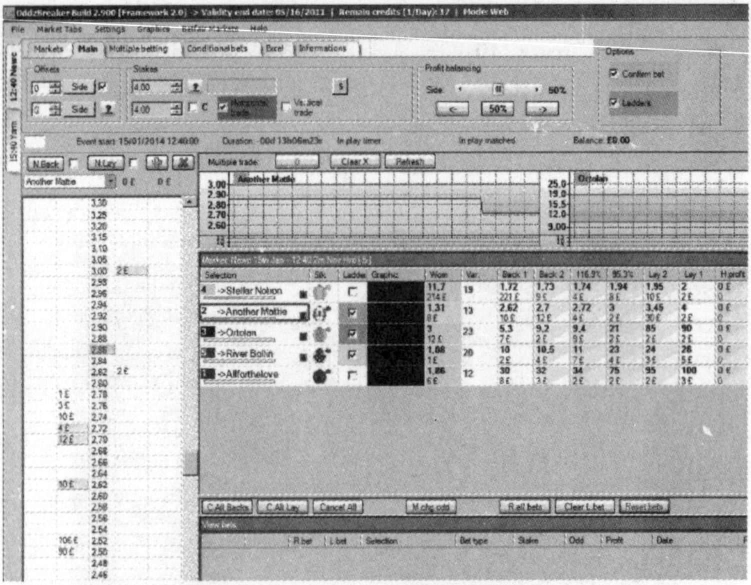

Fig. 8. Image of e-book database

Source : http://images.directoryofshareware.com/full/oddzbreaker_home_e-books_information_databases-58924.gif

8. E-DATABASES

A database is an organized collection of data or information in a machine- readable form that can be accessed by computer or any other supporting electronic devices. According to Chambers Science and Technology Dictionary the definition of database is "*A collection of structured data independent of any particular application*". The information of an e- database can be searched and retrieved electronically. Its main objective is to keep record and maintain information so that it can make the search easy and fast. It comprise of records in a particular subject or multidisciplinary subject areas.

Database mainly divided into 2 types- Full text Databases and Bibliographic Databases. Full- text databases contain the whole content of an article such as citation information, text, illustration, diagrams and tables. Bibliographic databases only contain citation information of an article, such as author name, journal title, publication date and page number. Figure 8 is an example of E- Database.

9. E-THESES AND DISSERTATIONS

A thesis or dissertation is a primary work for doctoral or master's degree respectively, which represents the research findings in a specific field. An ETD (Electronic Theses and Dissertations) is simply the digital representation of printed thesis or dissertations submitted, archived, or accessed primarily in electronic formats. It can be available in hypertext and multimedia formats. Figure 9 is an example of ETD.

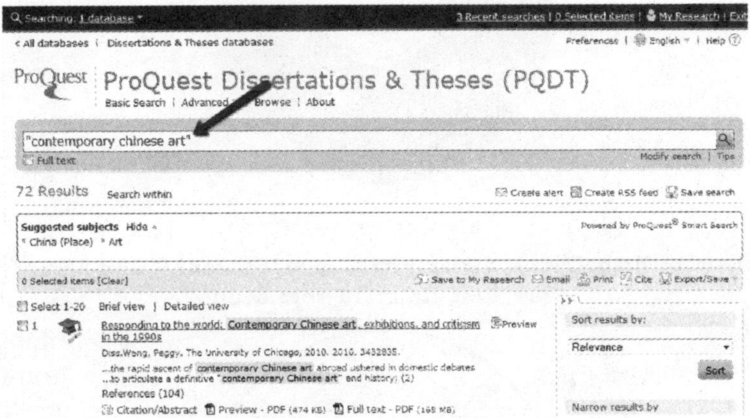

Fig. 9. Image of ETD

Source: http://nylibrary.sia.edu/sp/subjects/guide.php?subject=ChineseCont

10. CD/ DVD- ROM

CD/ DVD- ROM have become one of the best, powerful tools for storing and retrieving of huge amount of information in libraries and information centers. These are the offline form of e- resource. It was firstly introduced in 1985. The full form of CD- ROM is Compact Disk Read Only Memory. The 'ROM' part of the term means the data on the disk is read only or can't be altered or erased. It is the great media format for retail software. The capacity of CD-ROM is about 700 MB.

DVD stands for digital Video Disk or Digital Versatile Disk. It is an optical disk that can store large quantities of digital materials such as sound, images, and data. It stores large data as compared to CD. The capacity of DVD-ROM is about 4.3 GB.

Fig. 10. CD-ROM

Source: http://www.digiampietro.com/content/i_and_linux/my_first_linux_cd_rom.html

Fig. 11. DVD

Source: http://www.dpworkshop.org/dpm-eng/oldmedia/pages/dvd.html

11. CONCLUSION

Due to the changing and growing information environment most of the users will be in favour of e-resource due to its portability, convenience, small space and sharing of information from any part of the world within a small time. There is large no of e- resources are published so we should conscious about the relevancy of the matter. Copyright is one of the big issues in e-resources. Libraries are the essential central component of an education system. Different University libraries in world provide e- resources to their students. Some rare print materials, manuscripts are converted into electronic form due to easy long term conservation and preservation. In comparison to e- resources and print resources there are some advantages or disadvantages but if we analyses the readability of print and electronic, print (hardcopy) is maximum used anywhere in the world.

REFERENCES

1. Eason, K., Richardson, S. & Yu, L. (2000). Patterns of use of electronic journals, *Journal of Documentation*, 49(4), 356-69.
2. Mittal, P. &Bala, M. (2013). E-Resources selection principles. *International journal of advanced research in computer science and software engineering*, 3(3), Retrieved from www.ijarcsse.com/docs/papers/Volume_3/3_March2013/V3I3-0363.pdf
3. Rani, P. P. &Geetha, J. (2007). Electronic resources in the modern libraries: a new path. In *5th International CALIBER - 2007, Punjab University, Chandigarh*, 696- 701. Retrieved from http://ir.inflibnet.ac.in/bitstream/1944/1444/1/696-701.pdf
4. Chauhan, K. &Mahapatra, R. K. (2011). A Comprehensive Evaluation of Facilities and Features of free E- Resources in Library and Information Science. *VSRD-TNTJ*, 2(10), 505-524. Retrieved from http://www.vsrdjournals.com/vsrd/Issue/2011_10_Oct/Web/2_Koushal_Chauhan_491_Research_Article_Oct_2011.pdf

5. Sadeh, T. &Ellingsen, M. (2005). Electronic resource management system: the need and the realization. New Delhi: Emerald group publishing limited, 1- 12. Retrieved from www.exlibrisgroup.com/files/Publications/ERMSystems.pdf

6. Johnson, S., Evensen, O. G. & et.al. (Jan 2012). Key issues for e-resource collection development: a guide for libraries. *International Federation of Library Associations and Institutions*, 1- 31. Retrieved from www.ifla.org/files/assets/.../electronic-resource-guide-2012.pdf

7. Habiba, U. & Chowdhury, S. (2012).Use of electronic resources and its impact: a study of Dhaka University Library users. *The Eastern Librarian*, 23(1), 74- 90. Retrieved from http://www.bdresearch.org/home/attachments/article/nArt/371_USE%20OF%20ELECTRONIC%20RESOURCES%20AND%20ITS%20IMPACT.pdf

6

E-Resources of Central Library at Central University of Bihar Patna Campus: A Case Study

Md. Arshad Ali
Junior Professional Assistant Central Library, University of Bihar, (CUB) Patna - 800 014, Bihar

Asheesh Kamal
Assistant Librarian, School of Planning and Architecture (SPA), Vijayawada - 521104, A.P.

ABSTRACT

This paper focuses on utility of e-resources for academic library users at Central University of Bihar; Patna campus. Now a day library serves knowledge communication through e-resources, in the Academic era, very strong relationship between user and e-resources for research, study and new innovations purpose. E-resources can save the time and increase the ability of research the new information. E-resources are one of the best assets for research scholars and faculty. The explosion of e-resources and increased use by the end users in the field of education, research, teaching-learning and find new facts. In this case study to examine the usage of e-resources at Central Library, Central University of Bihar. The study revealed that research scholar respondents the first position of searching e-resources, faculty respondents the second position, PG students respondents the third position and UG students respondents the forth position. In this study access facilities improve with high speed internet.

Keywords : Researcher Perception, User study, Databases, e-resources, CUB Patna.

1. INTRODUCTION

A survey is conducted to assess the E-resources of the users of Central Library, CUB (UG students, PG students, faculty and Research Scholars), to understand awareness of information sources among users, methods of searching information systematically from print and e-resources by the users, information mining, information evaluation, information usage etc. To analyze the E-resources of Central Library user's questionnaires were prepared for UG students, PG students, faculty and Research Scholars were distributed in the Central Library, CUB. This survey helped in analyzing the E-resources of users. The questionnaire for the library staff was also prepared and circulated to library professional of Central Library, CUB to understand the status of the Central Library. Today traditional library become modern library as well as virtual library, paperless and Digital library due to e-resources.

2. WHAT ARE E-RESOURCES?

The document that are in electronic form are said to be electronic resources. The term electronic resources came into usage in late 1980's when first electronic journals came into being. The electronic resources are not single entities. It includes various types of resources such as e-books, e-journals, e-databases, digital archives and internet resources. Thus, those resources are available in the electronic form and access through intranet/internet/standalone computer known as e-resources or electronic resources.

2.1. Categories of e-resources

E-resources distributed into various categories, At Central library of central university of Bihar e-resources. Like e-journals, e-books, e-databases, e-reports, e-newspapers etc. These e-resources are very useful for users and easy to access and dissemination.

Table 1. Categories of e-resources

Name of e- resources	*Uses*
Electronic journals	Researcher/faculty can find new concepts for research purpose
Electronic books	latest books can find through e-books
Electronic Databases	Full text database
Electronic Reports	Report on Census, NSSO or others available through electronically
E-Thesis	All the thesis available online through OPAC
CDs & DVDs	Some CDs available for data collection
Digital Library	D-Space (Institutional Repositories)
Electronic Newspapers	CUB OPAC have links of freely e-newspapers available

3. CENTRAL LIBRARY OF CENTRAL UNIVERSITY OF BIHAR (CUB) PATNA CAMPUS-BRIEF STORY

The Central University of Bihar (CUB) is one amongst the newly founded fifteen Central Universities by the Government of India under the enactment of the Central Universities Act, 2009 (Section 25 of 2009). The University is presently located at the premises of Birla Institute of Technology- Patna (BIT Campus, P.O.- B. V. College, Patna – 800 014). Permanent location of the University is under consideration of the Central Government. The University made its beginning by establishing the Centre for Development Studies under the School of Social Sciences and Policy and launched a two years Masters Programmed in Development Studies in the academic session 2009 – 2010.

3.1. Resources of Central Library, CUB Patna Campus

The University believes that Library is the most important element in the facilities of an educational institution and hence the Central University of Bihar has developed a well-equipped Central Library for both the campuses (Patna and Gaya) to cater the information requirements of students and faculties for their academic accomplishments.

The Library has built a balanced collection of more than 18,800 books (Patna and Gaya) to support academic curricula, teaching and research in various science and social science subjects. All the books are barcoded and are organized on shelves using Dewey decimal classification scheme. An Online Public Access Catalogue (OPAC) of library books is made available for students, faculties and officials on every computer in the University premises. The Central Library is presently having 10 staff working in both the campuses.

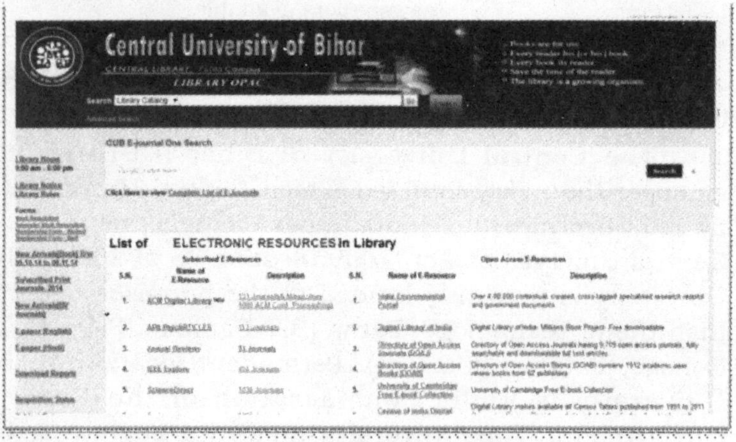

Fig. 1. OPAC of Central Library, CUB Patna campus.
Source: www.cub.ac.in

3.2. E-Resources of Central Library, CUB Patna Campus

The library subscribes renowned publishers from across the world and more than 8,500 online journals. Being a member of UGC-Infonet Digital Library Consortium, more than 4000 e-journals are available to the Central library from Springer, Taylor & Francis, Annual Reviews, Project Muse, Wiley-Blackwell, Oxford University Press, Cambridge University Press and ScienceDirect's 10 subject collections from Elsevier Inc. Library also subscribed to various e-journals packages i.e. IEEE (ASPP+ POP) from IEEE and ACM Digital Library Package from ACM, USA for Computer Science, PsycARTICLES from American Psychological Association (APA) for Psychological Sciences. Besides, library also subscribes many online databases, MathSciNet–a bibliographic database for mathematical sciences; JSTOR - full-text database mainly for social sciences,Manupatra-full text database for Law, Indiastat – a statistical databasefor development studies and JCCC – a general purpose bibliographic database.

This Central Library have *CUB E-journals one search* like Goggle and find out any e-Journals /Articles which subscribed by library just given keywords or terms which you want to search. This is really very helpful and convenient for all the users and easily retrieves their information.

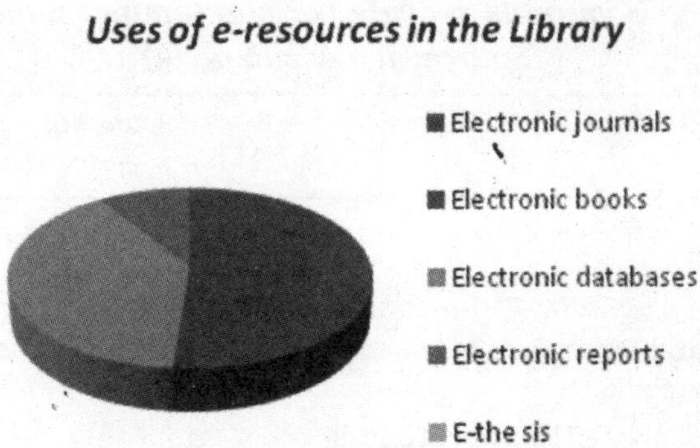

Fig. 2. Uses of e-resources in the library
Source: www.cub.ac.in

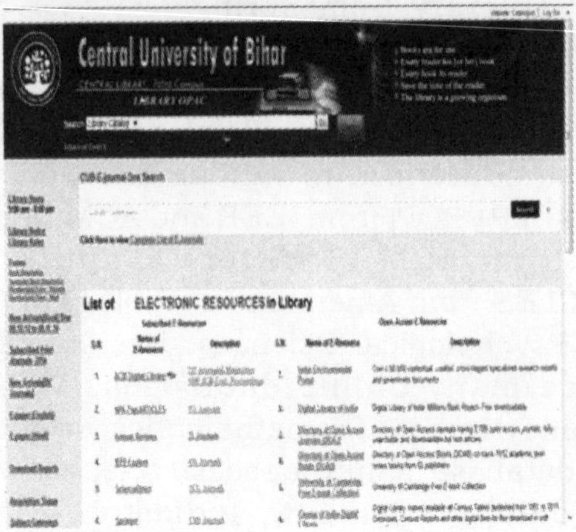

Fig. 3. CUB E-journals one search (Screenshot of OPAC from www.cub.ac.in)

The Research Scholars and faculty are aware of e-resources like e-books, e-journals, e-databases availability in libraries.

4. CENTRAL LIBRARY SUBSCRIBES MORE THAN 8500 E-JOURNALS FROM VARIOUS REPUTED PUBLISHERS AS MENTIONED BELOW:

Table 2. e-journals provide various reputed publishers (Source: www.cub.ac.in)

Sl. No.	*Name of the E-Resources*	*Quantity*	*Total downloaded*
1.	ACM Digital Library	131 Journal and 1000 Conference Proceedings	72
2.	Annual Reviews (33 Full Text E-Journals)	33	0
3.	APA PsycARTICLES (113 Full Text E-Journals)	113	83
4.	Cambridge University Press (224 Full Text E-Journals)	224	0
5.	Economic and Political Weekly (1 E-journal)	1	0

6.	IEEE Explore (ASPP+POP - 416 full text e-journalsand Conference Proceedings)	416	0
7.	JSTOR (2072 full text E-journals)	2072	2141
8.	Oxford University Press(202 full text E-Journals)	202	0
9.	Portland Press (10 e-journals for Science)	10	3699
10.	Project Muse (493 full text E-journals)	493	0
11.	ScienceDirect (1036 full text E-journals)	1036	0
12.	Sage HSS Package (Access to 482 e-journals for 2013 only)	482	0
13.	SIAM Journals (17 full text E-journals)	17	0
14.	Springer (1389 full text e-journals)	1389	0
15.	Taylor & Francis (1173 full text e-journals)	1173	0
16.	Wiley Blackwell (908 full text E-journals)	908	3161
17.	Nature Biotechnology (1 full text E-journal)	1	1585
18.	Journal of Immunology (1 full text E-journal)	1	1418
19.	The Plant Cell (1 full text E-journal)	1	0
20.	The Plant Physiology (1 full text E-journal)	1	0
21.	Transactions of the American Mathematical Society (1 full text E-journal)	1	0
22.	Journal of Biological Chemistry (1 full text E-journal)	1	0
23.	Cell Stem Cell (1 full text E-journal)	1	0
	E-Resource Management package	8576	12159

Average number of e-resources downloaded/printed are download per month are 529.

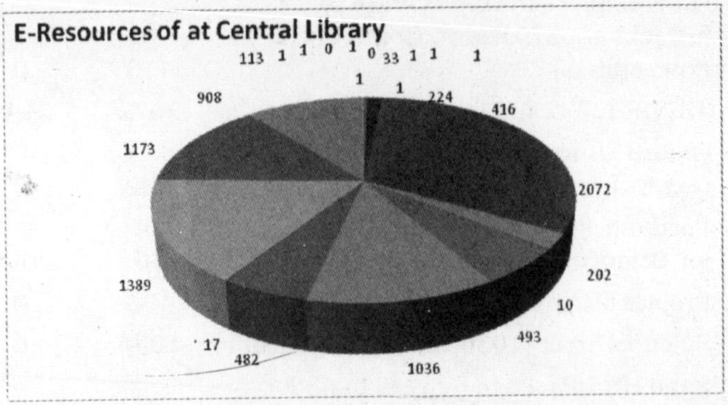

Fig. 4. E-Resources of Central Library
(Source: www.cub.ac.in)

Portland Press, Wiley Blackwell, JSTOR e-journals are mostly downloaded whereas Annual Reviews, Cambridge University Press, Oxford University Press etc. not to be single downloaded during this period.

4.1. Central Library subscribes Online Databases from various reputed publishers as mentioned below:

1. JGATE- An E-Journals Gateway to Indian Universities and Colleges [Bibliographic Database]
2. MathSciNet [Bibliographic Database]
3. indiastat.com [Full text Database]
4. Manupatra [Full text Database for Law]

5. STUDY REPORT ON EXAMINATION TIME NO. OF ARTICLES DOWNLOADS/PRINTED CENTRAL LIBRARY, CUB

E-Resources of Central Library of Central University of Bihar Number of Articles downloads/Print status monthly But at the time of examination *May and June (321 & 456)* number of articles downloaded more than other month. Statuses of the downloaded Articles are as follows with graph.

Table 3. No. of articles downloads / Print
(Source from www.cub.ac.in)

Month	*No. of Articles downloads/Printed*
January,14	0
February,14	0
March,14	147
April,14	258
May,14	321
June,14	456
July,14	90
August,14	254
September,14	112
October,14	213
November,14	128
December,14	106

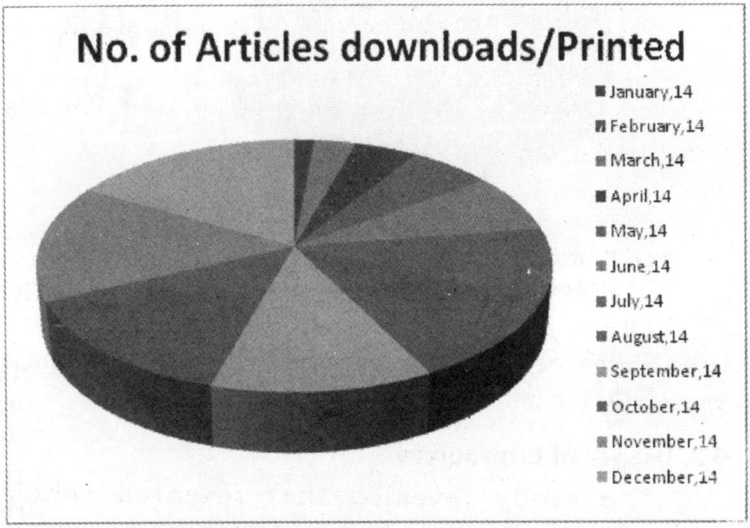

Fig. 5. No. of Articles downloads/Printed
(Source from www.cub.ac.in)

Maximum number of articles mostly downloaded and printed in the month of May and June, 2014, whereas in the month of January & February, 2014 no download was resported as mentioned in the Table 3.

5.1. Open Access

Table 4. Open Access

Open access to users	*No. of respondents*	*%*
Yes	80	100
No	0	0
Total	80	100

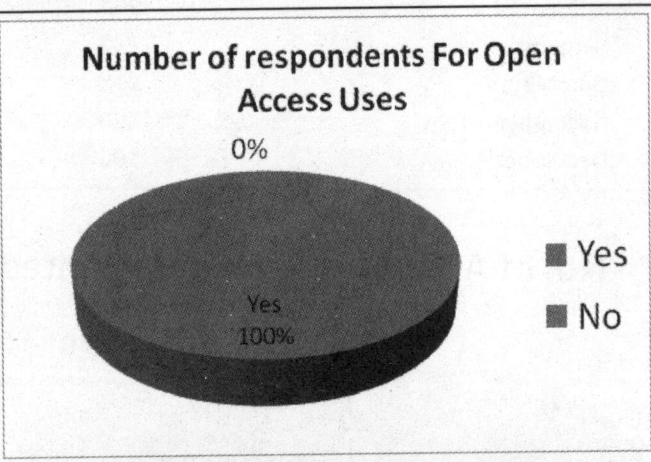

Fig. 6. Number of respondents for open Access uses (Source: e-journals from www.cub.ac.in)

All the faculty of management institutes surveyed uses open access resources available for various purposes especially for teaching and research.

5.2. Usages of E-resources

The study revealed that research scholar respondents the first position of searching e-resources, faculty respondents the second position, PG students respondents the third position and UG students respondents the forth position.

Table 5. Usage of E-resources (source: www.cub.ac.in)

Respondents	*Usage of e-resources (%)*
Research Scholars	45
Faculty	32
PG Students	16
UG Students	7
Total	100

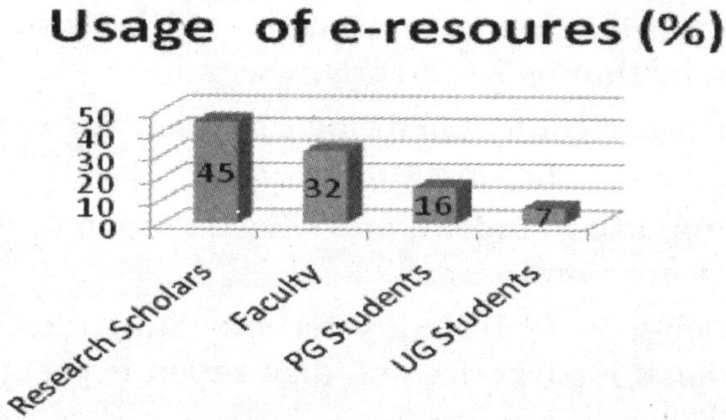

Fig. 7. Usages of E-resources (Source: www.cub.ac.in)

The Research Scholars and faculty are aware of e-resources like e-books, e-journals, e-databases availability in libraries.

5.3. Digital Library of Central Library, CUB, Patna Campus

Fig. 8. Digital Library of Central Library, CUB (Source: http://10.0.3.200/xmlui/)

Digital Libraries are generally found on the Internet. Materials in a digital library may have been digitized using a scanner.

The objectives of an institutional repository are:

- Managing and measuring research and teaching activities;
- Facilitating the development & sharing of digital teaching materials.
- to provide open access to create global visibility for an institution's scholarly research
- to collect content in a single location and to store & preserve other institutional digital assets.
- Supporting student, providing access to theses and dissertations

Therefore, CUB library recently start the D-space institutional repositories and digitization is going on.

6. ADVANTAGE OF E-RESOURCES

- E-journal can be searched quick and easy often through the complete full text of articles.
- Electronic Journals are speedy scientific communication process, Interactive, easy to search for articles by a particular author or on a particular topic or any specific information anywhere in the text, Available 24 hours a day, 7 days a week.
- Ability to do full text search across a huge number of resources in one Search
- Ability to download, print, or send the desired document instantly (easily manipulate data to suit your need as long as you acknowledge source. i.e. can cut/paste/undo/redo)
- Currency, quality and timeliness of the information
- Convenience of accessing articles any time from your own computer/Home/anywhere

- Ability to link directly to additional resources or related content.
- The ability to deliver video, animation, 3-D images, and links to the abstracts or full text of other journals articles.
- They can easily be merged with alerting services, Support multimedia and Link to other pages on the internet.
- They don't need library space nor shelving costs nor can they be stolen from the library.

7. CONCLUSION

The Central University of Bihar, Patna is the highly established institute which is well known for quality research and academic activities. The study sought to get the overview of researcher perception on e-resources by taking sample from various sections. The choice of collection should meet the need and requirements of the end user. Consequently, Assistant librarians must be aware of how the researchers seek information utilizing e-resources. The libraries should develop necessary tools to provide such services to their users satisfactorily. It is recommended that library staff or Assistant librarians focus on assisting users to develop a better image for the library. Staff should help researchers to improve their electronic based information and in finding the types of information they need.

REFERENCES

1. Sinha, M., Singha, G., & Sinha, B. (2011). Usage of Electronic Resources Available Under UGC-INFONET Digital Library Consortium by Assam University Library Users. In *8th International CALIBER 2011,* 490-510. doi: http://ir.inflibnet.ac.in/bitstream/1944/1642/1/50.pdf
2. Thanuskodi, S. (2011). Usage of Electronic Resources at Dr. T.P.M. Library, Madurai KamarajUniversty: A Case Study. *DESIDOC Journal of Library & Information Technology, 31*(6),

437-445. doi : *http://www.publications.drdo.gov.in/ojs/index.php/djlit/article/download/1318/566*

3. Kumar, A. (2012). Researcher Perception on E-Resources at BabasahebBhimraoAmbedkarUniversty (A Central University), Lucknow: A Study. *International Refereed Research Journal,* 3(1)), 85-91. doi: *http://www.publications.drdo.gov.in/ojs/index.php/djlit/article/download/1318/566.*
4. CUB Patna. (2015). Retrieved January 06, 2015 from *http://www.cub.ac.in.*
5. CUB Patna. OPAC. (2015). Retrieved 06, 2015 from *http://10.0.3.8/ .*
6. CUB Patna. Digital Library. (2015). Retrieved 06, 2015 from *http://10.0.3.200/xmlui.*

Effective Searching and Discovery

7

Dubai Electricity & Water Authority (DEWA)'s Smart Library: A Case Study on Customized Electronic Library for Government Authority

Renukaradhya N. Shivanna
Senior Executive Knowledge Management
Dubai Electricity & Water Authority (DEWA),
Government of Dubai, UAE

ABSTRACT

DEWA's Smart Library provides its staff with 24-hour access to external technical and business information from the world's leading publishers. Established by DEWA's Knowledge Management (KM) Section, the Smart Library (E-Library) supports the Smart Government initiative launched by HH Sheikh Mohammed bin Rashid Al Maktoum, Vice President and Prime Minister of the UAE and Ruler of Dubai.

The Smart Library provides a wide range of resources in different fields including: power and water, science, engineering, management, training, environment, health and safety, and quality. The content has been selected to meet the needs of DEWA's employee and the business. The selection was made after consultations with key subject matter experts from across the organization and will be reviewed annually to ensure that it remains current and relevant to DEWA and its changing needs.

Any users can search and view bibliographic details, but for the time being accessing/ downloading of complete e-books, e-journals and articles is restricted to registered DEWA employees only. DEWA Employees can access the Smart Library (E-Library) using desktops, laptops, tablets, and other smart devices inside and outside of DEWA's offices to help them with their work and professional development.

Keywords : Smart Library, Electronic Library, Discovery, Authentication, Knowledge Resources

1. INTRODUCTION

DEWA was established in 1992 by a degree issued by H.H. Sheikh Maktoum bin Rashid Al Maktoum to merge the Dubai Electricity Company and the Dubai Water Department, which had been operating individually. Both these organizations were established in 1959 at the initiative of H.H. Sheikh Rashid bin Saeed Al Maktoum, as government-supported bodies with the objective of providing an adequate and reliable supply of electricity and water to the people of Dubai (DEWA, 2012).

Since its incorporation DEWA has become an inspiring success story; known for its efficiency and reliability in every facet of its operations. Constant planning and forecast to meet growing demands of customers has always been DEWA's central philosophy. This enabled the Authority in coming a long way to serve the customers, making its own contribution to the economic growth of Dubai.

The decision to launch the Smart Library (E-Library) is based on DEWA's direction toward becoming a smart organization when providing its services to all stakeholders, which include its employees. As of now, downloading/accessing full text document from DEWA Smart Library is restricted to employees only, the general public still can do search and view bibliographic records.

DEWA's Smart Library initiative was linked to one

of the DEWA's Strategic Objective - "Skilled and experienced workforce with effective KM" under the Perspective - "Support, Learning & Growth" of DEWA's Corporate Strategy Plan for the years 2014 to 2018 (DEWA, 2014).

Establishment of DEWA's Smart Library was also based on the employees' long term demand to access the latest and the best knowledge resources, information, standards and technical reports, and to reach the highest level of development both professionally and personally in order to contribute to the organizational creativity and innovation.

2. BACKGROUND

The idea for Smart Library was emerged out after a team comprising of employees from Knowledge Management, Benchmark and Partnership Sections of DEWA jointly conducted several benchmark visits to University Libraries namely United Arab Emirates University, Al Ain, American University of Dubai and Sharjah, as well as Dubai Health Authority, Dubai Municipality and ENOC (Emirates National Oil Company).

Apart from the understanding of how these Universities and Organizations manages both their physical and electronic knowledge resources, these bench mark visits also provided key contacts of relevant vendors who are in the UAE market dealing with such products and services.

DEWA invited these vendors to its office to conduct their product demonstrations and also asked them to provide proposals for Smart Library for DEWA.

3. SMART LIBRARY CORE COMMITTEE

The first major hurdle faced by the KM Section was to select the appropriate Electronic Resources for this Smart Library. Hence, a "Smart Library Core Committee" was formed; where key 2-3 Subject Matters experts across all divisions of DEWA were carefully chosen. As these Committee members were nominated by their respective divisional heads, thus providing the complete authority to them to select all relevant Electronic Resources required for their divisions.

Fig. 1. View of Exclusive trial session for committee member

Exclusive trail sessions were organized for these Committee members as well as provided 1 to 3months of testing of various electronic resources and products, wherever it was possible. Finally, these Committee members provided their recommendation on the following:

1. Types of Resources
2. Subject Areas
3. Electronic Resources

4. LICENSING

Being a Government entity, any products or services procured for DEWA should have proper license agreement. This has become second major hurdle faced by the KM Section. Fortunately, the DEWA's Legal Section came into help and reviewed each license from respective intended Electronic Resources providers and modified those terms and conditions which enabled these

Electronic Resources providers to conduct business with DEWA.

5. TENDERING AND PURCHASE

Although the required types of resources and Electronic Resources providers were selected by the "Smart Library Core Committee" members, the third major hurdle faced by the KM Section was to follow the tendering procedure to procure these resources and products. The KM Section successfully did the call for tendering and completed the procurement of the Smart Library products and services.

6. IMPLEMENTATION OF DEWA SMART LIBRARY

Fig. 2. A snapshot of DEWA Smart Library portal

DEWA Smart Library was established jointly in partnership with one of the leading knowledge service provider in UAE. This partner acted as a mediator between DEWA and Electronic Resources providers. Although DEWA had a license agreement with each of the Electronic Resources providers, all technical issues and final payments were done through this partner.

As soon as the purchase order was issued to the partner, a project team was formed representing from members of KM and IT Section of DEWA and members from partner.

The entire implementation of DEWA Smart Library was carried out as a Project by following the fundamentals of Project Management Principles. The project was initiated with a Project Kick-off meeting, where the project team gathered to discuss and approved the project plan. The project was executed as defined in the approved plan, with regular weekly meeting and interactions among the project team members.

As a part of the DEWA Smart Library, a Portal (*http://www.dewa-elibrary.ae/*) was developed, which acted as a gateway to the world of information for the end user. The Portal consists of following sections:

1. E-Resources : This section lists out all the publishers, with whom DEWA has purchase/ subscriptions for eBooks. DEWA employee can directly go to the any of the respective publishers by clicking on them. However, in order to access the full text document, they need to register first.

2. E-Journals : All the electronic journals subscribed DEWA, could be browsed alphabetically by title from this section. There are 2 search options, where in the 1st option, one can enter their search keyword and also select any of the 4 dropdown filters, namely "Title begins with" or "Title equals" or "Title contains all words" or "ISSN equals". In the 2nd option, one can search by selecting subject category of their interest.

3. DEWA KM : This section was dedicated to provide all details about KM Section of DEWA. Apart from providing brief information on various initiatives/activities on Knowledge Management, this section also provides DEWA's KM Section strategies, policies and approaches.

4. FAQs : As the name suggests, this section

provides answers to the most frequently asked questions such as How to register and login?", "How to browse and search?" and much more.

5. Support : This section provides users with the "Submit form" to inform about any technical issues or problems that they are facing while using DEWA Smart Library. For example, they are unable to access or download the full document from the DEWA Smart Library even after entering all the correct credentials.

6. KM Updates : Weekly news updates related to the DEWA's KM Section, Knowledge Center and E-Library activities are provided under this section.

7. Contact Us : DEWA employee could get in touch with the KM Section regarding any general queries on DEWA Smart Library using the "Submit form" in this section.

Apart from the above sections, the Home page of the Portal provides options the following:

1. Registration : DEWA employee, who has official DEWA e-mail ID could do one time registration by filling up the "Submit form" available in this page. There is a proper authentication system built in order to avoid any unauthorized users would be able to register and get access to the full documents. In this page, also "Copyright" related information is provided so that the DEWA employee can read and safeguard themselves against any breach or infringement.

2. Search : One of the important features of the DEWA Smart Library is its "Search". By entering any keyword of user choice and clicking on the "Search" button, then the search engine (discovery service) will search for that keyword from all DEWA subscribed collections (Electronic Resources) from all the publishers at the same time. Once the search result page appears, the user will have lots of filters to further refine the search such as "Content Type/Format", "Discipline/Categories",

"Publication Date Slider" to name a few at the left side of the search result page. On the right side of the search result page, user can see definition of the search term from Wikipedia as well as Related Topics. In the middle of the search result page, there will be list of search result titles. Upon clicking on the title of choice, the user will be asked to provide his/her credentials to download the complete full text document. User has the option of downloading the PDF version of the document or viewing the HTML version of the full text.

3. Recommended Reading : This section highlights important books from a particular publisher once in a month.

4. Ask a Librarian : This section enables user to ask questions on anything related to content on this Smart Library and/or Knowledge Centers (Libraries) of DEWA.

Once the DEWA Smart Library Portal was developed, customized as per the requirement, and all the contents were uploaded, a proper user testing was conducted. After rectifying the issues faced during the testing, the DEWA Smart Library was officially launched to all the employees of DEWA. Further, the entire project activity was closed, lessons learnt were documented and final payment was made to all the Electronic Resources providers through the DEWA partner for this project.

7. PROMOTION OF DEWA SMART LIBRARY

1. Launch e-mail : The first major promotion activity was done by circulating the official e-mail to all the DEWA employees about the launching of DEWA Smart Library.

2. Brochure and Registration Guides : A brochure on DEWA Smart Library and registration guides were developed and circulated to all the DEWA employees through e-mail. Also hard copies of these materials were kept in all the Knowledge Centers (Libraries) of DEWA.

3. Awareness sessions : Conducted awareness

campaigns across all major DEWA divisions and locations.

Fig. 3. Register window for promotion

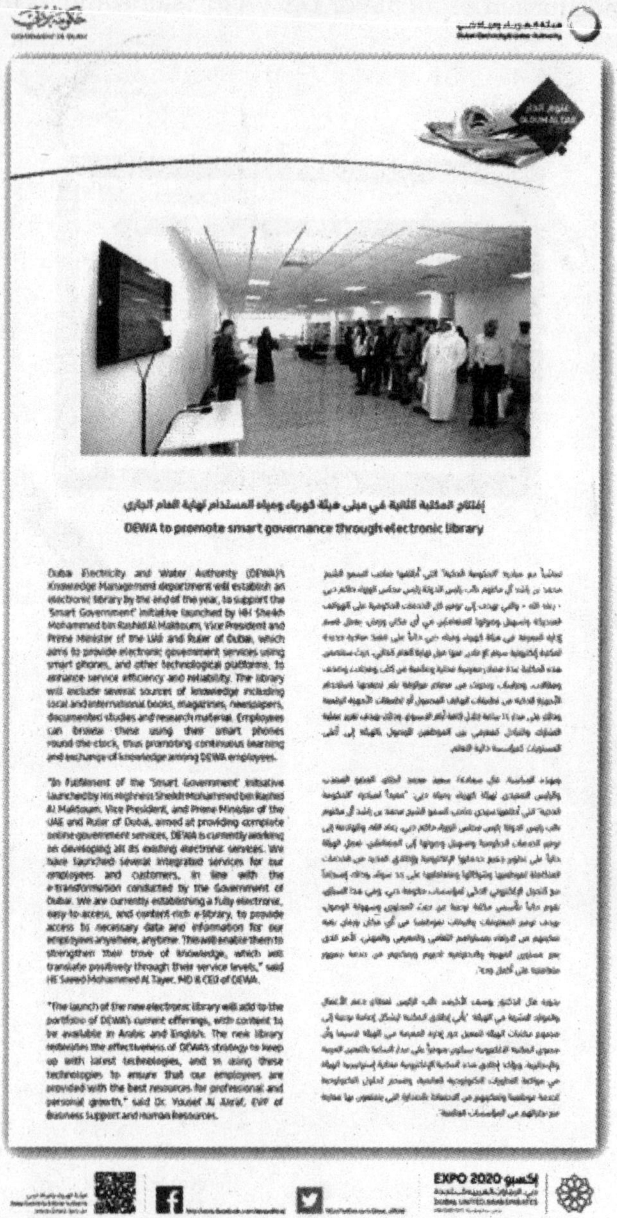

DEWA to promote smart governance through electronic library

Dubai Electricity and Water Authority (DEWA)'s Knowledge Management department will establish an electronic library by the end of the year, to support the 'Smart Government' initiative launched by HH Sheikh Mohammed bin Rashid Al Maktoum, Vice President and Prime Minister of the UAE and Ruler of Dubai, which aims to provide electronic government services using smart phones, and other technological platforms, to enhance service efficiency and reliability. The library will include several sources of knowledge including local and international books, magazines, newspapers, documented studies and research material. Employees can browse these using their smart phones round the clock, thus promoting continuous learning and exchange of knowledge among DEWA employees.

"In fulfilment of the 'Smart Government' initiative launched by His Highness Sheikh Mohammed bin Rashid Al Maktoum, Vice President, and Prime Minister of the UAE and Ruler of Dubai, aimed at providing complete online government services, DEWA is currently working on developing all its existing electronic services. We have launched several integrated services for our employees and customers, in line with the e-transformation conducted by the Government of Dubai. We are currently establishing a fully electronic, easy-to-access, and content-rich e-library, to provide access to necessary data and information for our employees anywhere, anytime. This will enable them to strengthen their trove of knowledge, which will translate positively through their service levels," said HE Saeed Mohammed Al Tayer, MD & CEO of DEWA.

"The launch of the new electronic library will add to the portfolio of DEWA's current offerings, with content to be available in Arabic and English. The new library reinforces the effectiveness of DEWA's strategy to keep up with latest technologies, and in using these technologies to ensure that our employees are provided with the best resources for professional and personal growth," said Dr. Yousef Al Akraf, EVP of Business Support and Human Resources.

Fig. 4. A snapshot of Exclusively articles on DEWA Smart Library

4. Internal Communications : Exclusively articles on DEWA Smart Library were written and published on several DEWA's internal magazines as well as messages were communicated as internal media releases.

5. Surveys : Division wise surveys were conducted to assess and promote the usage of DEWA Smart Library.

6. Usage statistics : Monthly usage statistics in-terms of "Number of registered users per divisions", "3 Top Publishers", "10 Top Search Queries", "Popular downloads", etc... were generated and communicated to top management as well as to all the divisions to build healthy competition among them to outsmart other divisions.

Fig. 5. Snapshot of awareness session

8. RESULT

Within a short span of 9 months, the DEWA Smart Library has witnessed tremendous growth both in terms of registered users and document downloads as given in the below graph.

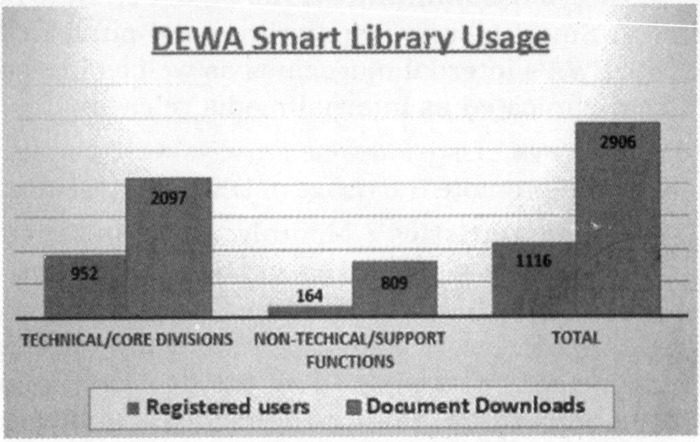

Fig. 7. DEWA Smart Library Usage

9. THE ROAD AHEAD

The early success has encouraged the DEWA Smart Library project team to take this journey further as follows:

1. Enhance the DEWA Smart Library by having more document collections both in terms of subjects and numbers, i.e., addition of new content as well as new Electronic Resource providers.
2. Include Arabic language content also in addition to the existing English language contents.
3. Integrate the DEWA Smart Library with that of International Standards such as IEEE, IEC, ASTM, BSI, and much more.
4. Finally build DEWA Smart Repository, which includes both the External Knowledge Resources and Internal Knowledge Resources.

REFERENCES

1. DEWA (2012). *Employee Handbook: Your Guide Book at DEWA.* Dubai, UAE: Dubai Electricity & Water Authority.
2. DEWA (2014). *DEWA Strategic Plan 2014 -2018.* Dubai, UAE: Dubai Electricity & Water Authority.

8

Essential Skills for Searching Information from Electronic Resources in the College Libraries: A Survey

Mahantesh Ajagond

Librarian , ICLES' MotilalJhunjhunwala College of Arts, Science and Commerce, Vashi, Navi Mumbai, Maharashtra.

Sarita Wadekar

Assistant Librarian ICLES' MotilalJhunjhunwala College of Arts, Science and Commerce, Vashi, Navi Mumbai, Maharashtra.

ABSTRACT

Drastic changes are taking place in the academic libraries as a result of Information Communication Technology (ICT) revolution. The dawn of the Internet has impacted the library and information services enormously and made the present libraries more a centers of learning resources and multimedia centers. With the continuous expansion of ICT and internet resources libraries have been greatly benefited and also activated in democratizing information. Day by day the content and coverage of the e-resources are expanding. The generation of the present day has been greatly influenced by tremendous amount of academic information available in the format of e-resources for the effective teaching and learning program. It has been observed that using the e-resources for the purpose of accessing the required information is not an easy task. In order to evaluate the information available in the form of e-resources requires some well-defined search strategies. The so called information skills developed over a period of time have been successfully tested and practiced. In order to understand the information search skills of the college students a small survey was conducted in some selected NAAC accredited colleges in Mumbai. This paper gives briefly the result of the survey to highlight the essential information skills and their operations in the college library environment.

Keywords : E-resources, Search Skills, Information skills, Academic Library.

1. INTRODUCTION

E-resources represent an increasingly important component of the collection-building activities of libraries. "Electronic resources" refer to those materials that require computer access, whether through a personal computer, mainframe, or handheld mobile device. They may either be accessed remotely via the Internet or locally. Some of the most frequently encountered types are:

E-journals, E-books, Full-text (aggregated) databases, indexing and abstracting databases, Reference databases (biographies, dictionaries, directories, encyclopaedias, etc.), Numeric and statistical databases, E-images, E-audio/visual resources.

2. LIBRARIES IN THE CURRENT CHANGING ENVIRONMENT

As the information technologies are changing day-today and growing at a tremendous speed, the knowledge society is becoming more complex, competitive and dependent on technological changes and information explosion. The need for e-information services to the users are also growing and becoming very essential. The impact of web based e- learning and teaching environment has influenced every facet of library and information services in academic libraries and providing new opportunities and challenges to the library professional for involvement in the knowledge based society including electronic and multimedia publishing, Internet based-information services, global networking, web based digital resources etc.

Librarians are charged with selecting and organizing resources and instructing patrons on how to locate and use these, and preserving information regardless of format or technology. The information revolution and the knowledge that is available on the Web have created new challenges to these traditional professional ethics. The emerging challenges of acquiring and providing access to electronic knowledge resources require librarians to change their role from traditional librarian to information scientist by learning and applying new skills to understand the evolving technologies to manage and provide quality on-line information service to the knowledge society. So the vision of the future academic library professional must be to create a World Class Networked Global Library and Information Centre to provide timely web based quality information service to the user in time in the e-learning environment. The future visions need for changes in academic libraries, trends and challenges before the library professional in the e-learning environment and the various changing roles of the academic library professional also have been discussed in this study.

3. ICT AND ITS IMPACT ON THE ACADEMIC LIBRARIES (COLLECTION & SERVICES)

The information atmosphere around the world is changing every minute and growing at a tremendous speed due to the emergence of the web based Information and Communication Technologies (ICT), globalization of networks and Internet. Hence ensuring and organizing access to educational materials in the electronic environment is an important factor in determining realistic requests for development and advancement of education. The information revolution and the pervasive thinking that everything is available on the Web have created new challenges to the traditional library professional ethics. Acquiring and providing access to electronic knowledge resources require library professional to change their role from traditional librarian to information scientist by learning and applying new skills to understand the evolving technologies to manage and provide quality on-line information service to the patrons of the knowledge society. Since, almost all the educational institutions, organizations, universities and academic associations have created their own websites with the digital repositories on Internet; the global networked environment has paved the way and opportunity to e-literacy. The impact of web based e-learning and teaching environment has influenced very much on every facets of library and information services in Academic Libraries and providing new opportunities and challenges to the library professional.

4. ELECTRONIC RESOURCES AND ITS IMPACT ON THE ACADEMIC LIBRARIES

Libraries have witnessed a great metamorphosis in recent years both in their collection development and in their service structure. Over the last several years, a significant transformation has been noticed in collection development policies and practices. Print medium is increasingly giving way to the electronic form of materials. As a greater number of electronic resources become available, retrieving relevant and authoritative information has become progressively more challenging and time consuming. Locating relevant information in a timely manner is critical for both the researcher and the information professional. Electronic resources are one way to enhance the digital library with global 24-hours-a-day and 7-days-a-week access to authoritative information, and they enable users to quickly retrieve and access specific research material easily, quickly, and effectively. It is crucial to not only provide these electronic resources, but to integrate them into library systems to streamline library operations, as well as promote user adoption.

5. INFORMATION SEARCHING SKILLS FOR SEARCHING INFORMATION FROM ELECTRONIC RESOURCES

Information explosion is very high and information overload is experienced by the scholars. The information is now published in print and electronic media and the rate of information generation is very high. For the scholars and researchers searching proper information from the ocean of information is very difficult task. Librarian and users have to search the information properly and pin pointedly. Information is vital entity and without information it is difficult even a common man to survive. Everyone needs information for different purposes. Information searching is very complex task and need searching skills. The proper information retrieving form the knowledge base is task of experienced person. Librarians are well versed in information handling and information searching. But due to increased e-publications the information searching needs different skills. There is a need to reviews the skills applied to effectively search information sources using the variety of information tools available.

6. A BRIEF SURVEY OF INFORMATION SKILLS IN THE SELECTED COLLEGE LIBRARIES OF MUMBAI

In this survey the outset taken the strength of the students from the Colleges of Mumbai city and randomly selected the samples from library users for the distribution of questionnaires. The following table 1 elaborates the analysis of the total population surveyed and responded. The survey is conducted by selecting twenty NAAC “A” Grade accredited colleges situated in Mumbai metropolitan city. It is also taken into consideration the availability of e-resources and internet facility provided by the libraries and use of e- resources by students for learning, studying and project / Seminar works.

6.1. Response to Survey

Table 1. Population of Study

Faculty	*Respondents*	*Boys*	*Girls*
Arts	457	343 (75.05%)	114 (24.94%)
Science	494	287 (58.10%)	207 (41.90%)
Commerce	769	412 (53.58%)	357 (46.42%)

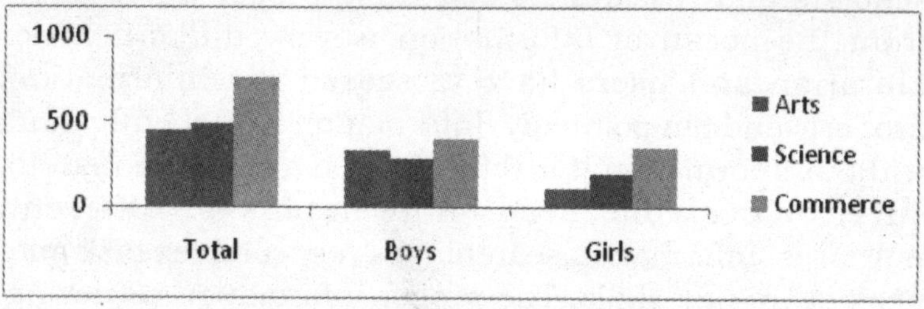

Fig. 1. Population of Study

It is observed from the table 1 that 2000 questionnaires were distributed randomly to selected population sample. The response to the survey was 86% i.e. 1720 questionnaires received duly filled in. In the succeeding paragraphs an attempt is made to tabulate the data collected and also presented the analysed data under the respective headings.

6.2. Method Used to Collect Desired Information (information seeking habits)

Table 2. Access to Desired Information

Collecting Desired Information	*Respondents*	*Arts*	*Science*	*Commerce*
Using library resources	1419 (34.17%)	421 (29.67%)	452 (31.85%)	546 (38.48%)
Using internet and web resources	1011 (24.34%)	241 (23.84%)	350 (34.62%)	420 (41.54%)
Using friends notes	801 (19.29%)	250 (31.21%)	270 (33.71%)	522 (65.19%)

Discussion with teachers	795 (19.14%)	210 (26.42%)	261 (32.83%)	324 (40.75%)
Any other	126 (03.03%)	31 (24.60%)	40 (31.75%)	52 (41.27%)

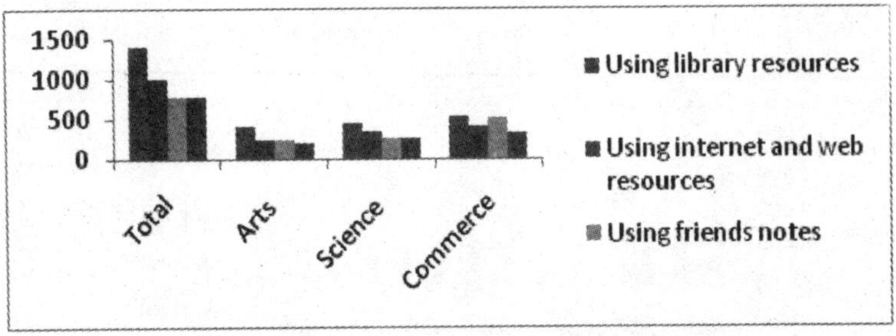

Fig. 2. Access to Desired Information

The students collect the information required for study purpose through various means. The data revealed that 34.17% students collects information from libraries, 24.34% using internet and web, 19% each from friends and teachers. The analysis of faculty wise information collection in which 65% Commerce students rely on notes shared with friends and 41.54% from internet and web resources. Same is not the case with arts and science students; they use more or less similar percentage in accessing the desired information from all the listed sources equally.

6.3. Information Resources Used

Table 3. Preferred Sources of Information

Information Resources	*Respondents*	*Arts*	*Science*	*Commerce*
Textbooks and general Books	1545 (29.97%)	385 (24.92%)	410 (26.54%)	750 (48.54%)
Reference books (like encyclopaedias)	834 (16.18%)	215 (25.78%)	382 (45.80%)	237 (28.42%)
Journal and magazines	675 (13.09%)	154 (22.81%)	328 (48.59%)	193 (28.59%)
Internet resources (Like Wikis)	1062 (20.60%)	265 (24.95%)	324 (30.51%)	473 (44.54%)

Electronic databases	591 (11.46%)	130 (22.00%)	269 (45.52%)	192 (32.49%)
Web tools	345 (6.69%)	81 (23.48%)	105 (30.43%)	159 (46.09%)
Any other	102 (1.97%)	21 (20.59%)	32 (31.37%)	49 (48.04%)

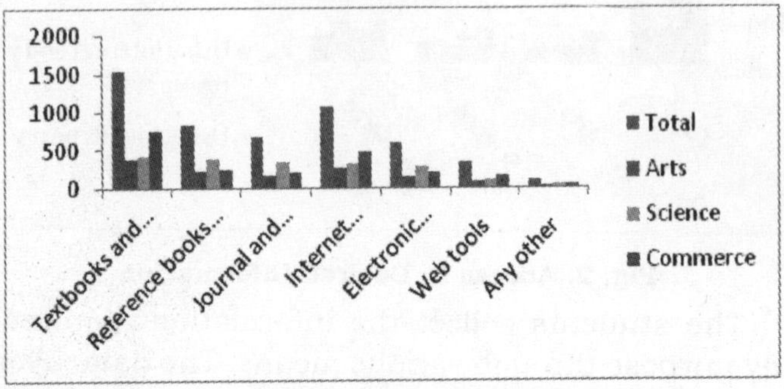

Fig. 3. Preferred Sources of Information

It is found that students use internet resources, databases and web tools (38.75%) comparatively more, and followed by use of textbooks and reference books (29.97%). This indicates that young generation is inclined towards use of digital resources and internet usage. Table 6 presents an interesting picture that science students (48.59%) prefer to refer Journal and magazines where as 48.54% of the commerce students prefer the textbooks and general books. Web tools and internet tools have made an impact on commerce students more than the science and arts students. It is heartening to note that arts students have very least preference to all the sources. It is inferred that commerce students and science students in general refer all the resources of information better than the arts students.

6.4. Use of E-Resources

Table 4. Preference for Using E- resources

Choice	*Total*	*Arts*	*Science*	*Commerce*
Yes	1365 (79.36%)	3109 (22.71%)	421 (30.84%)	634 (46.45%)
No	355 (20.64%)	137 (38.49%)	73 (20.56%)	135 (38.03%)

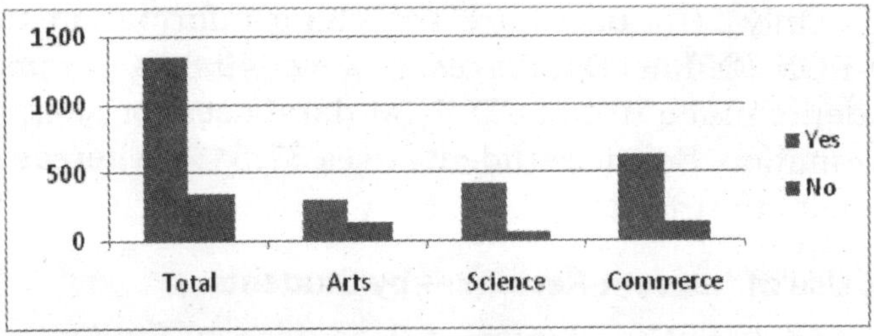

Fig. 4. Preference for Using E- resources

Nearly 80% studetns opined that they use E-resources and also prefere to use new media e-publicatoons, interent resources, databases etc. Though commerce students (46.45%) are more conversant in using e-resources than science students (38.84%) and arts students (22.71%), but science students whenever find leisure time they rush for using internet. It is true that those libraries containing e resources have made better impact on the students than the libraries not having enough of resources. This calls for offering a orientation to develop familiarity with e- resources by the respective libraries.

6.5. Use of Databases (Offline)

Table 5. Searhing Information Using CD ROM Database

Choice	*Respondents*	*Arts*	*Science*	*Commerce*
Yes	333 (19.36%)	42 (12.61%)	125 (37.54%)	166 (49.85%)
No	1387 (80.64%)	415 (29.92%)	369 (26.60%)	603 (43.48%)

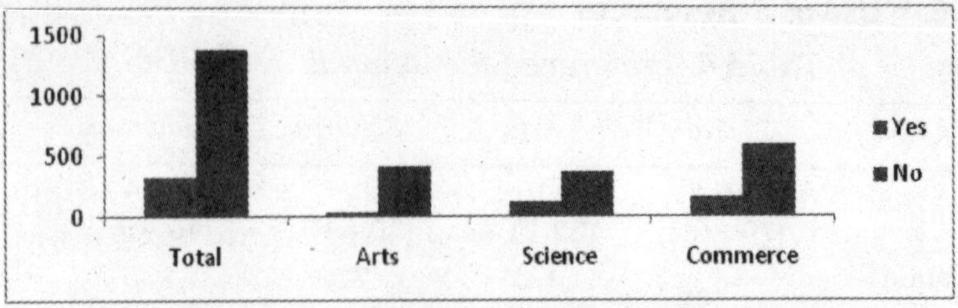

Fig. 5. Searhing Information Using CD ROM Database

Only 20% users are searching information using CD-ROM (Offline) Databases. however 49.85% Commerce students make use of CD-ROM databases for searching information. Science students uses 37.54%, whereas Arts are reluctant to use.

6.6. Use of Interent Resources by Students

Table 6. Use of Internet Resources by Students

Choice	*Respondents*	*Arts*	*Science*	*Commerce*
Yes	1419 (82.5%)	367 (25.86%)	395 (27.84%)	657 (46.30%)
No	301 (17.5%)	90 (29.9%)	99 (32.89%)	112 (37.21%)

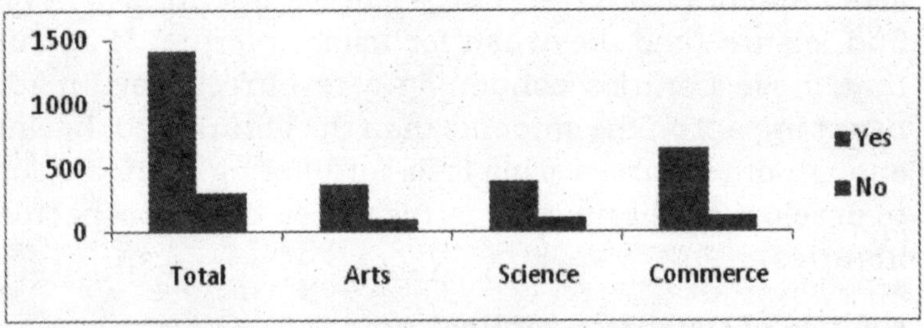

Fig. 6. Use of Interent Resources by Students

It is observed that in all 82% studets uses interent resources for different purposes. Use of interent resourecs by science and arts stuents is less as compared to science (46.3%).

6.7. Techniques used for Searching Internet

Table 7. Techniques used for Searching Internet

Techniques used for Searching Internet	*Respondents*	*Arts*	*Science*	*Commerce*
Simple search	1695 (36.17%)	446 (26.31%)	490 (28.91%)	759 (44.78%)
Complex search	708 (15.10%)	128 (18.08%)	294 (41.53%)	286 (40.40%)
Advance search	981 (20.93%)	247 (25.18%)	319 (32.52%)	415 (42.30%)
Field search	642 (13.70%)	198 (30.84%)	268 (41.74%)	176 (27.41%)
Free text search	660 (14.08%)	174 (26.36%)	195 (29.55%)	291 (44.09%)

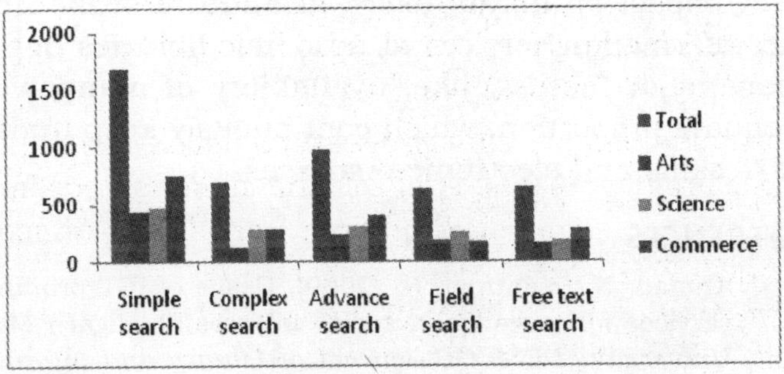

Fig. 7. Techniques used for Searching Internet

Simple search is very common among the students (36%) and very few undertake advance searches (Expert search) 15.10%. Field and free text searches are not common or might not know to students. Science students perform more complex and field searches, Commerce student's uses simple, complex and advanced searching Techniques. Arts students are moderate in applying all techniques.

7. CONCLUSION

The impact of e-resources in the academic libraries is a complete revolution in the status of collection development and services of the library. As Information communication Technology (ICT) advances, the emphasis of academic libraries has focused upon the intrinsic excellence of collection development suitable to e-resources.

Information Literacy Programs for the users of the library impart skills to users in accessing the e-resources. The present survey also provides scope to study in detail the need for developing the required information skills in using electronic information resources in academic libraries.

The study also explains that e-resources have a great impact on library users. The future of the library and information services at academic libraries depends upon major factors, like, availability of manpower in adequate proportion, which continuously keep updating its IT skills and electronic resources.

REFERENCES

1. Ahmad, N. & Fatima, N. (2009). Usage of ICT products & services for research in social sciences at Aligarh Muslim University. *DESIDOC Journal of Library and Information Technology*, 29(2), 25-30.
2. Chinnasamy, K., et al. (2008). E-resource usage by Management Institute students: A study. *PEARL: A Journal of Library and Information Science*, 2(1), 35-41.
3. COUNTER (Counting Online Usage of Networked Electronic Resources) Codes of Practice, (n. d.), Retrieved May 30, 2011 from http://www.projectcounter.org/code_practice.html
4. Dadzie, P. S. (2005). Electronic resources: access and usage at Ashesi University College. *Campus-Wide Information Systems*, 22(5), 290-297.
5. Dhanavandan, S., Mohammed, E. S. & Mani, V. (2008). Use of CDROMs and Internet in Engineering Colleges in Uddalore District: A Study. *PEARL: A Journal of Library and Information Science*, 2(3), 21-25.

6. Hadagali, G. S., Kumbar,B. D., Nelogal, S. B. &Bachalapur, M. M. (2012). Use of electronic resources by post-graduate students in different universities of Karnataka State. *International Journal of Information Dissemination and Technology,* 2(3), 189-195.

7. Kumbhar, R. (2009). Use of E learning in library and information science eductaion. *DESIDOC Jounral of Library and Information Technology,* 29(1), 37-41.

8. Others, S. J. (2012). Key issues for e-resource collection development: a guide for libraries. USA: IFLA.

9. Rawtani, M. R. & Yusuf M.(2002). Professional manpower needs of libraries with special refernce to skills. *ILA Bulletin,* 38(2), 81-83.

10. Thamaraiselvi, G. (2009). Vision and the Changing Roles of the Future Academic Library Professional in the E-Learning Environment: Challenges and Issues. ICAL, 139-145.

9

Use of Federated Search in Libraries for Effective Information Retrieval

Anupama Meher
Library Professional Trainee
National Institute of Technology, Rourkela

ABSTRACT

Today in the cyber world, most of the libraries try to provide relevant information as per the information need of the users. So in this condition most of the incredible libraries use federated search to provide the suitable information to the end users. Federated search is playing a significant role in today's library. This article focuses on the basic concept of federated search, its advantages, work and architecture of federated search. The climax of this article lies with open source federated search tools and Commercial tools used in different libraries. Federated search enables users to search multiple resources in one box. At the end of this paper, proposes a model on federated search for Biju Patnaik Central Library (BPCL) using single search interface to enhance the usage of its resources.

Keywords : Federated Search, Cross Search, Harvested Search, Open Source Tools and Commercial Tools

1. INTRODUCTION

Internet search is one of the most important weapons of the today's world. Large numbers of users depended on the search engine for finding and access their information. The rapid increase in the number of web document and the web search engine does not provide the relevant result for the need of the users. In the scenario most of library is indexing the electronic resources together single platform called portals. A portal is a gateway site where users can search for information on the web. Federated search is also often refers to as a portal, where users to search multiple information sources simultaneously through one search query.

2. FEDERATED SEARCH: AN OVERVIEW

Federated search is a powerful way to comprehensively search multiple databases in real time. It is also known as multiple databases searching, meta searching, cross searching, poly searching, database searching and a variety of other names (FAQ's, n.d.). Federated information retrieval also called distributed information retrieval it allows users access multiple database through one search interface. It is use software connects to access information sources. The federated search engine first collects the user's search query, then transforms the search terms to match each content source requirement and submit the query to each of the sources simultaneously. When the search result comes back from each of the sources, the federated search engine merges them together into a single set of results pages. The work of a successful federated search, deliver to users what they want, easily access relevant information in less time. It helps the libraries to maximized the resources and save money.

2.1. Work and Architecture of Federated Search

Federated search system depend some independent collection search for a query. And finally effectively merge the result they return for query. Bellow Figure- 1 highlights the details work flow of federated search.

The architecture and work of federated search first receive the query from the users and index the result into a single centralized search index. In many cases index is failure to provide relevant result. In this case, a federated technique called Meta search is the only option to provide relevant results. And finally combine the indexing result and Meta search result and collect the relevant information. The final result is merging in the federated search session.

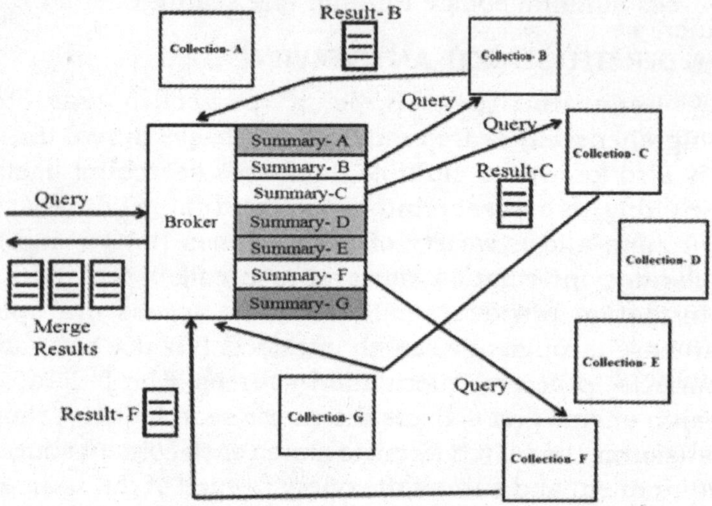

Fig. 1. Work and Architecture of Federated Search
Source: Federated Search by M. Shokouhiand L. Si (2011)

In this figure A (Broker) is the central section to receive the query from the users it is called the search federator, sent them to collection that is considered the relevant results. In this figure focus some collection those select for the query, in this collection Broker gather some important information about available collection. Then Broker typically compares each query the summary each of collection and estimate the goodness of collection. Once the collection summary is generated, the broker has sufficient knowledge of collection section. The broker selects a few collections that are most likely to relevant document based on their summaries. The selected collection runs the query and returns their results to the broker. In final steps Result merging the collection, rank, the result returned by multiple collections and presents them to the user. (Shokouhi and Si, 2011).

2.2. What makes Federated Search different from Normal Search

Now in the 21st century everyone gets their answer quickly and easily. Large number of users depends on the search engine for getting their result in internet. In these cases Google and other search engine are facing some difficult problems. Google and other search engines use programs called crawler or spiders to download web documents. Crawling is a technique that doesn't find everything. Google cannot easily index un-crawlable hidden web collection while federated search system can search the contents of hidden web collection without crawling. In certain scenarios federated search engine builder has to be customized to their search software for each web from every encounter. Google search engine retrieves quicker result than using a federated search but that may be relevant and non-relevant result. But in the federated search engine use their own relevancy search algorithms that ensure that result are meaningful and relevant and searches are done in the real time. Federated search can be configured to search merge and remove duplicates during the ranking process.

2.3. Advantages of Federated Search

- Efficiency and huge time saver.
- It provides relevant and real time information.
- Simultaneously searching across all searches.
- It is mapping result list navigators into a common form.
- Removing duplication.

- Direct links to the native source for further searching.
- Direct links to the native source for further searching.
- It is integrated with open URL.

2.4. Disadvantages of Federated Search

- Hard to go deeper in collection.
- Slow in response to time.
- Users have difficult to identify appropriate databases.
- Uses present too many choices will only look at few.
- Complex de-duping is difficult.

3. FEDERATED SEARCH TECHNOLOGY

Federated search technology can be deviated into two major categories: Cross Search and Harvested Search.

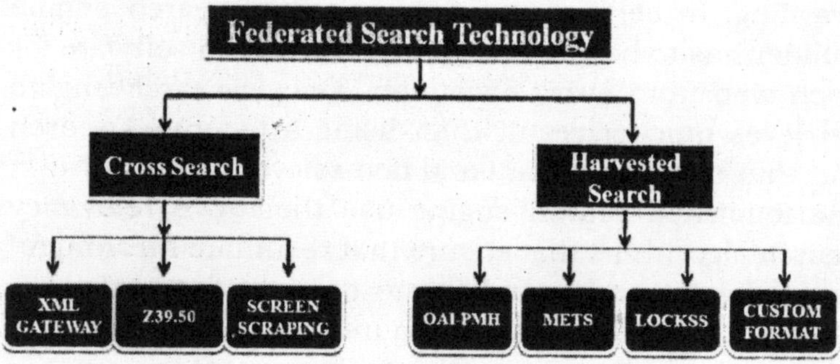

Fig. 2. Federated Search Technology

3.1. Cross Search

Cross search is a discovery tool designed to provide a fast and simple way to begin researching a topic

a. XML Gateway : XML gateway, a web application that enables a federated search using XML tags. XML gateway, a web application that enables a federated search using XML tags (Frequently Asked Questions, n.

d.).

b. Z39.50 Protocol : Z39.50 is an international standard client–server, application layer communications protocol that define how a client can communicate with a database of content to perform information retrieval that to search for and retrieve document.

c. Screen Scraping : screen scraping is sometimes called advanced terminal emulation. Screen-scraping, which is a way of translating data found on non-structured HTML pages through the use of special mappings called HTTP connectors or translators. It is used when the target database does not support any of the other search protocols. Relevant elements are parsed out of the HTML code underlying the native interface.

3.2. Harvested Search

Harvest search will harvest all of the relevant sources of data, normalize them into a single metadata schema, and index all of them together in one large union index. This approach offers huge advantages in speed and in the logic that can be applied to the presentation and sorting of results.

a. OAI-PMH : OAI-PMH Open Archives Initiative Protocol for Metadata Harvesting allows a service provider to send an http request to a data provider, who returns an XML-encoded data stream containing the metadata for a specific collection of objects or articles.

b. METS : METS (metadata encoding and transmission standard) schema is a standard for encoding descriptive, administrative, and structural metadata regarding objects within a digital library, expressed using the XML schema language of the World Wide Web Consortium. Similar to OAI-PMH in purpose and function, METS supports XML-encoded metadata harvesting, but unlike OAI-PMH, METS can harvest both metadata and object.

c. LOCKSS : LOCKSS collects content by crawling a web site and downloading each page it finds there. The data provider must implement a "manifest" page for each collection, explicitly granting permission for LOCKSS crawlers to visit. The owner of the LOCKSS box maintains "plugging" that instruct the LOCKSS software how to crawl and audit content from each provider.

d. Custom Format : a vendor might prefer to supply metadata or content in an agreed-on custom XML or delimited text format.

4. FEDERATED SEARCH IN LIBRARIES

Online resources are the bread and butter for todays scholars. Around 24 hours they find their resources on the internet. Today, most of the library resources are available in the digital format. The library is the vast collection of the digital information, but it is not purely satisfying needs of the users. In the context of library federated search is one of the most important tools for providing the relevant information to satisfy the users. Federated search provide multiple information into a single searchable point. For example- A student come to the library for their research work, he/she needs books, journals, reference books in this case you will first send students to the OPAC terminal to find books in your collection, but to another computer to look for periodical article, Sent another computer to send internet access. In this case the end user confuses to search the result and less his/her interest to find the information. In this situation federated search help the end user identify appropriate resources, find the record or article and directly access available resources. Federated search portals, provides for library resources either commercial or open access. Library catalogue (OPAC), WorldCate, Amazon and Google scholar allows users to search across multiple resources. Here in this paper analyses some vendors who offer a similar service for searching across their subscription database.

Table 1. Library Site Using Open Source federated Search Tools

Sl. No.	*Open Source Tools*	*Libraries using these tools*
1	Library Find (Oregon State) libraryfind.org/	• Deschutes public library www.dpls.lib.or.us/ • Oregon state University http://osulibrary.oregonstate.edu/
2	dbWiz (Simon Fraser University) dbwiz.lib.sfu.ca/dbwiz/	• Simon Fraser University Library http://www.lib.sfu.ca/
3	Masterkey (Index Data) • www.indexdata.dk/masterkey/	• NA
4	Care Affiliates: Open Translators Open source friendly • www.care-affiliates.com	• NA

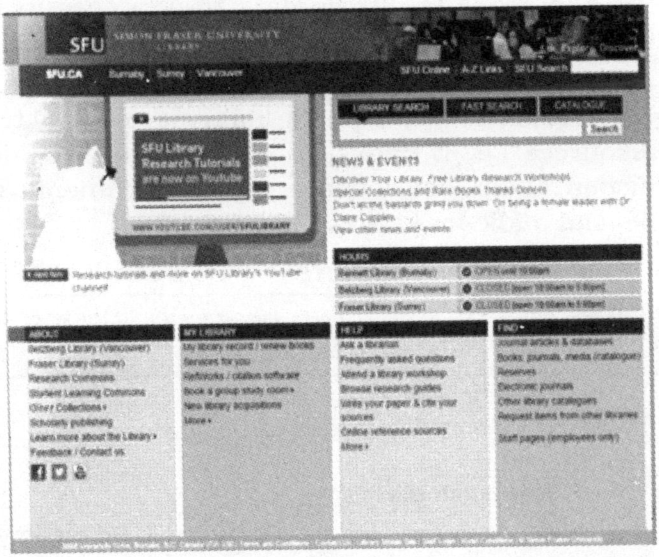

Fig. 3. Demo by Simon Fraser University Library

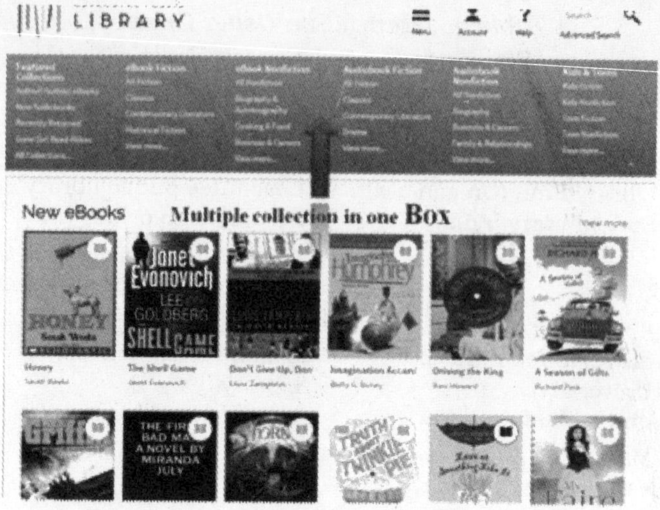

Fig. 4. Demo by Deschutes public library

Dbwiz was originally developed by Simon Fraser University Library (SRU) to help students determines the best starting point. dbwiz open source software for database management, Electronic journal management, Books and other resources data base access in one platform (Figure 3).

The typical example of Demo by Deschutes public library. It is Is one type of public library it collect all types of resources i.e. E-Books, E-Books fiction, E-Books nonfiction, audio book fiction, and audio book nonfiction, Books and audio for kids etc. (Figure 4)..

Table 2. Use of Commercial Federated Tools in Libraries

Sl. No.	*Commercial Tools*	*Libraries using these tools*
1	Deep Web Technologies http://www.deepwebtech.com/	
2	First Search: https://firstsearch.oclc.org/	
3	Ex Libris: http://www.exlibrisgroup.com/	• Vanderbilt University: www.library.vanderbilt.edu/

		• University of Iowa: www.lib.uiowa.edu/ • Emory University: http://web.library.emory.edu/ • University library System http://www.library.pitt.edu/
4	WebFeat: http://www.webfeat.net/	
5	Serials Solution: https://clientcenter.serialssolutions.com/CC/Login/Default.aspx	• Dartmouth College Libraries: http://library.dartmouth.edu/ • University of Calgary: http://library.ucalgary.ca/ • University of Sydney: www.library.usyd.edu.au/
6	VTLS http://www.iii.com/	• Demo-Networked Digital Library of Thesis and Dissertations: http://thumper.vtls.com:6080/visualizer/ • Demo: http://thumper.vtls.com:7080/visualizer/ • Upper Arlington Public Library: www.ualibrary.org/index.php
7	PROQUEST: http://www.proquest.com/	
8	Muse Global Inc: http://www.museglobal.com/	
9	EBSCO: http://www.ebscohost.com/	
10	Knimbus: http://www.knimbus.com/user/auth.do	
11	JGATE/FEDGATE: http://jgateplus.com/search/login/	

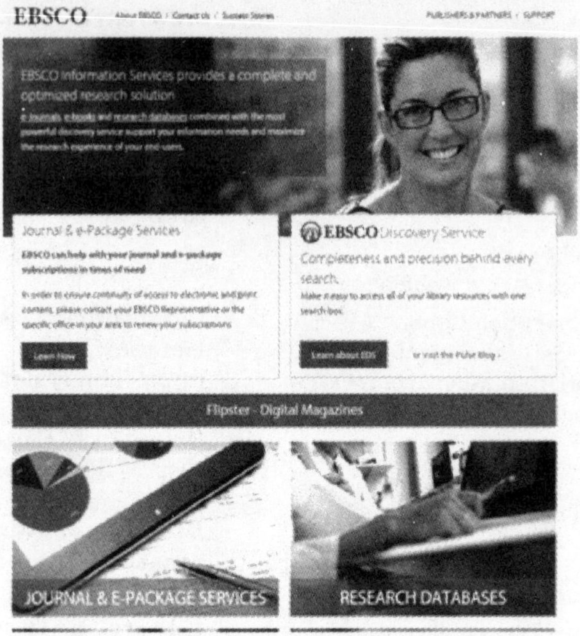

Fig 5. EBSCO

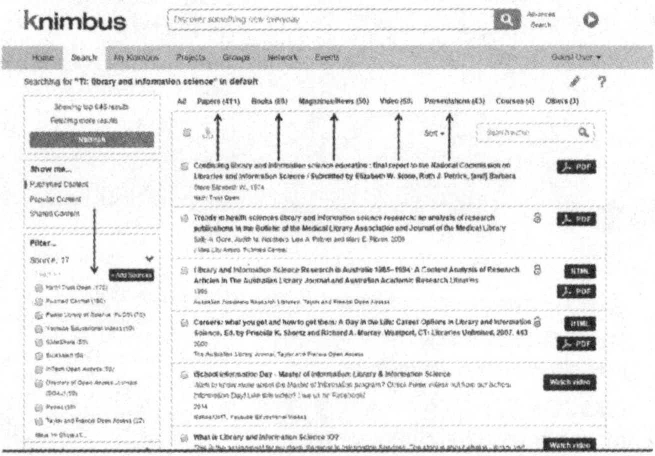

Fig. 6. KNIMBUS

Ebsco host is a next generation approach to federation allowing users to search multiple resources within one familiar interface. It provides journal and E-package services, Research database, E-Book, Digital archives, Health Resource, Corporate Resources and reader advisory (Figure 5).

Knimbus is a collaborative platform that helps you discover and share knowledge globally. It provides Agriculture, Engineering and Technology, Science, medical science; Art and Social Science cover all area of research. In one database you will access different database pub med center, DOAJ, Sodhganga. And it filters all the results in one database (Figure 6).

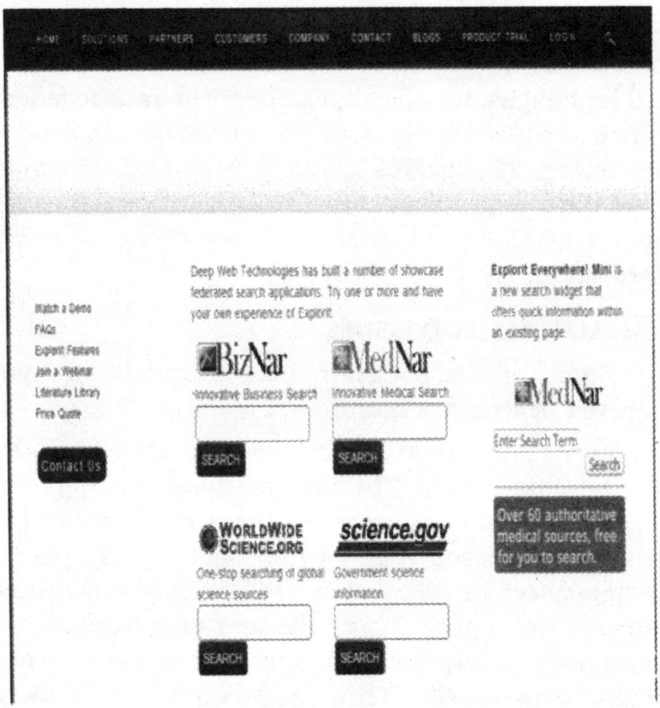

Fig. 7. Deep web Technology

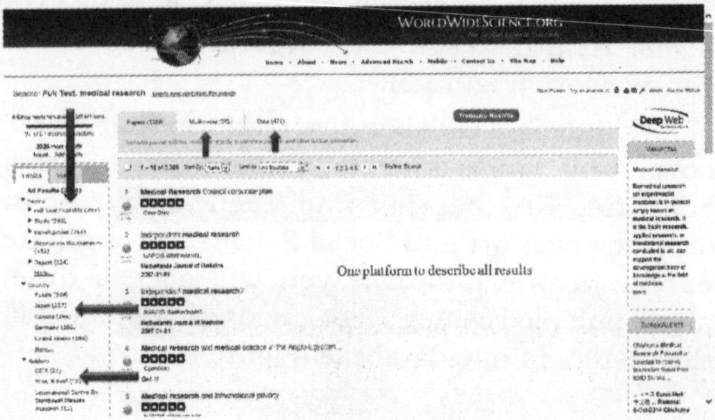

Fig. 8. WorldwideScience.org

Deep web technology is one of the most commercial federated search tools. It provides 100 different sources in 10 languages. It builds a number of showcase federated search application, i.e. Science.gov, worldwide science.org. It provides globally scientific information. Worldwide science.org is the one of the important commercial federated search tools searching the scientific information.

5. CHALLENGES AND ISSUES

Some of the common issues and challenges of federated search are mentioned below.

Access issues with federated search engine do not hold the data locally. The federated search engine must be able to access multiple results a single interface. In the security reason it gives the login ID and password one time users can show their result easily. It is password protected database. The challenges of federated search vendor are to make sure that only license user can access database properly. This may require a library or corporation to setup multiple areas where only certain license users can access a federated search

Second one is search query and interface issues. Federated search vendor allows Client to create their own look and feel for Search each interface and result page. In this case they will decide who will be the audience, how mush staff resources are available for designing the interface. Most of the vendor allows to customize the database of search field i.e. keyword, title, publisher, subject, ticker symbol etc. In this case facing some challenges. Data is not standardized, customer are modify and changes the sources.

One of the important issues for federated search is it eliminate the duplicity and provide the relevant results to the need of the users. Search engine provides in the first page of URL mostly 10 hits understand that audience. But in the federated search engine provides highest quality of results hits return first. Challenges true de-duplication provides it is impossible because it take more time, database provide 10 to 20 results at a time (Federated Search Engine Article, n. d.).

To overcome these issues and challenges, a well-planned access strategy need to plan for accessing the subscribed resource.

6. PROPOSED MODEL OF FEDERATED SEARCH FOR BPCL

The amount of online scholarly information is rapidly increasing and available on various platforms and in diversified sources which requires a single search interface like Google. With the proper use of Federated search tools enable librarians to meet these challenges in an efficient, effective manner to provide relevant result to their patron. Federated search reduce the time it takes to search and usually display result in a single platform. In library users need to refers the catalogue to find particular books from vast collection of the library. Similarly the other collections on different platforms needs to be accessed on single platform at the time. Information retrieval. Following the same federated search helps users to find all type of information i.e. e-journal, subscription database, electronic print collections, other digital repository in one search.

In this regard, an attempt has been made here to propose a model on federated search for Biju Patnaik Central Library (BPCL) using single interface to enhance the usage of its resources. Bellow this figure describe the services provides by BPCL.

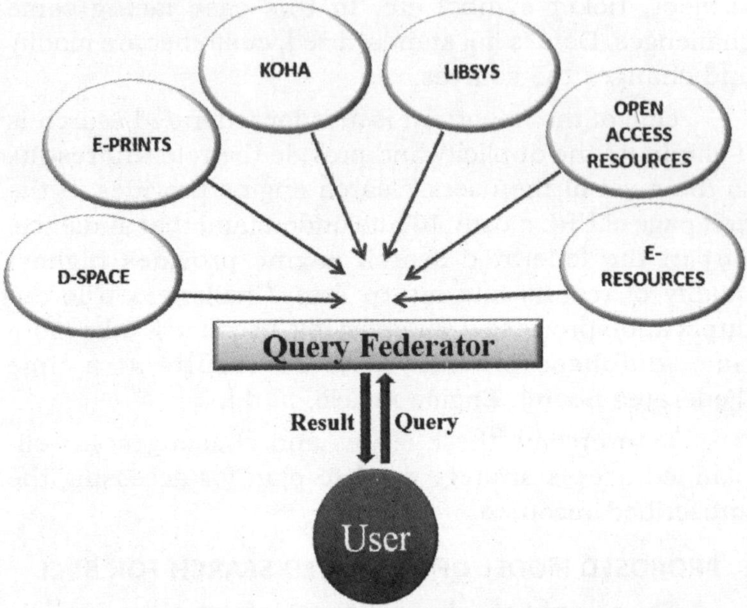

Fig. 9. Proposed model on federated search for BPCL

7. CONCLUSION

In conclusion, federated search has played a vital role in providing a technology for aggregate search and crawling the hidden web. Federated search is simultaneously searching multiple online database and an emerging feature of automated, web based library and information retrieval systems.

In this work this article has highlighted the basic concept of federated search, its work and architecture and lastly it is desirable some open source federated search tools and commercial tools that are using in different library. The application of federated search is not limited to the web search engine, most of the digital library uses successfully federated search for searching multiple collection independently. And lastly it proposed model on federated search system for Biju Patnaik Central library (BPCL).

ACKNOWLEDGEMENTS

I would like express my sincere gratitude and respect to my all Teacher for keen interest, constant encouragement, and immense help were instrument in the successful completion of this paper. Special thanks to my dear friends for their love, Cooperation and understanding.

REFERENCES

1. Cervone, F., & Wisniewski, J. (n.d.) What's New in Federated Search?. Retrieved January 7, 2015, from http://www.cervone.com/Whats_New_In_Federated_Search.pdf.
2. Deshmukh, S., Bhavsar, S., &Bhavsar, S. (2012). Open source software for federated search. *DESIDOC Journal of Library and Information Technology,* 32(5), 427–430. Retrieve From *http://publications.drdo.gov.in/ojs/index.php/djlit/article/view/2653/1323.*.
3. Gibson, I., Goddard, L., & Gordon, S. (2009). One box to search them all: Implementing federated search at an academic library. *Library Hi Tech,* 27(1), 118–133. doi:10.1108/07378830910942973.
4. Kumar, S., &Sanaman, G. (2008). Federated Search: New Option for Libraries in the Digital Era. In *Proceedings of the 6th International CALIBER 2008,* 267–285. Retrieved from *http://ir.inflibnet.ac.in/dxml/handle/1944/1233.23.12.2014.*
5. Lederman, S. (n.d.). Federated Search Primer. Retrieved January 7, 2015, from *http://www.deepwebtech.com/wp-content/uploads/2010/12/Federated-Search-Primer-1.pdf.*
6. Shokouhi, M., & Si, L., (2011). Federated Search.Foundations and Trends in Information Retrieval, 5(1), 1-102. Retrieve From *https://www.cs.purdue.edu/homes/lsi/FnTIR_2011.pdf.*
7. WebFeat, Inc., (2005). Evaluating Federated Search Engines What's the difference between federated search vendors/ ?

Retrieve From http://www.caul.edu.au/content/upload/files/datasets/webfeat-evaluation.pdf.

8. Yang, S. Q., & Wagner, K. (2010). Evaluating and comparing discovery tools: how close are we towards next generation catalog? *Library Hi Tech*, 28(4), 690–709. doi:10.1108/07378831011096312.
9. Federated Search Engine Article. (n.d.). Retrieved December 22, 2015, from http://www.searchitright.com/federated-search-engine-article.asp.
10. Federated search. (n.d.). Retrieved December 23, 2014, from http://en.wikipedia.org/wiki/Federated_search. 12/23/2014.
11. Federated Search for your library and in your Enterprise. (n.d.). Retrieved January 10, 2014 from *http://www.infotoday.com/cilmag/may08/FederatedSearch_White Paper_CIL0508.pdf*
12. Science.gov mobile app among 10 best according to GCN. (n.d.). Retrieved December 22, 2014, from *http://federatedsearchblog.com/*
13. Vendor Info. (n.d.). Retrieved January 6, 2015, from *http://federatedsearchblog.com/vendor-information/*
14. The Library of Congress Portals Applications Issues Group: Federated Search Portal Products & Vendors. (n.d.). Retrieved January 10, 2015, from *http://www.loc.gov/catdir/lcpaig/portalproducts.html.*
15. Try Explorit Now. (n.d.). Retrieved January 9, 2015, from *http://www.deepwebtech.com/product-trial/try-it-now/*.
16. FAQ's. (n.d.). Retrieved January 10, 2015, from *http://www.deepwebtech.com/company/resource-center/faqs/*.
17. Home. (n.d.). Retrieved January 9, 2015, from *http://www.bainsight.com/federated-search*
18. Home | University Library System (ULS). (n.d.). Retrieved January 9, 2015, from *http://www.library.pitt.edu/*
19. Deschutes Public Library. (n.d.). Retrieved January 18, 2015, from *http://www.deschuteslibrary.org/*
20. DbWIZ: Open Source Federated Searching. (n.d.). Retrieved January 18, 2015, from *http://researcher.sfu.ca/dbwiz*
21. Frequently Asked Questions. (n.d.). Retrieved January 18, 2015, from *http://help.galileo.usg.edu/faqs/what_is_a_metasearch_federated_search/*

E-Resources Organizational Strategies

10

ERM : A Strategic Management Technique

V. M. Bankapur
Associate Professor, DLISc, RCUB

"Without a strategy, execution is aimless, without execution strategy is useless" –Moris Chang

ABSTRACT

E- Resources are the future and fastest growing sources of information. These resources have changed the landscape of the libraries. "ERM" has become a new science of information management associated with a strategy converging with library policy, procedural and rules to achieve its goals. It is an effective management technique. An attempt is made to explore these strategies for electronic resource management useful for libraries.

1. INTRODUCTION

As per AACR2, 2002 edition glossary "Electronic resources defined as any work encoded and made available for access through use of computers. Here Acquire, Archive, collect and link are the elements associated with ERM. Electronic resources consists of data (Information representing numbers, text graphics, images, maps, moving images,music,sounds etc,.), programs (instructions etc., that process the data for use), or combinations of data and programs.- AACR Rule 9.0

A1. Electronic resources are the future of the libraries. We are in the mist of transformation. The main reason for this transformation if the change in form of information. Technologies have compelled to redefine the library concepts and roles into a new dimension of collection development, access and services to keep intact the users in the competitive world. The reviewing of the policies and procedures of the libraries in the electronic world is essential component. Reframing the policies may entail a new strategy of library dominance and acceptance in the real world search engines. They tend to be threat and may cause breach between library and the patrons. By definition "Strategic Management of electronic resource is continues process of tactical planning of resources required of the libraries and focusing on achieving the objectives of the Libraries". The library strategy has to look into the areas as:

- Electronic forms are the next generations information products for the library (Content Management);
- Dissemination of information is the goal where we converge a new role of access management ;
- Collection development is based on storage and retrieval systems;
- Handling of information is art to be redefined by training the manpower as per skill development policies;
- Usage of resource are the real challenge to reach the patrons with their preference study applying metrics options and preference study;
- Promotional needs are always a concept to influence users. Marketing tools and techniques are more predominate for this study.

2. CONTENT MANAGEMENT : REDEFINING LIBRARY COLLECTION

Electronic forms are the next generation information products for the library. Today all resources are procured in the form of digital contents. The content can are:

- Procured content &
- Produced content.

The volume of information grows. The varieties of information increases and libraries are becoming more visible. Now there are ways and means of managing this content as libraries have become a resource rich hub which houses varieties of options of content dissemination. Thus has become a very important with competitive world and changed environment of digital access:

- Computation with search engines;
- Users behavior towards e-resources;
- Meta content organization;
- E-publishing ;
- Multimedia and formats options;
- Building relevant collection;
- Copy right and others issues;
- Infrastructure for content browsing.

3. ACCESS MANAGEMENT: INFRASTRUCTURE FOR ACCESSING RESOURCES

Access to content is the complex activity looking into many facets of digital content form open and commercial resources. Managing access to the resources will be challenging job for libraries. Strategically the access management tools have to be developed for the library. Cooperative measures have to be taken with library, publishers and online service providers. License agreements are must for the resources clearly defining the access and use of these resources. The other issues are making the accessibility less simple and less complex, user privacy and good faith. Solutions may be an option by giving a password based access/ IP and /or campus based access are the priorities.

- Designing access facility to the users
- Limiting direct access to resources which are paid
- Networked access to all resources with many options of accessibility
- Supporting users with their preferred way of access points.

4. COLLECTION DEVELOPMENT: STRATEGIC COLLECTION POLICY

This is a major art to be learned by libraries, as it is not just one day activity. Handling and building resources for the library are guided by the policy matters of the library is a regular process. People, place and products are to be promoted with collaboration, collation, collection and connecting them to the users. Collection development is process of library building block of resources. Referring to the B-Model of the collection development is activity of selection and deselecting. It is also helps in space management.

- Building resources is long process;
- Policies play a vital role in building collections;
- Adds values with rich collections;
- Helps in space management;

5. SKILL DEVELOPMENT: TECHNOLOGY USAGE

Technical skill development plays a vital role in library. The Library personnel's has to perform and stand with environmental changes happening in the library. The Library has moved from traditional print to digital environment. Constant leverage of training is need of the hour. The Library staff has to:

- Aptitude of Learning;

- Ability to adopt to change;
- Develop a new medium of digital environment;
- Ability of adding new technology in the library;
- Developing Library search engine.

6. METRIC MONITORS: DECISION MAKING

Today metrics is being more used as decision making tool for every activity and services library provides. From mere feedback to access to resources all count makes a measure of validity. It acts a performance Indicators including benchmarking and best practices. The numerous data sources are generated in the library which acts as an input operations like:

- Users Numbers;
- Resource Usage data;
- Facilities (Hours/ Computers/ Learning space etc,)
- Services (Circulation statistics)
- Time
- Cost
- Quality
- Quantity

7. PROMOTIONAL NEEDS: MARKETING APPROACH

Library has to indulge in promotional activities like application of marketing concepts for library services and products. Design the services as per the requirement of users and library stake holders. The environment in which the services are to be designed should match the needs of the users.

- Strategic Promotional and marketing practices of digital content offered by the library;
- Identify tools for promotions of library services and products;
- Ways and means of communication tools have to be designed, and

- E- Advertising can be media for extensive promotion.

8. CONCLUSION

ERM is the future of library collection building process. It is continues process of content building in digital era and challenging task. Consolidating all factors of managing e- information is strategy which we define it as ERM (Electronic resource management). Today the theory revolves around not just the collection building process applied earlier in the traditional libraries. It is beyond the scope of print resources. Managing e-resources is clubbed with hardware, software, network and digital content. It never stops here many aspects of prompting and designing services as per the requirement of the customer's plays a vital role. In digital era there new concepts emerging like Content Management Systems, Collection development, Access Management, skill development, promotional aspects and metrics application has to be strategically applied in managing the e-resources.

REFERENCES

1. Bankapur, V. (2012). Managing E-Resources strategically (ERM) In Engineering College Libraries. In *Proceedings of the national conference on Trends in Developing and Managing E-resources in libraries* (pp. 375-378).
2. Library of congress collections policy statements supplementary guidelines. (n.d.). Retrieved December 30, 2014, from http://www.loc.gov/acq/devpol/electronic resources.pdf
3. Paschoud, J. (2009). Access Management for Libraries: the Issues and the Future. In *Proceedings of the 7th International Convention on Automation of Libraries in Education and Research.*
4. Schmidt, J. (2007). Promoting library services in a Google world, *Library Management*, 28(6/7). 337 – 346.
5. Sreekumar, M.G.(2012). Strategies on e-resources management for smart information systems. *Annals of Library and Information Studies*, 59, 155-169.

11

Consortia is a Boon to Libraries: A Study of Indian Initiative

Md. Muzaffar Iqbal
Librarian, Vikash College of Engineering for Women, Bargarh

Srikanta Sahu
Technical Assistant, National Institute of Technology, Rourkela, Odisha

Ajay Kumar Sahu
Technical Assistant (Library), NSHM Knowledge Campus, Kolkata

ABSTRACT

The information explosion, fiscal strains and the publication deluge have stood as an impediment in the path of information center and libraries to quench the increasing information thirst of its varied user community. It is not possible on the part of any single library or information center to be self-sufficient in holdings that can meet query of knowledge of its users. As a remedy to this malady, the library consortia have emerged as a vital concept. It implies to collaborative efforts among the member libraries for the prime motive of sharing of information and resources. This paper discusses the concept of consortia and focuses on few consortium initiatives taken in India like INDEST, CSIR, UGC INFONET, FORSA etc.

1. INTRODUCTION

With the advancement of science and technology in one hand and information explosion on the other, it is nearly impossible for any institution or organization to quench the thirst of the user community. No one can declare of possessing all the information available at every corner of the world as new information is being produced at every stroke of the clock. It has been very difficult on the part of library professional to manage with the users and their need of information. The present era has compelled the information professionals to change their role of library document keeper to that of navigator of information. In this connection, library consortium may work wonders by giving some helping hands to the participating libraries in sharing their resources that under one umbrella are willingly ready to get and provide support to others.

2. DEFINITION

Consortium can be defined as "an.amalgamation or association or group of libraries who join together to achieve the common goal of 'optimum user satisfaction' with the participation in a common activity and sharing the resources among two or more institutions, organization or companies".Consortium comes from the Latin word, means 'partnership,association or society' and derives from consort 'partner', itself from con- 'together' and sors 'fate',meaning owner of means or comrade.

A library consortium is a group of libraries who partner to coordinate activities, share resources, and combine expertise. The International Coalition of Library Consortia is an informal discussion group of such consortia. Library consortia offer significant advantages to increasingly strapped libraries. The sharing of resources and collaboration on shared goals often enables libraries to deliver higher quality services than they would be able to deliver on their own.

According to American Heritage Dictionary of the English Language, a consortium is said to be "A cooperative arrangement among groups or institutions: a library consortium."

Library consortium is a group of libraries, preferably with some homogeneous characteristics by subject, or institutional affiliation, or affiliation to funding authorities, who join together with the primary objective of providing expanded access to information resources needed by its user community through a process of pooling and sharing information and infrastructure resources with due adherence to copyright compliances.

Consortia may be formed at a local, regional, national or international level, on a functional or format basis, or on a subject basis. The majority of the libraries, particularly in developing countries like India are thinking about the co-operative purchasing for any group of libraries. Thus, Consortia are constituted for often being useful for establishing a formal structure regarding sharing of resources and services with formal agreement by each participating library.

According to Allen Kent "the success and survival of libraries will much depend on how much and to what extent the libraries cooperate with each other in future".

3. CONCEPT OF LIBRARY CONSORTIA

The concept of library consortia first came up by the academic libraries that formed consortia for a common aim of sharing of printed materials. With the passage of time and change in the scenario of science and technology, many consortia have been formed at different levels with the prime motive of cooperation and coordination among the member libraries. They began to acquire information in stabilizing and reasonable prices and disseminate through internet.

The consortia provide various facilities like inter-library loan, document delivery services, union catalogue and even sharing of expertise. The concept gained momentum when large numbers of libraries got automated and also where web based resources were provided with a single click.

4. NEED OF LIBRARY CONSORTIA

Development in the field of technology, change in format of scholarly journals, price based models of publishers for consortia grant ample of opportunities for libraries to provide quick access to information resources. Here are the few factors that describe the need of library consortia in modern day society:

a. Lack of finance : The lion share of the budget allocated to library goes for procuring of information. Consortia exist with a common aim and objective to boost the purchasing capability of the member libraries in this decisive situation of the major financial crisis faced by the libraries.A consortium makes possible for the member libraries to entertain the benefit of wider access to resources at reasonable price.

b. Information explosion : There is a sudden information explosion in the world where every now or then a new piece of information is being produced or generated. The existing information is also changing its media i.e. print to electronic. The internet plays a vital role in this. A consortium, with the combine, potency of resources of different member libraries available to it, is in an enhanced pose to determine the problems of supervision, managing, organizing, archiving and dissemination of the electronic assets (resources) among themselves.

c. Impossibility of self-sufficiency : In the present world no library can declare of being self-sufficient in procurement of documents and catering the need of the users. Fiscal constraints, space curb, lack of skilled human resources also pressurize upon the need for the libraries to go for a consortium.

d. User requirement : The technology has altered the outlook and vision of the users, their endurance, approach and willingness to acknowledge services that are accessible on demand. The Web-based electronic resources are an apt response to the expectations of the user community. They yearn for access to the desired information resource as quickly as possible, and many of them would like to have information at their fingertip.

e. Rapid Access : With new technologies, electronic resources are widely and remotely accessible round the clock. The document delivery is done at rapid speed and at a cheaper price.

f. Standard of research : Consortia procure many resources available throughout the globe which enriches their collection which ultimately helps in raising the standards of user's research and findings.

g. Future developments : Infrastructure becomes obsolete in due course of time. Therefore, consortia has to run with the pace of development to acquire, process, disseminate information, train staff and user in much faster rate with accuracy.

5. FEATURES OF CONSORTIA

- Library consortia help in building a good collection of resources
- It reduces the cost incurred in the procurement of information resources
- It gives ample of opportunities to all the member institutions, organization to share and receive resources among themselves
- Consortia encourages the user community in their research and findings
- New tools, techniques and technology are shared resulting in the development of staff and library professionals

- Interlibrary loan, document delivery services in minimal cost incurred is an added feature

6. TYPES OF CONSORTIA

Consortia are based on different models depending upon the nature, agreement, participation and funds.

Open group consortia : Open group consortia are open ended. Here any library can join and leave as per their will. Ex INDEST consortium run by the Ministry of Human Resource Department, Government of India

Closed group consortia : Closed group consortia are having a defined group of members. They are formed by coalition, affiliation and collaboration among them. Their guidelines and administrations are easy and simple. Ex DAE, CSIR, IIM Consortium

Centrally funded consortia : These consortia are generally dependent on central funding agency, by its parent body. Ex INDEST, UGC INFONET, CSIR, ICMR Consortia

Shared budget consortia : Here the participating libraries form the consortium and the management of funds is handled individually. Ex FORSA

Publisher initiative consortia : In these consortia the members get heavy discounts from the publishers. Ex Emerald Full Text Library published by Emerald Publishing Group

Institutional head quarter funded consortia : ex TIFR and its branches

National consortia : Theses have national level licensing of products. Ex INDEST, UGC INFONET

International consortia : In this, libraries across the globe are its members. Here an individual or a group of consortia can become a member. Ex OCLC, International Coalition of Library Consortia

7. ADVANTAGES

- Consortia based subscription of electronic resources provides wider range of resources and that too at very low cost which are normally not possible for a single institution.
- Maximum utilization of funds from the parent organization or participating libraries for procurement of resources
- Building a comprehensive collection, access and preservation round the clock
- Interlibrary loan and document delivery service among member libraries
- Facilities to build a digital library, union catalogue, checking of duplication of resources
- Exchange of ideas, tools, techniques and technology among the consortia members
- Reduces storage space and cost

8. DISADVANTAGES

- High finance involved at the initial stage of consortia
- Absence of printed copy of journals
- Lack of technical knowledge among staff and users in using electronic resources
- Violation of copyright
- Archiving and backup problems
- Requirement of infrastructure for access of electronic resources
- Insufficient bandwidth and unreliable telecommunication links
- Lack of awareness as user community prefers hard copy instead of electronic journals

9. CONSORTIA INITIATIVES IN INDIA

INDEST : The "Indian National Digital Library in Engineering Sciences and Technology (INDEST)

Consortium" was set up in 2003 by the Ministry of Human Resource Development (MHRD) on the recommendation of an Expert Group under the Chairmanship of Prof. N. Balakrishnan appointed by the Ministry having its headquarter in IIT Delhi. It is the leading consortium in terms of number of member institutions in Asia.It receive grants required for subscription to electronic resources for 62 centrally - funded Government institutions including IITs, IISc Bangalore, NITs, ISM, IIITs, IIMs, NITTTR's and few other institutions that are considered as core members of the Consortium. 60 Govt./Govt.-aided engineering colleges are provided access to selected electronic resources with monetary support from the AICTE and 102univeristies/institutions have joined the Consortium under its self-supported category in 2012. The total number of members in the Consortium has now grown to 1235. The Consortium subscribes to over 12,000 electronic journals from a number of publishers and aggregators.

CSIR : Council of Scientific and Industrial Research (CSIR) established in 1942, is an autonomous body and India's largest research and development (R&D) organization, with 37 laboratories and 39 field stations or extension centers spread across the nation. The consortium was formed in June 2002 in Pune with Elsevier and Springer Kluwer to provide access to electronic journals.

UGC INFONET : The UGC-Infonet Digital Library Consortium was formally launched in December, 2003 by Honorable Dr. A P J Abdul Kalam, the President of India soon after providing the Internet connectivity to the universities in the year 2003 under the UGC-Infonetprogramme. It is overlaid on Education and Research Network (ERNET) infrastructure to provide assured quality of service and optimal utilization of Bandwidth resources. On behalf of the UGC, the INFLIBNET is executing the UGC-INFONET project in collaboration with the ERNET. The Consortium provides current as well as archival access to more than 7500+ core and peer-reviewed journals and 10 bibliographic databases from 26 publishers and aggregators in different disciplines. These e-resources covers almost all subject disciplines including arts, humanities, social sciences, physical sciences, chemical Sciences, life sciences, computer sciences, mathematics and statistics, etc. The programme is wholly funded by the UGC and executed by the INFLIBNET (Information and Library Network) Centre, Gandhinagar which is the nodal agency for coordination of UGC-INFONET.

FORSA : FORSA stands for the Forum for Resource Sharing in Astronomy and Astrophysics, established in the year 1981. It includes members from Raman Research Institute, Indian Institute of Astrophysics, Physical Research Laboratory (PRL), National Center for Radio Astrophysics and Inter University Centre for Astronomy and Astrophysics, where the resources in common areas for research and development are being shared among themselves.FORSA has realized four consortia, viz. Nature Online Consortium; Indian Astrophysics Consortium for physics/astronomy journals of Springer/Kluwer; Consortium for Scientific American Online Archive (EBSCO); and Open Consortium for Lecture Notes in Physics (Springer).

IIM Consortium : IIM Library consortia is a Digital Library network system based on internet technology to provide the IIM community (faculty, students and staff) an online web enabled access to the information resources available in all the IIMs without any barriers of time and distance. It will be a simple, efficient and cost effective system. The fundamental operating theory of this system is decentralized acquisition and processing but centralized utilization.

ICICI Knowledge Park : TheICICI Knowledge Park is now IKP Knowledge Park, located at Hyderabad. Four

Hyderabad based and one Pune based Research and Development Institution are receiving access to the J-Gate Custom Contents for Consortia service as per the agreement signed with Informatics India Ltd. These services are free to the members at the initial stage to make them self-sustainable at the later stage.

ICMR : The Indian Council of Medical Research (ICMR) is the apex body in India for the formulation, coordination and promotion of biomedical research. It is one of the oldest and largest medical research bodies in the world. It receive grants by the Government of India through the Ministry of Health and Family Welfare. To cope up with the change in information technology, ICMR formed a consortium and entered for electronic resources. It subscribes resources from Nature, Lancet, BMJ, Science and NEJM which are shared among all the institutes of ICMR.

HELINET : HELNET stands for Health Science Library and Information Network. It was implemented to accomplish the mission to network all the Health Science libraries for minimizing the cost of acquisition and maintenance of learning resources and maximizing their utilization among the faculty, students and researchers in the health science colleges and institutions. With a vision to enhance the education and research quality in the Health Science institution, HELINET was formed. Its goal was to convey information without any time barrier. The consortium made possible to access more than 600 journals which are very difficult for a single library to do so.

Apart from the above mentioned names there are still many more consortiums like ISRO, CeRA, ERMED, National Medical Library Consortium, DAE, NTR MEDNET, and MUHS.

10. CONCLUSION

In Indian scenario, numerous library consortia have been developed and also functioning successfully which help the participating institutions to provide better and effective library services with minimum library budget. The leading members of the consortium need to clearly frame their policies involved, consultation of all participating member libraries and also take steps to provide training programs for library professionals and user community for successful use of e- resources etc, so that libraries can achieve better benefits of these consortia and the movement of consortia can be more effective.

REFERENCES

1. Islam, A. &Mezbah-ul-Islam, M. (n.d). Concept, issues and importance of library consortium: Problems and prospects of university library consortium in Bangladesh. Retrieved from http://pdf.aminer.org/000/264/832/developing_a_digital_ resources_consortium_for_university_libraries_in_bangladesh.pdf
2. Indian Institute of Technology Delhi (2012). INDEST-AICTE Consortium. Retrieved from http://paniit.iitd.ac.in/indest/downloads/brochureforcoremembers.pdf
3. Library consortium (n.d.). Retrieved from http://en.wikipedia.org/wiki/Library_consortium
4. Yernagula, R. &Kelkar, P. K. (2007). Library consortia: benefits and models of ejournals Consortia." In *Resources of CBSOR*. Retrieved from www.isical.ac.in/~serial/consortia/CBSOR-11.pdf
5. Singh, K &Rao,V. (2008). An Overview of the Library Consortia in India. Retrieved from http://ir.inflibnet.ac.in/bitstream/1944/1124/1/10.pdf
6. Birdie, C. (2005). Library consortia and open access initiatives: collaboration at different level. Retrieved from http://prints.iiap.res.in/handle/2248/5606
7. Yadav, M. & Kale, V. (n.d). Consortia: A Boon To Medical Libraries. Retrieved fromhttp://www.journal.mimsr.edu.in/

download/02_Dec-2011/3.1_Consortia-A-Boon-To-Medical-Libraries.pdf

8. Birdie, C. &Alladi, V. (2002). The Future of Consortia among Indian Libraries - FORSA Consortium as Forerunner? Retrieved from https://www.eso.org/sci/libraries/lisa/lisa4/proceedings/Birdie.pdf

Evaluation and Review of E-Resources

12

Use of E-Resources by University Faculty Members of Chhattisgarh, India: A Study

Sunil Kumar Satpathy
Deputy Librarian, National Institute of Technology, G.E./Road, Raipur, (C.G)-492010

S. R. Kashyap
Sr. Asst. Professor, SOS in Library & information Science, PT. Ravishankar Shukla University, Raipur, (C.G.) – 492010

ABSTRACT

E-resources in any type of libraries more specifically academic libraries of higher learning institutions have become a center of attraction for users, particularly faculty members. The quality of a library and its services are now a day's mostly calculated on the basis of availability and usage of e-resources. This paper defines e-resources, objectives, scope and limitations of the study. Data are collected through questionnaire and collecteddata are analyzed and interpreted. The major findings of the study are summarized which reveals an encouraging picture of the use of e-resources buy the faculty members of various universities of Chhattisgarh. Concludes with the remarks that keeping pace with the development of information technology and demands of users, the universities libraries of Chhattisgarh need to acquire more and more e-resources and develop necessary facilities to access the e-resources, so that maximum uses of e-resources will be possible return on investment can properly made and justified.

Keywords : E-resource, Faculty members, Universities, Chhattisgarh

1. INTRODUCTION

E-resources in any type of libraries more specifically academic libraries of higher learning institutions have become a center of attraction for users, particularly faculty members. The quality of a library and its services are now a day's mostly calculated on the basis of availability and usage of e-resources. Users of this generation are also more comfortable in using these resources in comparison to their print counterparts. In the opinion of Appleton "E-resources and services refer to the variety of electronic and digital sources of information available to teachers and learners within an academic context. The change in traditional document delivery services from print to electronic has come about very quickly and libraries and information services have undergone significant transformation in order to effectively deliver electronic resources to the academic community (Appleton, 2006).With the changes in library environment, a new type of resources i.e. e-resources have entered into the library collection and is gradually occupying a major portion of library collection and library budget. Users' inclination towards e-resources is also increasing day by day due to its multifarious advantages over its print counterparts. In any academic setup faculty members are the main mentor of all academic activities and the quality of education primarily depends upon their skill and knowledge. Hence they need to be well versed will all types of library resources including e-resources (Sapathy & Kashyap, 2014).

There are numbers of Universities in Chhattisgarh excluding NIT, IIM, which are autonomous organization of MHRD, Government of India. The present study confined to six numbers of Universities which have regular teaching departments and have collection on e-resources. These are Gurughasi Das Central University, Bilaspur;

Hidayatullah National Law University, Raipur; Indira Ghandhi Agriculture University, Raipur; Indira Kala Sangeet University, Khairagarh; Kushabhau Thakre Patrakarita avam Jansanchar University, Raipur and Pt.RavishankarShukla University, Raipur. All these universities have established libraries and faculty members regularly use their libraries and e-resources. The present study is an attempt to access the use of e-resources by the faculty members of Universities of Chhattisgarh.

2. REVIEW OF LITERATURE

A good number of studies on use and usage of e-resources and its related subjects, case studies have been carried out by students, research scholars, and teachers of various institutions all over the world. (Satpathy& Rout, 2010) in their paper found that faculty members are aware of the e-resources and various types of e-resources, e-database, and e-journals, and highlights the suggestions for the improvement in the access facilities with high Internet speed and subscription to more e-resources by the Central Library of CVRCE. (Tahir, Mahmood & Shafique, 2010) in their paper found that humanists still stick to the printed information sources but they pay good attention to electronic resources. Most of them have access to computer and Internet at office and home. They are regular users of a variety of electronic technologies. Although faced with many problems, the humanists perceive that modern technology made their work easier. (Madhusudhan, 2010) in his paper found that electronic resources have become an integral part of the information needs of research scholars at Kurukshetra University. Further, he identified that e-resources can be good substitutes for conventional resources, if the access is fast and more computer terminals are installed to provide fast access to e-resources. (Zhang , Ye & Liu, 2011) in their paper found that that most NSTL users are graduate students and young staff members and the number of male users surpasses female ones slightly. The purpose of the utilization of electronic resources for customers is scientific research, teaching and the need for self-development. (Zabed Ahmed, 2013) in his study found that faculty members are not generally satisfied with the current level of university subscribed e-resources. The faculty members identified that limited number of titles, limited access to back issues, difficulty in finding information, inability to access from home, limited access to computers and slow download speed are major constraints. These constraints do affect e-resources use in the public universities.

3. OBJECTIVES OF THE STUDY

The basic objectives of the present study are to make a study on the use of e-resources by the faculty members of different government universities of Chhattisgarh. However the other objectives of the study can be summarized as below.

a) To Know the types and media of e-resources used by faculty members

b) To find out the purpose of use e-resources by faculty members

c) To Know the preferred place of faculty members for searching the e-resources

d) To examine the effect of e- resources on study and research activities of faculty members

e) To find out the advantages of e-resources felt by the faculty members.

f) To identify various problems/barriers in using e-resources by faculty members

4. SCOPE AND LIMITATIONS OF THE STUDY

The Study is confined to the use of e-resources by the regular faculty members of 06 universities of

Chhattisgarh such as, G. G. Central University, Bilaspur, Hidayatullah National Law University, Raipur, Indira Gandhi Agricultural University, Raipur, Indira Kala Sangeet University, Khairagagrh, Kushabhau Thakre Univeristy of Journalism and Mass Communication, Raipur and Pt Ravi Shankar Shukla Unversity, Raipur. The various limitations of the study are:

a) The study is limited to the neither universities of Chhattisgarh state having regular teaching departments and e-resource collection and neither any other universities of Chhattisgarh nor universities of any other states.

b) Among different categories of users of libraries of these universities, the study is confined to regular faculty members only.

c) Among various aspects of these libraries, the study is limited to the use of e-resources by the faculty members only and not any other aspects.

5. METHODOLOGY FOLLOWED

The study was based on cross sectional survey method. Among various techniques of Survey method, Questionnaire technique was selected for the study. Accordingly a structured questionnaire was designed to collect data from the regular faculty members of various universities of Chhattisgarh under the scope of the study, keeping in mind the basic objectives of the study. The entire population i.e. all regular faculty members were taken as sample for the study which was 555 in numbers.

6. DATA ANALYSIS AND INTERPRETATION

A structured questionnaire was prepared and was distributed to 320 faculty members of various states of Chhattisgarh who were physically available in the Universities and excluded others who were absent due to various official and personal assignments. Out of 320 faculty members, 202 responded with the filled in questionnaires (63.12%).Hence in all cases the total number of respondents for the present study will be 202. Further all the respondents were computer literate and were using Internet regularly. The collected data were edited, tabulated and analyzed with the help of statistical techniques and graphical representation.

Table 1. Purpose of using e-resources by the faculty members

S.No.	*Purpose*	*# of Respondents*	*% of Response*
1	Teaching	166	82.17
2	Research	200	99
3	Paper publication	192	95.04
4	Update knowledge	98	48.51
5	Other	69	34.15

The purpose of using e-resources varies from person to person. The analysis of data of Table-1 reveals that out of 202 respondents, as high as 200 respondents having 99% of response opined that the basic purpose of using e-resources is research. It is followed by responses on other purposes such as paper publication (95.04%), teaching (82.17%),update knowledge on their subject(98%) and other purposes such as entertainment, accessing e-resources for other etc.(34.15%).

Table 2. Places used by faculty Members for accessing e-resources.

S. N	*Place*		*# of Respondents*	*% of Response*
1.	University central library	Yes	190	94.05
		No	12	5.95
2.	Departmental library	Yes	50	24.75
		No	152	75.25
3.	Constituent college library	Yes	10	4.95
		No	192	95.04
4	Other places	Yes	29	14.36
		No	173	85.64

The faculty members use different places for accessing e-resources. The analysis of data of Table-2 reveals that the faculty members mostly use Central library for accessing their required e-resources with a response rate of 94.5% ,followed by Departmental library(24.75%) , constituent college library(4.95%) other places(14.36%) which includes ,official chamber, home, Internet cafe etc.

Table 3. Types of e– resources used by faculty members

S.N	Types of e-resources	# of respondents	%
1.	e-Bibliography	170	84.1
2.	e- Journals	187	92.5
3.	e- thesis	133	65.8
4.	e- report	132	65.3
5.	e- book	76	37.6
6.	e- encyclopedia/dictionary	136	67.3
7.	e- News paper	108	53.4
8.	Other	74	36.6

The analysis of data of Table-3 shows the various types of e-resources used by the university faculty members of Chhattisgarh. It indicates that e-journals are mostly used by faculty members i.e. 187 out of 202(92.5%). It is followed by use of other types of e-resources such as e-bibliography (84.1%), e-encyclopedia/dictionary (67.3%), e-thesis(65.8%), e-report(65.3%), e-newspaper(53.4%), e-book(37.6%), and other types of e-resources (36.6%) which include e-magazines, e-maps, other e-reports etc.

Table 4. Mode of e – resources used by Faculty of C.G.

S.N	Mode	# of Respondents	%
1.	Online	140	69.30
2.	Offline	04	1.98
3.	Online & Offline	64	31.68

The e-resources can be assessed both online and offline mode. The analysis of date of Table- indicates that most of the faculty members use online e-resources (69.30%), followed by use of both online and off line e-resources (31.68%) and only offline e-resources (1.98%).

Table 5. Effect of e-resource on faculty Members

Effective	*Decreasing Effect*		*Increasing Effect*	
	# of Respondents	*%*	*# of Respondents*	*%*
Searching time	160	79.2	42	20.8
Utilization of Study time	51	25.25	151	74.75
Speed in work	8	3.96	194	96.04
Publication of Research Papers/Articles	6	2.97	196	97.03
Publication of book	5	2.48	197	97.52
Participation in Seminar/Conf./ Workshop	12	5.4	190	94.6
Improvement in teaching quality	7	3.47	195	96.53
Update subject Knowledge	10	4.95	192	95.5

The study attempted to find out the effect of e-resources on various works of faculty members. The analysis of data on this has been tabulated in Table- which explains the effect of e-resources on various works of faculty members. Regarding searching time to find required information, out of 202 repondents,160(79.2%) respondents were in the view that the time for searching information is decreasing due to use of e-resources whereas 42(20.85) were in the view that the searching time is increasing. Similarly the majority of the respondents were in the view that various aspects such as utilization of study time, speed in work, publication of research papers/articles, publication of books, participation in seminar/conference/workshop, improvement in teaching quality, update subject knowledge has increased due to the effect of e-resources with the rate of responses such as 74.75%, 96.04%, 97.03%, 97.52%, 94.6%, 96.53%, 95.5% respectively.

Table 6. Advantages of e- resource by faculty of C.G.

S.N	*Advantages*		*# of Respondents*	*% of Responses*
1.	Save Time	Yes	165	81.68
		No	37	18.32
2.	Speed in access	Yes	120	59.40
		No	82	40.60
3.	Easy to use	Yes	164	81.18
		No	38	18.82
4.	More informative	Yes	167	82.68
		No	35	17.32
5.	More useful	Yes	169	83.66
		No	33	16.34
6.	Less expensive	Yes	141	69.81
		No	61	30.19

The present study attempted to analyze various advantages of e-resources opined by the faculty members. The data collected on this as per the analysis of Table- reveals that maximum respondents opined the main advantage of e-resource is that it is more useful with a response rate of 83.66%. It is followed by other advantages expressed by faculty members such as more informative (82.68%), save time (81.68%), easy to use (81.18%), less expensive (69.81%) and speed in access (59.40%).

Table 7. Problems in using e- resource by faculty Members

S.N	*Problems*	*# of Respondents*	*% of Response*
1.	Unfamiliar to e-resources	34	16.83
2.	Lack of knowledge/guidance to access e-resources	105	51.98
3.	Uncomfortable to Study on screen	88	43.56

4.	Unavailability of required information	44	20.29
5.	Slow downloading	106	52.47
6	Language	97	48.01

Regarding various problems faced by the faculty members in accessing e-resources, the analysis of data of Table indicates that slow downloading is the major problem in accessing e-resources (52.47%). The other problems as indicated by the faculty members are lack of knowledge/guidance to access e-resources with a response rate of 51.98%, language (48.01%), uncomfortable to study on screen (43.56%) and unavailability of required information (20.29%).

7. MAJOR FINDINGS OF THE STUDY

On the basis of data analysis and interpretation and also on the basis of personal interaction with the faculty members, the major findings of the study can be summarized as below.

a) The basic purpose of using e-resources by the faculty members is to carry out research work with a response rate of 99%.

b) The main place for accessing e-resources by the faculty members is the Central library of their respective universities as opined by 94.05% of respondents. Further departmental library is used by very few numbers of respondents (24.75%) which indicates that either the absent of departmental libraries or the departmental libraries lack necessary infrastructure facilities to access e-resources. Also poor rate of response i.e. 14.36% for other place like departmental chamber indicates that the e-resources may be of single user or may be of user ID and password based instead of IP based. Similarly low response to use e-resources from outside the institute indicate the absence of remote user facilities in these universities.

c) E-journals are the main e-resources used by the faculty members with a response rate of 92.5%. Surprisingly use of e-theses as opined by 65.8% seems to be due to Sodhaganga project of UGC and availability of various open access and commercial Electronic Theses and Dissertation (ETD) databases. Surprisingly as opined by respondents e-books are of lowest use by the faculty members (37.6%) which indicate that e-books are not procured by all universities libraries.

d) Most of the faculty members preferred to use e-resources online (69.30%)

e) Due to the effect of e-resources, the various works of faculty members such as utilization of study time, speed of work, publication of research papers/ books, participation in seminar/conference/ improvement of teaching quality, update subject knowledge etc. has increased remarkably as per the opinion expressed by them. Further the searching time to find out the required information of faculty members has decreased (97.2% response)

f) The main advantages of e-resources as expressed by the respondents is "more informative" with a response rate of 82.68%.However another advantages "speed in access" is opined by lowest rate of response i.e. 59.40% which is little surprising since the main essence of e-resource is the speed in access. It indicates that faculty members are not fully aware of the search techniques of e-resources.

g) The main problems faced by faculty members in using e-resources as opined by them are slow down loading (52.47%) and lack of knowledge/guidance to use e-resources (52.47%). Further language of e-resources is another problem expressed by the respondents, which is due to the Hindi medium educational system of the Chhattisgarh state.

8. SUGGESTIONS AND CONCLUSION

E-resources are gaining popularity day by day among faculty members and gradually they are becoming more comfortable in using e-resources. Accordingly the libraries of academic institutions more particularly the university libraries need to continuously access the electronic information need of faculty members and their information seeking behavior so that they can develop a good collection of e-resources .Further simply acquiring e-resources is not enough ,the libraries must ensure its smooth access through development of necessary infrastructure, promote the use of e-resources through proper notification of availability of e-resources through personal mail, website etc and conduct regular training programs about the technicalities and effective ways to use e-resources. The present study reveals an encouraging picture about the use of e-resources by the faculty members of universities of Chhattisgarh. However keeping pace with the development of information technology and demands of users, the universities libraries of Chhattisgarh need to acquire more and more e-resources and develop necessary facilities to access the e-resources ,so that maximum usages of e-resources will be possible and return on investment can properly made and justified.

REFERENCES

1. Appleton, L. (2006). Perceptions of electronic library resources in further education. *The Electronic library*, 24(1), 54-63.
2. Madhusudhan, M.(2010).Use of electronic resources by research scholars of Kurukshetra University. *The Electronic Library*, 28(4), 492–506. doi: http://dx.doi.org/10.1108/02640471011033684
3. Satpathy,S. K. &Kashyap, S. R. (2014). A study on use of e-resources by the faculty members of Pt. Ravishankar Shukla university (PRSU), Chhattisgarh. In M. Pandey, P. K. Joshi, B. C. Jain, T. Choudhury & R. P. Kujur (Eds.), *Agricultural*

Inforamtion Management in Digital Era (pp. 270-273). Indira Gandhi KrishiViswavidyalaya: Raipur.

4. Satpathy, S. K. & Rout, B. (2010). Use of e-resources by the faculty members with special reference to CVRCE, Bhubaneswar. *DESIDOC Journal of Library & Information Technology,* 30(4), 11-16.

5. Tahir, M., Mahmood, K. &Shafique, F. (2010). Use of electronic information resources and facilities by humanities scholars. *The Electronic Library,* 28(1), 122–136. doi: http://dx.doi.org/10.1108/02640471011023423

6. Zabed Ahmed, S. M. (2013). Use of electronic resources by the faculty members in diverse public universities in Bangladesh. *The Electronic Library,* 31(3), 290–312. doi:http://dx.doi.org/10.1108/EL-05-2011-0081

7. Zhang, L., Ye, P. & Liu, Q. (2011), A survey of the use of electronic resources at seven universities in Wuhan, China. *Program,* 45(1), 67–77. doi: http://dx.doi.org/10.1108/00330331111107402

13

SWOT Analysis of Electronic Library Resources

Vijayakumar M.
Central Library, Birla Institute of Technology, Deemed University, Mesra, Ranchi, Jharkhand - 835215

Saket Kumar
Central Library, National University of Study & Research in Law, Ranchi, Jharkhand

Debojyoti Nath
Central Library, Birla Institute of Technology, Deemed University, Mesra, Ranchi, Jharkhand - 835215

Premraj Mishra
Manager, Information Services, Tata Steel Limited, Jamshedpur, Jharkhand, PIN: 831001

ABSTRACT

Due to information explosion through electronic format, we can find some many changes in our library especially. Usage of print library resources is declined in most of academic and research libraries. Even usage of electronic library resources is increased in most of the libraries, may it be academic or research libraries. Regarding budget, the majority of the library resource budget in most of the libraries is spent on electronic library resources, and even this trend will continue in future also. With the advent of cloud computing technology there will be reduce in the overall number of technical personal required for technical services. This paper addressed using the SWOT tool may itself be thought of in terms of phases or a life cycle. And employ a strategy to match strengths and opportunities; and employ those strategies for converting the weaknesses and threats into strengths and opportunities for electronic library resources.

Keywords : SWOT Analysis, Application of SWOT, E-Library Resources

1. INTRODUCTION

Access to electronic library resources has been major boon all libraries users, may it be academic library user, research/special library user and public library user. Electronic library resources are considered to be one of note harmony of hybrid library collection. Even it become essential tool in all academic and research activities. Electronic Library Resource means, any library resources that can be accessed electronically or digitally are called electronic library resources. Due to advantage of information technology, electronic library resources are exploding in its growth with all dimensions.

2. TYPES OF ELECTRONICS LIBRARY RESOURCES

We can find wide and varied electronic library resources in the market some the following are the common Electronic Library Resources that can be accessed by our library users.

- Journals, Magazines, Newspaper
- Books
- Patents
- Paintings/Pictures
- Maps/Graphs
- Sounds/Videos
- Zine
- Thesis & Dissertation
- Website
- Link
- Reference sources

  - Dictionaries
  - Treasures
  - Encyclopaedias
  - Gazetteers
- online database
  - Bibliographic—references to published material
  - Numeric—e.g. statistical tables
  - Full text—complete publications
  - Audio—collections of music
  - Image—e.g. collections of slides
  - Multimedia—audio-visual, animation etc.
- Reference tools
  - Plagiarism checking
  - Grammar checking
  - Remote access

3. SWOT ANALYSIS APPLICATION

The SWOT analysis is not a procedure in itself, such as strategic planning for ICT tools in library, opportunity analysis for automation, networking &digitization or others. Instead it's a tool used to structure a particular task internally (Strength and Weakness) and externally (Opportunity & Threat). As a result, a task that's addressed using the SWOT tool may itself be thought of in terms of phases or a life cycle. However, the SWOT analysis, is simply a tool that may be used one or more times to gain a collection of ideas regarding a particular task.

3.1. SWOT Analysis of Electronic Library Resources

So there is an urgent need to structured planning to evaluate the electronic library resources in terms of their Strength, Weakness, Opportunity and threats which commonly known as SWOT analysis electronic library resources. This swot analysis will helpful to develop a strong strategy to procure electronic library resource for the benefit of library users which can be used on 24x7 basis.

3.2. Strength of Electronic Library Resources

While procuring the electronic library resources, we should think about its strength how it will be benefit the library and its users. We may feel, the following are some the strength of the electronic library resources.

- beyond Google/Wikipedia
- Access to premium content
- Anytime anywhere access
- Return on Investment
- Accessible
- Easily searchable
- Speed
- Interactive
- Links
- Added Value
- Inexpensive
- Flexibility
- very up-to-date
- Embargo of research articles

3.3. Weakness of Electronic Library Resources

For the cost effectiveness we should overcome the weakness of any electronic library resources. So the following are the points that we may feel as a weakness of electronic library resources.

- In adequate information literacy
- Cost/ Budget
- Management
- Lack of awareness on business model

- Disintegrated technology
- Techno stress,
- No guarantee of archival
- Perishable citation - once online, if websites change URLs citations disappear
- Authenticity - authors concerned about establishing the source, authority of material in general, convinced reader for their credibility

3.4. Opportunity for Strength of Electronic Library Resources

We should grab the all the benefits of electronic library resources for the benefit of our library and library users. The following are some of the points that we may consider as a great opportunity for library community.

- Integration of web 2.0
- E-Marketing of Services
- 24x7 access
- High impact
- Cross domain mingling
- Multi-platform
- currency of content
- Multi users
- Easy Sharing
- Easy to publish
- Find resources for your subject
- Keep up-to-date with the latest research in your area

3.5. Threats for Electronic Library Resources

We can have chance to reverse threats into opportunity, so following threats should be reverse back to opportunities.

- Google mind set
- Distancing user

- Disintermediation
- Publisher dependency
- Invisibility of e-resources
- Health aspect
- Easy plagiarism
- Not habituated to read in the screen
- Often not included in indexing and abstracting services
- Search engines ignores PDF files
- Fee-based access
- Standard very variable
- No physical collection development, if we go for non-perpetual access (subscription based)
- Format that a large proportion of e-journal use

4. ADVANTAGES OF SWOT ANALYSIS OF ELECTRONIC LIBRARY RESOURCES

We know well SWOT Analysis is active in policy formulation. It is one of a powerful tool, SWOT analysis of ERS is fine when it used as a channel, and not as a suggestion or recommendation. Success of all libraries will be depend upon on their strengths, they have to correct their weakness and protect against external threats.

The main advantages of SWOT Analysis is as it helps in strategic planning like

- It will be bible for strategic planning to acquire E-resources.
- It will helps to build the potential of e-resources
- It will be helpful to overcome the weaknesses e-resources.
- It may be helpful to capitalize on its opportunities.
- It may be helpful to overcome e-resources threats.

- It may be helpful to classify core competencies of e-resources.
- It may be helpful to lay down the pre plan to procure e-resources.
- The entire process of SWOT analysis may act as a beacon to strengthen e-resources

5. LIMITATIONS OF SWOT ANALYSIS ELECTRONIC LIBRARY RESOURCES

Every process or analysis has its own merits/ demerits or opportunity/threats. Even SWOT Analysis is not free from its limitations. Normally SWOT Analysis does pressure upon the consequence of Strength, Weakness, Opportunity and Threats. It is quite well known to all that SWOT analysis having its own limitation that are not in control of organization.

The factor that includes

- financial atmosphere;
- penetrating an innovative e-resources
- inadequate financial budget and expansion amenities;
- No access to e-resources due to adequate infrastructure and deprived worth;
- underprivileged relations between library and user community;
- If inappropriate strategies is used then, proper decisions can't be made
- Exterior aspects are not in our control
- The process of SWOT analysis varies time to time and organisations to organisation
- The SWOT analysis may be treated as genuine, if internal teams desire to showcase only their t strengths.

6. CONCLUSION

Due to information explosion through electronic format, we can find some many changes in our library especially. Usage of print library resources is declined in most of academic and research libraries. Even usage of electronic library resources is increased in most of the libraries, may it be academic or research libraries. Regarding budget, the majority of the library resource budget in most of the libraries is spent on electronic library resources, and even this trend will continue in future also. With the advent of cloud computing technology there will be reduce in the overall number of technical personal required for technical services. So SWOT analysis will helps us to employ a strategy to match strengths and opportunities; and employ those strategies for converting the weaknesses and threats into strengths and opportunities for electronic library resources.

REFERENCES

1. DaulatJotwani. (2014). Marketing of Electronic Resources in IIT Libraries, *DESIDOC Journal of Library & Information Technology*, 34(2), 162-169.
2. Advantages & Disadvantages of SWOT Analysis. (n.d.). Retrieved January 20, 2015, from http://smallbusiness.chron.com/advantages-amp-disadvantages-swot-analysis-41398.html
3. John Paul Anbu K., Sanjay Kataria, and Shri Ram. (2013). Dynamics of Managing Electronic Resources: Electronic Resource Management System (ERMS) Initiatives, *Defence Scientific Information & Documentation Centre*, 33 (4), 300-305.
4. Mahabaleshwara Rao, Baikady, Jessy A., and Shivananda Bhat K. (2014). Off Campus Access to Licensed E-resources of Library: A Case Study, *Defence Scientific Information & Documentation Centre*, 34 (6), 486-490.
5. Jalal, Samir Kumar and Vijayakumar M. (2008). Strategies for E-Learning: An Overview. *INFOLIB: A Quarterly Bulletin of Jharkhand Information & Library Association*, 1(1-2), 18-22.

6. Thomas B. Hickey. (1996). The Impact of Electronic Publishing on Academic Libraries, *Defence Scientific Information & Documentation Centre*, 16(1), 9-16.
7. Vijayakumar M. and Manjunath B. (2007). Exploring the Availability and Effective utilization of Electronic Resources in Dental Science Libraries in the State of Karnataka. *Indian Journal of Information Science and Services*, 1(1), 18-25.

14

Usage of e-Journals Among Research Scholars of NIT Rourkela : A Survey

SK Abdul Gaffar
Library Trainee

Bhojaraju Gunjal
Head, Biju Patnaik Central Library, NIT Rourkela

ABSTRACT

Libraries are investing huge amount on subscription or renewal of e-journals every year, in this scenario there is a need of study to understand and analyses its usage from the users w.r.t. different perspectives. This study is tried to investigate different perspectives such as awareness, access and usage of E-journals among the research scholar's at National Institute of Technology Rourkela, Orissa along with the problems they encounter during the usage of the same. Based on the study, it was also recommended that user education programme; stable high speed internet supply and adequate no. of computers should be provided to ensure constant, consistent access to available e-journals services. This study explains the detailed analysis of this survey on these different aspects; findings and solutions and also recommends a probable solution for improvising the usage of e-journals.

Keywords : Electronic Journals, E-journals, E-database, online journals, Virtual Journals, Library Consortia.

1. INTRODUCTION

Electronic journals (e-Journals) as one type of Electronic resources have become a major resource for research community for their information gathering that can play an important role in their research work. There is no standard definition for E-journals. As a result they have called by various names such as E-journals, network journals, paperless journals, virtual journals and CD-ROM journals etc. Libraries are investing huge amount on subscription or renewal of e-journals every year, in this scenario there is a need of study to understand and analyses its usage from the users' w.r.t. different perspectives. This study is tried to investigate different perspectives such as awareness, access and usage of E-journals among the research scholar's at Biju Patnaik Central Library (BPCL) of National Institute of Technology Rourkela (NITR), Orissa along with the problems they encounter during the usage of the same.

2. E-JOURNAL : AN OVERVIEW

The phrase electronic journal or e-journal is used to signify a broader category of electronic publications that may or may not have a print counterpart.

2.1. Definition

The Encyclopedic Dictionary of Library and Information Science define a journal as "the record of proceeding of transactions of a learned society".

According to Harold's Librarian's Glossary it is a journal for which the full end product is available on optical disk, over a network or in any other electronic form, strictly a journal in which the entire process is carried out electronically. In other word, an electronic journal is one where writing, editing, refereeing and distribution of item are carried out electronically without paper intermediaries.

According to (Pullinger, Brain & Schkel, 1990) "e-journal is one whose input text may be entered directly by a computer or by other file transfer mechanisms in a machine readable form, whose editorial processing is facilitated by a computer and whose articles are thus made available in electronic form to readers. According to Lancaster "an e-journals are those journals which are available in electronic medium and is available only in this medium. In general a journal that is available in electronic form through online host is called e -journals."

2.2. Characteristics of e-journals

According to (Dash, 2006), several characteristics are there of E-journals, some are given below:

i. Printing and distribution of E-journals are almost different.

ii. It is established network communication between authors, editors, referees and users.

iii. Reader can access their urgent articles or full issues of the journals, without no time if required or printout of the relevant pages can obtain.

iv. Different sections within individual journals or articles can link to related resources on internet through the Hypertext links.

v. Though it is multimedia capacities it is provides an edge over the conventional journals available in print form.

vi. Immediacy is one good feature of E-journals.

vii. It is allow to remote access, so it is save the time to the users.

viii. It can use at the same time more than one user.

ix. Provide time access and at 24x7 formula.

2.3. Advantages of e-journals

As explained by (Jones & Cook, 2000) and (SOAS, n.d.), e-journals are becoming quite popular because the cost of electronic equipment is falling down significantly, therefore making e-publishing costly. Due to low cost of electronic publishing and distribution; it is more economic than paper printing. So e-journals have large numbers of advantages:

i. User can browse the contents pages or the full text of journals to find articles on their required subject.
ii. User can read journal articles on their respective desktop; no need to be go physically in the Library.
iii. User can e-mail articles to their self or download E-journals for printing.
iv. User can read articles 24/7 hours be available, even when library is closed.
v. User can move different sections within individual journals or articles can link to related resources on internet through the Hypertext links.
vi. E-journals can include more audio-visual and images.
vii. User can e-mail the author or editor with their respective comments.
viii. Maximum E-journals provides indexing and abstracting services.
ix. It is also providing Security (therefore e-journals cannot be lost)

2.4. Disadvantages of e-journals

Similarly (Jones & Cook, 2000) provides certain disadvantages of e-journals as given below :

i. Though it is less cost but first time investment is very high. For equipment of computers and printers are required to read electronic journals.
ii. Technological and hardware support may vary from one publication/publisher to another.
iii. E-journals have different format and different price level so sometimes it is making confuse to subscribe for an organization.

iv. It is take some time to display its pages and images on computer screen.

v. It is related to legal and copy right issues.

3. ACCESS TYPES OF E-JOURNALS

According to (Jones & Cook, 2000) different types of access of e-journals provided by the publisher are as follows:

i. Free access : In which publishers from time to time provides access to those e-journals, which are subscribed in print format.

ii. Exclusive subscription : Those institutions can get whole the journals bought out by the publisher without subscription to the print counterpart.

iii. Selective access : That subscriber chose a few e-journals from the publisher and pay for agreement.

iv. Fee-based access : The publisher provides access to its complete e-holdings.

v. Institution Vs consortium access : Though few institution having common interest and requirement can for consortia for e-journals access.

vi. Consortium-based access model : That the member in institution need not subscribe to e-journals on ownership basis.

4. OBJECTIVES OF THE STUDY

Following objectives have been framed for this study:

i. To study the level of awareness among the research scholars about the existence of the e-journal resources subscribed by the central library.

ii. To find out the purpose of the using of e-journals by the research scholars.

iii. To analyses the frequency of using of e-journals among research scholars.

iv. To find out the problems encountered by the research scholars.

v. To determine the importance of e-journals among research scholars.

5. STATEMENT OF THE PROBLEM

The Biju Patnaik Central Library (BPCL) at NIT, Rourkela invests huge amount every year on e-journals, in this scenario there is need for a study to understand and analyses the usage of it from the users in different perspectives. This study investigated different perspectives such as awareness, access and usage of E-journals among the research scholar's.

6. SCOPE OF THE STUDY

For this study, the following scope has been defined.

Respondents : Only Research scholars are taken into consideration.

Questionnaires : 150 questionnaires collected from 700 research scholars.

E-Resources : only e-Journal is considered among the various types of e-resources subscribed by library.

7. RESEARCH METHODOLOGY

In this paper, the methodological issues that are applied to carry out the empirical investigation are described in detail below. According to the theoretical studies, there are supposed to be difference in the purpose to using, awareness and access of e-journals among research scholars viz. M. Tech(R) and Ph. D students of NIT Rourkela. Based on the above assumptions, a frame work is adopted using Questionnaire and Observation methods by applying appropriate statistical tool.

7.1. Survey Data Collection

A survey will be the most appropriate method for this study. The present study, primary data are collected through survey method by preparing Close-ended and Open-ended Structured Questionnaire. Method of collecting data – (i) Group mail sent to all research scholars with questionnaire and (ii) Personal meeting with the scholars.

7.2. Site, Population of Study and Sampling Procedure

The research population of this study was selected among research scholars of M. Tech(R) and Ph. D. of NIT Rourkela adopting convenient sampling. Convenience sampling technique is non probability technique where all the elements in the sample frame do not have an equal opportunity of getting selected and the method of selection is through expediency (Yu, & Cooper, 1983). A questionnaire, was administered and collected from various scholars both the hostellers and day scholars of NIT Rourkela. The questionnaire was divided in some sections on the basis of various objectives.

7.3. Statistical Tools and Data Analysis

There are many statistical tools available with new features. Among them, one of the most popular MS-Excel was used as the main statistical tool to analyses, manipulate and calculate the collected primary data. The gathered data were analyzed and interpreted with the help of table and figures for easy and lucid understanding.

8. DATA ANALYSIS AND DISCUSSION

Here provides the results obtained by using statistical tools namely MS-Excel is used to meet the objectives of the study. Nos. of questions were prepared in different category viz. awareness (04), access (08) and usage (05) aspects. Similarly the data analysis is carried our based on these categories of the questions made are explained below. Few important aspects are explained with diagrams in below sub-sections.

8.1 Respondent's profile

The respondents were belong to Ph.D. and M.Tech (R) courses from different departments.

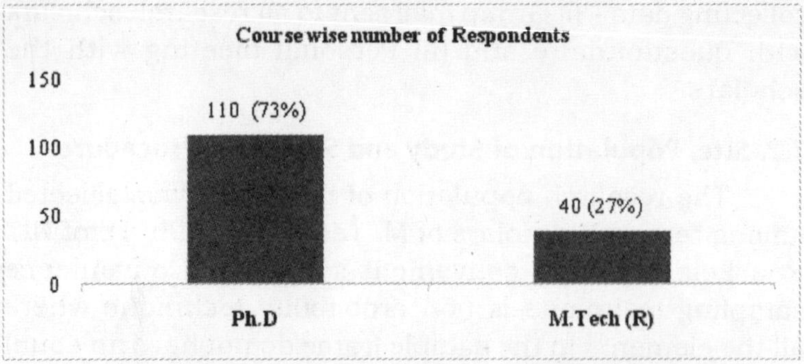

Fig. 1. Course wise number of Respondents

From the total 700 questionnaires distributed among scholars and 150 scholars responded back. Ph.D.110 (73%) and M. Tech(R) 40(27%) that consisted of the scholars of NIT Rourkela irrespective of their courses and discipline.

8.2. Awareness Aspects

Here the data analysis pertaining to awareness aspects has been explained as below:

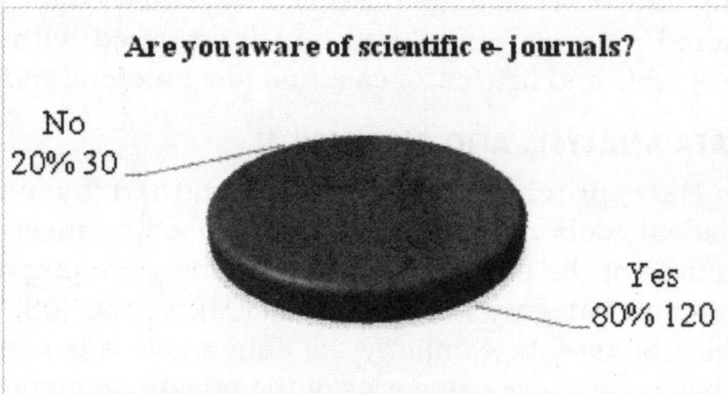

Fig. 2. Awareness level of online scientifice-journals of the respondents.

Fig. 3. Awareness level of online databases subscribed from library of the respondents.

Figure 2 represents that 120 (80%) of the respondents they have good awareness level about online scientific e-journals, but while 30 (20%) of the respondents they are not aware of online scientific e-journals.

Figure 3 shows that 105(70%) of the respondents they have knowledge of online databases and they also subscribed from the library (BPCL), while 45(30%) of the respondents they are not aware of online databases.

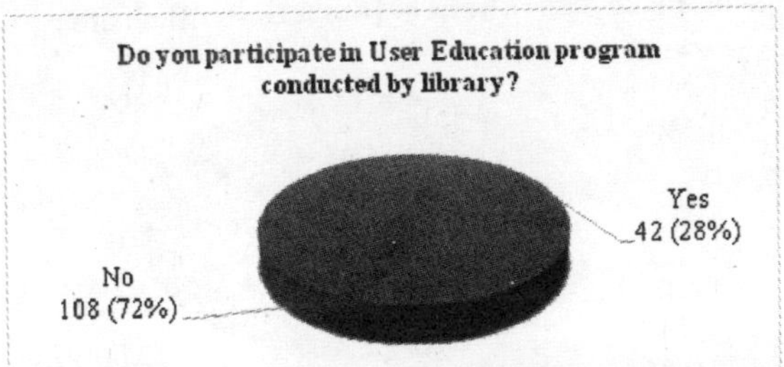

Fig. 4. Awareness level of User Education program conducted by library of the respondents.

Figure 4 represents that 108 (72%) of the respondents they are not participate in User Education program conducted by the library (BPCL) and even they are not aware of user education program but only 42 (28%) of the respondents they participate in User Education program conducted by the library (BPCL).

8.3. Access Aspects

In this section data analysis pertaining to access aspects has been explained to following:

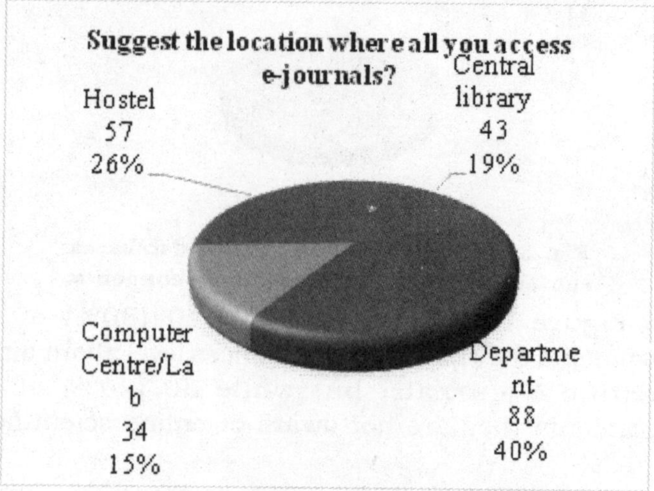

Fig. 5. Accessing e-journals while using several location by the respondents

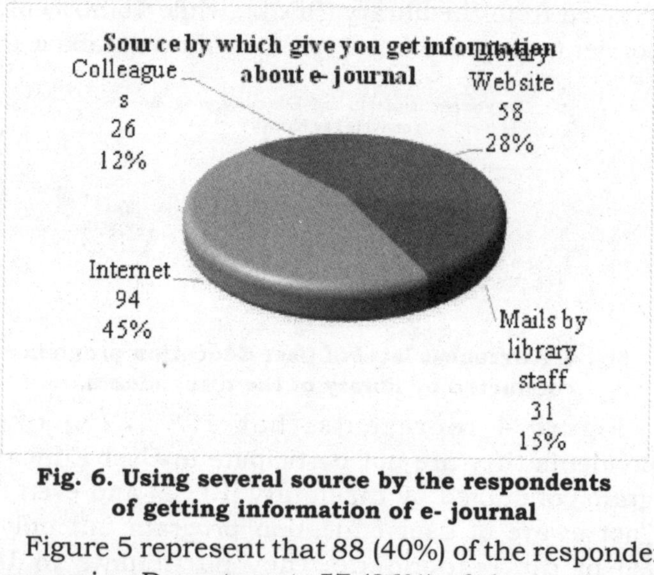

Fig. 6. Using several source by the respondents of getting information of e- journal

Figure 5 represent that 88 (40%) of the respondents are say using Department, 57 (26%) of the respondents are say using Hostel, 43 (19%) of the respondents are say using Central library and remain 34 (15%) of the respondents are say using Computer Centre/Lab for accessing e-journals.

Figure 6 shows that 94 (45%) of the respondents are using internet, 58 (28%) of the respondents are using library website, 31 (15%) of the respondents are using Mails by library staff and very few 26 (12%) of the respondents are using their colleagues help to getting information of e-journal.

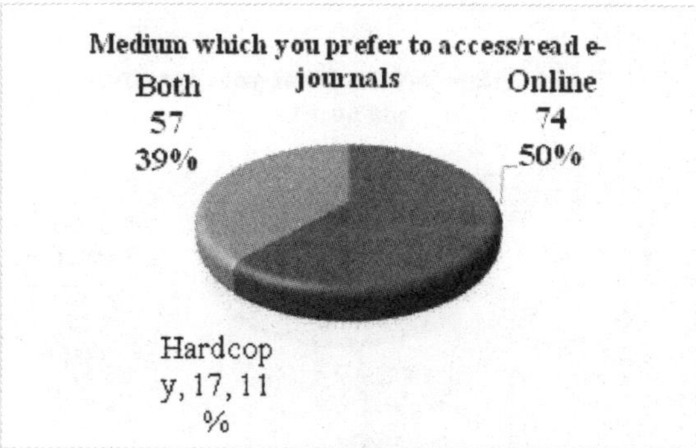

Fig. 7. Respondents prefer Medium to access/read e-journals

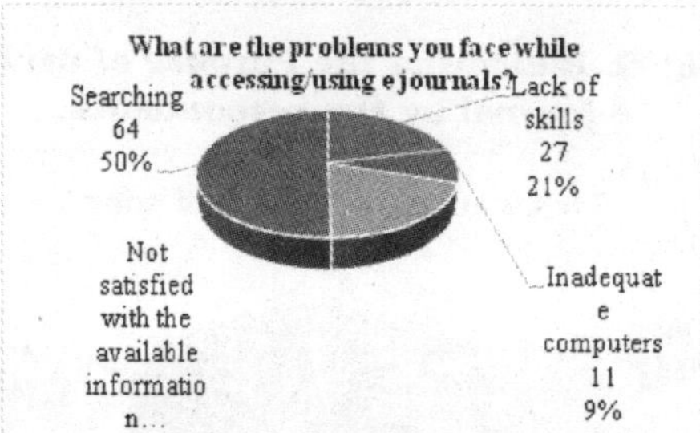

Fig. 8. Respondents face problems while accessing/using e journals

Figure 7 represents that 74 (50%) of the respondents are prefer online medium, 57 (39%) of the respondents are prefer both (Hard copy and soft copy) and only 17(11%) of the respondents are prefer only hard copy to access/ read e-journals.

Figure 8 shows that 64 (50%) of the respondents are prefer searching; 27(21%) of the respondents are prefer lack of skills; 25 (20%) of the respondents are not satisfied with the available of information and 11(9%) of the respondents are prefer inadequate computers problems facing, while they are accessing/ using of E-journals.

8.4. Usage Aspects

Data analysis pertaining to usage aspects has been explained to following:

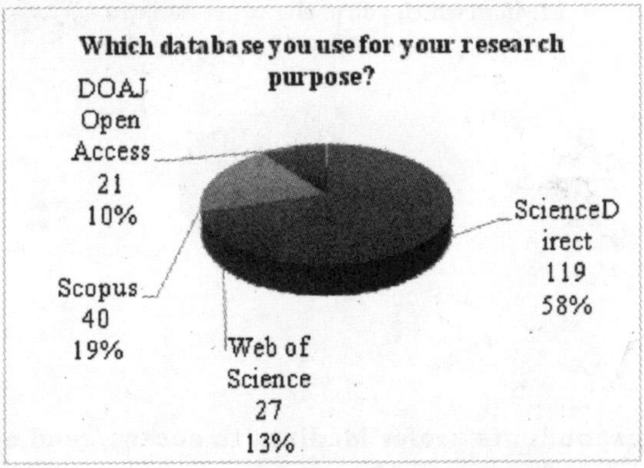

Fig. 9. Indicating the Purpose of using e-journal by the respondents

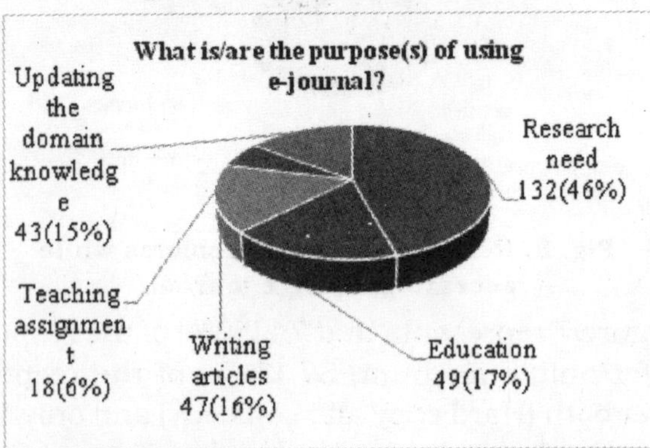

Fig. 10. Database use by the respondents

Figure 9 represents that 119(58%) of the respondents are using Science Direct, 40(19%) of the respondents are using Scopus, 27 (13%) of the respondents are usingWeb of Science and very few21 (10%) of the respondents are using DOAJ Open Access for their research purpose.

Figure 10 represents that 132(46%) of the respondents are say research need, 49(17%) of the respondents are say education, 47(16%) of the respondents are say for writing article, 43(15%) of the respondents are say updating knowledge and very few 18(6%) of the respondents are say teaching assignment Purpose they are of using e-journal.

9. FINDINGS

Following are the major findings of the study:

- 80% of the respondents have good awareness level of online scientific e- journals therefore; research scholars are regular user of e- journals.
- The respondents of the study came from heterogeneous group belonging to different departments. The majority of the scholars pursuing Ph.D.i.e.73% and 27% belongs to M. Tech(R)
- More than 70% of the respondents have good knowledge of online databases, and they also subscribed from the Central library (BPCL).
- The study also found that the most 72% of the respondents they are not participating in regular User Education program conducted by the library.
- 40% of the respondents are accessing e-journals from their respective department, 26% of the respondents' access from hostels; 19% of the respondents using Central library and remaining15% of the respondents using Computer Centre/Lab for accessing e-journals.
- The study found that the most 45% of the

respondents are using internet, 28%of the respondents are using library website, 15% of the respondents are using Mails by library staff and very few 12% of the respondents are using their colleagues help to getting information of e- journal.

- Almost 50% of the respondents prefer online medium; 39% of the respondents are prefer both Hard copy and soft copy whereas 11% of the respondents prefer only hard copy to access/read e-journals.
- This study also shows that 58% of the respondents are using Science Direct; 19%are using Scopus; 13%are using Web of Science and very few 10% of the respondents are using DOAJ Open Access for their research purpose.
- Purpose of using e-journals: Users access e-journals for different needs i.e.46% of the respondents uses for research need; 17%uses for education; 16%uses for writing article; 15%uses for updating their domain knowledge and very few 6% of the respondents uses for teaching assignment purpose.
- Some of the non-English journal likes chines journals are not understandable. So, library should be subscribe these journals in English language.

10. SOLUTIONS

Below are the probable solutions to overcome the problems analyzed in this study:

- Even though awareness about e-journals is 80%, but 72% of the respondents are not attending the regular User education programme (UEP). So study recommends scholars to attend the user education programme on regular basis conducted by library for more benefits.
- Organization in association with library needs to make some mandatory steps for all users to undergo UEP on regular basis to enhance its usage.

- Some respondents told that slow internet speed while downloading e- journals, so organization needs to take some positive steps to solve this technical problem.

11. CONCLUSION

The study was conducted among the research scholars of NIT Rourkela. Based on this study, it was observed that e-journals have great impact on the research scholars for their research work. The present survey also provides there is scope for developing the required information skills in accessing e-journals. Participation in User education programme and orientation to all library resources will greatly enhance the use of e-journals resources and imparting ethics of research. The further research should not be limited to a single Institute or University; rather it should be conducted on larger geographical and demographic among many Universities with wide scope of e-resources.

REFERENCES

1. Dash, S. & Panda, K. C. (2006). A challenge for the contemporary libraries. *Digital libraries,* 94-97.
2. Jones, S., Cook, C. (2000). Electronic Journals: Are They A Paradigm Shift?.*Online Journal of Issues in Nursing.* 5(1), Retrieved from www.nursingworld.org/Main Menu Categories /ANAMarketplace/ANAPeriodicals/OJIN/TableofContents/ Volume52000/No1Jan00/ElectronicJournalsAreThey AParadigmShift.aspx
3. Pullinger, D, Brain and Schkel (1990). The electronic journal research. *British library research report*
4. Yu, J. A. (1983). Convenience Sampling Technique Is Non Probability Technique.
5. SOAS, University of London. The School of Oriental and African Studies (n.d.). Retrieved January 18, 2015, from https://www.soas.ac.uk/library/resources/ejournals/ about/

15

Use of E-Learning Resources in Engineering College Libraries affiliated to JNTU-Kakinada

T. Venkata Rao
Librarian, GMR Institute of Technology
Rajam, Srikakulam Dt., Andhra Pradesh

K. Somasekhara Rao
Professor, DLIS, Andhra University
Visakhapatnam, Andhra Pradesh

ABSTRACT

The importance and concept of E-resources n libraries is mentioned. About 12 NBA accredited engineering college libraries are selected. The awareness of e-learning resources and the opinions of respondents on variable like NPTEL Video Courses, LAN Courses, Book CD's, Journal / Magazine CD's and Old Question papers are analysed.

1. CONCEPT OF E-RESOURCES

Electronic information serves as a motivating factor to students as it provides the opportunity to transmit, acquire or download and disseminate information on a subject of interest. Electronic information sources offer today's students opportunities different from their predecessors. (Brophy, 1993), details the advantages of networking for the user as being: "the information needed which can be delivered from the most appropriate source to the user; the user can express respectively his or her needs dynamically; the information is obtained when it is wanted, so it becomes 'just in time' rather than 'just in case'; the user selects only the information needed to answer the specific question and finally, the information is only stored by user wish." Other advantages according to (Ray and Day, 1998)include the fact that "electronic information sources are often faster than consulting print indexes, especially when searching retrospectively, can be searched using combinations of key words. They open up the possibility of searching multiple files at one time, a feat accomplished more easily than when using printed equivalents. Electronic resources can be printed and searches saved to be repeated at a later date; they are updated more often than printed tools." Related to these, Internet is used as a medium of expression to educate the learner, provide information needs at their desktop and send hitch-free and cross-referenced data to the appropriate location. It could be said that improved data transmission facilities will go a long way to reduce the incessant hardship faced by students in the acquisition and generation of data which serves as the basis for research and academic performance improvement. The use of electronic information by students enhances their performance in academic activities. Among the electronic information system student's lies to get most of their information are: Internet, e-mail, electronic journals, bulletin boards, telephone, telex, CD-ROM databases and electronic books.

2. METHODOLOGY

To conduct the survey on engineering college libraries, the list of Engineering College libraries affiliated to JNTU- Kakinada is obtained. As per the information obtained, there are 51 Engineering Colleges affiliated to JNTU – Kakinada (2005). And out of them 12 engineering colleges are selected for the present study. Due importance is given to NBA accredited and established Engineering College Libraries.

2.1. Awareness of different Learning Resources available in the library

All the 2498 respondents were asked to mention whether they are aware of the different learning resources available in their libraries and their responses are presented in the following Table.

Table 1. Awareness of different Learning Resources available in the library

Awareness of Learning Resources available in the library	*f*	%
Aware of the learning resources	1858	74.4
Not aware of the learning resources	640	25.6
Total	2498	100.0

Awareness about different learning resources available in the library is reported by about 74% of the respondents and the remaining 26% are not having any idea about the different learning resources.

2.2. Awareness of different Learning Resources available in the library by selected background variables

Information on the awareness of different learning resources available in the library as reported by the 2498 respondents is presented in the following Table by selected background variables.

The percentage reporting awareness of different learning resources is more among the females (78) than male students (72). This awareness is reported more by the older age group (20 years above) (80%) than the

Table 2. Awareness of different Learning Resources available in the library by different variables

Awareness of different Learning Resources available in the library by different variables

Variable		*n*	*Awareness of different Learning Resources* *Yes* *f*	*%*	*No* *f*	*%*	*Chi-square Value*	*df*	*Sig.*
Gender	Male	1543	1113	72.1	430	27.9	10.696*	1	0.001
	Female	955	745	78.0	210	22.0			
Age Group	< 20 yrs	1778	1284	72.2	494	27.8	15.152*	1	0.000
	> 20 yrs	720	574	79.7	146	20.3			
Academic level	UG	2153	1571	73.0	582	27.0	16.299*	1	0.000
	PG	345	287	83.2	58	16.8			
College	GMR	235	200	85.1	35	14.9	208.474*	11	0.000
	ADITYA_T	223	160	71.7	63	28.3			
	MVGR	224	162	72.3	62	27.7			
	VIGNAN	181	72	39.8	109	60.2			
	BVC	179	119	66.5	60	33.5			
	ADITYA_E	212	173	81.6	39	18.4			
	VASAVI	235	208	88.5	27	11.5			
	VISHNU	203	164	80.8	39	19.2			
	PVPS	183	143	78.1	40	21.9			
	GEC	220	193	87.7	27	12.3			
	LOYOLA	195	127	65.1	68	34.9			
	VRS&YRN	208	137	65.9	71	34.1			

* Chi-square value significant at 5% level.

younger age group (20 years or below)(72%); more by the PG students (83%) than the UG students (73%).

Among the 12 colleges, this awareness ranged from 40% in Vignan Engineering College to 89% in Vasavi Engineering College. Influence of variables like gender, age group, academic level and college on the reported awareness is evidenced by the computed chi-square values.

2.3. Awareness of different services helpful for Learning

All the 2498 respondents were asked to mention whether they are aware of different services helpful for learning. Here also, their responses are recorded in more detail as 'awareness'; 'knowledge' and 'use & evaluation'. These responses are shown in the following Table.

Table 3. Awareness of different services helpful for Learning

Learning Resources		*% Reporting*	
	Awareness	*Knowledge*	*Use & Evaluation*
NPTEL Video Courses	56.6	50.4	49.2
LAN Courses	32.4	30.4	28.0
Book CD's	64.8	63.8	62.0
Journal/Magazine CD's	74.1	65.9	64.7
Old Question papers	76.9	74.9	72.0

Note: n=1858 (Those who reported awareness of Learning Resources)

Most of the respondents are aware of 'Old Question Papers' (77%) and about75% reported detailed knowledge of it while 72% have reported use of it. This is followed by awareness about 'Journal / Magazine CDs' (74%) and knowledge of the same is reported by 66% and use is reported by 65%. About 65% are aware of 'Book CDs' and 64% reported knowledge of the same while use of it is reported by 62%.

Awareness of 'NPTEL Video Courses' is reported by 57% and knowledge of the same by 50% while 49% reported use of the same. Only 32% are aware of 'LAN Courses' and 30% reported knowledge of the same while use of it is reported by 28%.

2.4. Awareness of different services helpful for Learning by selected background variables

Information relating to the awareness of different services helpful for learning reported by the 1858 respondents who are aware of the resources is presented by selected background variables in the following Tables for each of the listed service.

(a) NPTEL Video Courses

The level of awareness and knowledge about NPTEL Video Courses and use of the same is reported more by the male students than the female students. These are reported more by the older age group (20 years above) than the younger age group (20 years or below) and more by the PG students than the UG students.

Among the 12 colleges covered, there is wide variation in these responses. The percentage reporting awareness ranged from 27 in Vishnu Engineering College to 79 in GEC Engineering College. Knowledge levels ranged from 14% in Vignan Engineering College to 69% in GEC and Aditya_E while the percentage reporting Use ranged from 11 Vignan Engineering College to 64 in GEC Engineering College.

Chi-square value indicates influence of gender on awareness and knowledge while influence of age group, academic level and college is found on the awareness, knowledge and use of NPTEL video courses.

Table 4. Awareness, Knowledge and Use of NPTEL Video Courses by selected background variables

Awareness, Knowledge and Use of NPTEL Video Courses by selected background variables					
Variable		n	% Reporting Awareness	Knowledge	Use & Evaluation
Gender	Male	1113	60.2	52.4	50.9
	Female	745	51.3	47.4	46.7
	Chi-square (df 1)				
		Value	14.465*	4.460*	3.063
		Sig	0.000	0.035	0.080
Age Group	< 20 yrs	1284	51.7	46.5	45.3
	> 20 yrs	574	67.6	59.1	57.8
	Chi-square (df 1)				
		Value	40.738*	25.047*	24.848*
		Sig	0.000	0.000	0.000
Academic level	UG	1571	54.1	47.3	45.6
	PG	287	70.4	68.6	67.2
	Chi-square (df 1)				
		Value	26.178*	38.646*	51.368*
		Sig	0.000	0.000	0.000
College	GMR	200	66.0	52.5	52.0
	ADITYA_T	160	70.6	48.8	45.0
	MVGR	162	65.4	64.2	58.6
	VIGNAN	72	62.5	13.9	11.1
	BVC	119	39.5	30.3	28.6
	ADITYA_E	173	68.8	53.8	37.6
	VASAVI	208	67.3	64.9	61.5
	VISHNU	164	26.8	25.6	23.8
	PVPS	143	58.7	51.0	42.7
	GEC	193	79.3	68.9	63.7
	LOYOLA	127	66.1	62.2	59.8
	VRS&YRN	137	35.8	35.8	32.1

Chi-square (df 11)				
	Value	210.462*	200.315*	165.855*
	Sig	0.000	0.000	0.000

Note : n=1858

* Chi-square value significant at 5% level.

(b) LAN Courses

The level of awareness and knowledge about LAN Courses and use of the same is reported more by the male students than the female students. These are reported more by the older age group (20 years above) than the younger age group (20 years or below) while awareness is reported more by the UG students and knowledge and use by the PG students.

Table 5. Awareness, Knowledge and Use of LAN Coursesby selected background variables

Awareness, Knowledge and Use of LAN Courses by selected background variables					
Variable		*N*	*% Reporting Awareness*	*Knowledge*	*Use & Evaluation*
Gender	Male	1113	33.2	33.2	27.9
	Female	745	31.1	28.2	26.2
	Chi-square (df 1)				
		Value	0.901	10.538*	0.025
		Sig	0.343	0.001	0.875
Age	< 20 yrs	1284	30.8	29.6	26.7
Group	> 20 yrs	574	36.1	32.2	30.8
	Chi-square (df 1)				
		Value	5.086*	1.301	3.345
		Sig	0.024	0.254	0.067
Academic	UG	1571	32.7	30.5	27.4
level	PG	287	31.0	30.7	30.0
	Chi-square (df 1)				
		Value	0.468	0.032	1.539

		Sig	0.494	0.859	0.215
College	GMR	200	75.5	73.0	69.0
	ADITYA_T	160	49.4	48.8	30.6
	MVGR	162	1.9	1.2	0.6
	VIGNAN	72	68.1	22.2	20.8
	BVC	119	18.5	17.6	16.0
	ADITYA_E	173	24.3	17.3	17.3
	VASAVI	208	30.3	27.9	26.4
	VISHNU	164	31.7	27.4	13.4
	PVPS	143	24.5	20.3	16.1
	GEC	193	32.1	29.5	28.0
	LOYOLA	127	47.2	39.4	35.4
	VRS&YRN	137	27.0	19.7	16.1
	Chi-square (df 11)				
		Value	299.173*	355.870*	300.427*
		Sig	0.000	0.000	0.000

Note : n=1858

* Chi-square value significant at 5% level.

There is wide variation in these responses among the 12 colleges covered. The percentage reporting awareness ranged from 2 in MVGR Engineering College to 76 in GMR Engineering College. Knowledge levels ranged from 1% in MVGR Engineering College to 73% in GMR Engineering Colleges while the percentage reporting Use ranged from 1 in MVGR Engineering College to 69 in GMR Engineering College.

Chi-square value indicates influence of gender on knowledge, age group on awareness while influence of college is found on the awareness, knowledge and use of LAN courses.

(c) Book CDs

The level of awareness about 'Book CDs' is reported more by the male students while knowledge and use of the same is reported more by the female students.

Awareness, knowledge and use of book CDs are reported more by the older age group (20 years above) than the younger age group (20 years or below) and more by the PG students than the UG students.

There is wide variation in these responses among the 12 colleges covered. The percentage reporting awareness ranged from 52 in GMR Engineering College to 89 in Vasavi Engineering College. Knowledge levels ranged from 33% in Vignan Engineering College to 85% in Vasavi Engineering Colleges while the percentage reporting Use ranged from 26 in Vignan Engineering College to 71 in VRS & YRN Engineering College.

Table 6. Awareness, Knowledge and Use of Book CDs by selected background variables

Awareness, Knowledge and Use of Book CDs by selected background variables

Variable		*n*	*% Reporting*		
			Awareness	*Knowledge*	*Use & Evaluation*
Gender	Male	1113	67.2	62.3	61.2
	Female	745	66.2	63.2	61.6
	Chi-square (df 1)				
		Value	7.038*	2.956	0.785
		Sig	0.008	0.086	0.376
Age Group	< 20 yrs	1284	61.4	61.7	59.2
	> 20 yrs	574	72.3	68.6	68.3
	Chi-square (df 1)				
		Value	20.477*	8.320*	13.951*
		Sig	0.000	0.004	0.000
Academic level	UG	1571	62.8	62.6	59.5
	PG	287	76.0	76.0	70.7
	Chi-square (df 1)				
		Value	18.525*	6.999*	28.061*
		Sig	0.000	0.008	0.000

College	GMR	200	52.0	50.0	45.0
	ADITYA_T	160	78.8	55.6	53.1
	MVGR	162	82.1	69.8	69.1
	VIGNAN	72	72.2	33.3	26.4
	BVC	119	63.9	61.3	61.3
	ADITYA_E	173	56.6	49.7	44.5
	VASAVI	208	89.4	84.6	47.6
	VISHNU	164	86.0	73.2	64.6
	PVPS	143	83.2	70.6	58.7
	GEC	193	63.7	61.1	54.9
	LOYOLA	127	68.5	58.3	57.5
	VRS&YRN	137	77.4	71.8	70.8
	Chi-square (df 11)				
		Value	128.546*	197.559*	126.000*
		Sig	0.000	0.000	0.000

Note : n=1858

* Chi-square value significant at 5% level.

Chi-square value indicates influence of gender on awareness and influence of age group, academic level and college is found on the awareness, knowledge and use of book CDs.

(d) Journal / Magazine CDs

Awareness, knowledge and use of 'Journal / Magazine CDs' are reported more by the female students; more by the older age group (20 years above) and more by the PG students than their counterparts.

Table 7. Awareness, Knowledge and Use of Journal / Magazine CDs by selected background variables

Awareness, Knowledge and Use of Journal / Magazine CDs by selected background variables					
Variable		*n*	*% Reporting*		
			Awareness	*Knowledge*	*Use & Evaluation*
Gender	Male	1113	73.0	63.7	62.8
	Female	745	75.7	69.3	67.7
	Chi-square (df 1)				
		Value	1.644	6.142*	4.595
		Sig	0.200	0.013	0.032
Age Group	< 20 yrs	1284	72.0	63.2	61.2
	> 20 yrs	574	78.9	72.6	72.1
	Chi-square (df 1)				
		Value	10.007*	14.188*	22.717*
		Sig	0.002	0.000	0.000
Academic level	UG	1571	72.9	65.1	62.5
	PG	287	80.8	77.0	70.4
	Chi-square (df 1)				
		Value	7.999*	2.995	22.339*
		Sig	0.005	0.084	0.000
College	GMR	200	72.0	48.5	46.5
	ADITYA_T	160	76.9	51.3	49.4
	MVGR	162	80.2	75.3	75.3
	VIGNAN	72	75.0	36.1	34.7
	BVC	119	67.2	58.8	57.1
	ADITYA_E	173	56.1	43.9	40.5
	VASAVI	208	92.8	91.8	91.2
	VISHNU	164	82.3	81.7	71.3
	PVPS	143	86.7	74.1	58.0
	GEC	193	62.7	60.6	59.6
	LOYOLA	127	87.4	85.0	81.1
	VRS&YRN	137	76.6	76.6	65.0

Chi-square (df 11)				
	Value	197.784*	226.034*	189.128*
	Sig	0.000	0.000	0.000

Note : n=1858

* Chi-square value significant at 5% level.

The percentage reporting awareness of the journal / magazine CDs ranged from 56 in Aditya_E to 93 in Vasavi Engineering College. Knowledge levels ranged from 36% in Vignan Engineering College to 92% in Vasavi Engineering Colleges while the percentage reporting Use ranged from 35 in Vignan Engineering College to 91 in Vasavi Engineering College.

Chi-square value indicates influence of gender on knowledge and academic level on awareness and use while influence of age group and college is found on the awareness, knowledge and use of journal / magazine CDs.

(e) Old Question Papers

Awareness, knowledge and use of Old Question Papers are reported more by the female students than the male students. Awareness of old question papers are reported more by the younger age group (20 years above) and UG students while knowledge and use are reported more by the older age group (20 years or below) and the PG students.

The percentage reporting awareness of the old question papers ranged from 56 in Aditya_E to 99 in MVGR Engineering College. Knowledge levels ranged from 54% in Aditya_E to 95% in MVGR Engineering Colleges while the percentage reporting Use ranged from 35 in Aditya_E to 94 in MVGR Engineering College.

Chi-square value indicates influence of college is found on the awareness, knowledge and use of the old question papers.

Table 8. Awareness, Knowledge and Use of Old Question Papersby selected background variables

Awareness, Knowledge and Use of Old Question Papers by selected background variables

Variable		*n*	*% Reporting* Awareness	Knowledge	Use & Evaluation
Gender	Male	1113	75.3	73.3	71.9
	Female	745	79.3	77.2	72.1
	Chi-square (df 1)				
		Value	4.095	3.544	0.009
		Sig	0.043	0.060	0.924
Age	< 20 yrs	1284	77.0	74.0	71.2
Group	> 20 yrs	574	76.8	76.7	73.7
	Chi-square (df 1)				
		Value	0.031	1.702	1.238
		Sig	0.861	0.192	0.266
Academic	UG	1571	77.0	74.5	71.2
level	PG	287	76.7	76.3	76.0
	Chi-square (df 1)				
		Value	0.070	0.578	2.690
		Sig	0.792	0.447	0.101
College	GMR	200	91.5	86.5	71.0
	ADITYA_T	160	65.6	63.8	53.1
	MVGR	162	99.4	95.1	94.4
	VIGNAN	72	95.8	58.3	54.2
	BVC	119	63.9	58.0	52.1
	ADITYA_E	173	56.1	54.3	35.3
	VASAVI	208	90.9	88.5	76.9
	VISHNU	164	83.5	70.1	68.9
	PVPS	143	88.8	75.5	64.3
	GEC	193	75.1	73.6	69.9
	LOYOLA	127	89.0	86.6	81.9
	VRS&YRN	137	80.3	75.9	74.5

Chi-square (df 11)				
	Value	186.085*	280.408*	174.679*
	Sig	0.000	0.000	0.000

Note : n=1858

* Chi-square value significant at 5% level.

3. CONCLUSION

It is found that female respondents, older age group and PG students reported more their awareness on learning resources available in libraries. The college wise picture on this aspect is also promising. It indicates, the users are using the learning resources to the expected level.It is found that more respondents reported their awareness, knowledge and use on old question paper database followed by Journal/magazine CDs, Book CDs and NPTEL video courses. The LAN courses are designed by faculty members, but not in all colleges.

The awareness, knowledge and use on NPTEL video courses is reported more by male students, older age group and PG students. It is found that three colleges reported less than fifty percent on this aspect. As stated earlier the NPTEL video courses offer a variety of knowledge on different branches of engineering and useful for their academic pursuits. So, it is necessary to train the users in such colleges on priority basis. The percentage reported on LAN courses by gender, age group and academic level is not promising. Except two colleges, the remaining reported low percentage on this aspect. Therefore, due emphasis be given in the forthcoming Information Literacy Programmes. The usage of Book CDs and journal/magazine CDs is promising in all variables. Regarding Old Question paper usage, it is found that all variables reported excellent to this aspect.

REFERENCES

1. Kaur, A. (2006). Use of E-resources by Teachers and Researcher of Science and Engineering and Technology

Faculties in Guru Nank Dev Univeristy: A Survey. In *NACLIN* (pp. 267-285).

2. Lenox, M. F. and Walker, M. L. (1993). Information Literacy in the Education Process. *The Education Forum,* 57(3).

3. Naqvi, S. H. (2007). Use of Electronic Resources at JamiaMillia Islamic: A Case Study. In *NACLIN* (pp. 320-324).

4. Ray, K., & Day, J. (1998). Students Attitudes towards Electronic Information Resources. *Information Research, 4*(2). Retrieved from http://information r.net/ir/4-2/paper54.html

16

Use of Electronic Resources by Library and Information Science Students of Babasaheb Bhimrao Ambedkar University (A Central University), Lucknow, Uttar Pradesh: A Study

Mahender Pratap Singh
Associate Professor
Department of Library and Information Science
B. B. Bhimrao Ambedkar University, (A Central University),
Lucknow, 226025

ABSTRACT

In present era E-resources have become most popular sources of information among the Research Scholars, Teachers, Professionals and Students. Today students have access vast amount of information through a variety of sources like E- journal, E- Books, Database, Institutional Repository and different format like Doc. File, PDF file, HTML file etc. The need of E-resources and on line services among the users are also growing day by day and becoming very essential. This study examines the need of E-resources for improve the effective information services among faculty, research scholar and students to achieve our goal. In this study questionnaire method was used as a tool for data collection. In this study 100 questionnaires was distributed among students of Department of Library and Information Science, BBAU. Out of 100 questionnaires 70 usable questionnaires were retrieved and utilized for the statistical analysis. The primary factor analyzed various variables determining the user behavior for the use of electronic resources. The statistical analyses indicate that 85 % students are aware about E-Resources with highly satisfaction level for using digital device.

Keywords: E- Resources, Digital Device, Information and Communication Technology, On-Line Database, Information Society.

1. INTRODUCTION

In the age of information technology, the traditional concept of acquiring information is gradually replaced by the accessing information online. Over the last decade electronic resources have become increasingly component of any academic library collection. Now it becomes the life line of any library. Libraries have witnessed a great metamorphosis in recent years both in their collection development and their services structure. E-resource is an electronic information resource that you can access on the web on/off campus. You can get any information anywhere any time.E-resources are those electronic products that delivers a collection of data, be it text referring to full text basis, e-journals, eBooks, online databases, image collection, other multimedia products and numerical, graphical or time based, as a commercially available till that has been published with an aim to being marketed. These resources include CD-ROM, on tap via the internet, electronic texts; bibliographic database, On-line databases, OPAC, CD-ROMS, online-databases, E-journals, E-books, Internet resources etc. So in the context the terms means any electronic product that delivers collection of data in text, numerical, graphical or time based as a commercially available resources. E-resources are basically divided in various types are:

E-Journals : E-journals are available in the electronic form and can be accessed using computer and communication technology. It could be available free or part of a paid services.

E-Books : E-Book is an electronic version of books that can be read by using a personal computer or by using e-book reader on the internet.

CD-ROM : CD-ROM is a non-volatile optical data storage medium using the same physical format such as audio, compact discs, readable by a computer with a CD-ROM drive.

Institutional Repository : Institutional Repository is a set of services that a university offers to the members of its community for the management and dissemination of digital materials created by the Institution and its community member.

Digital repository : Digital Repositories are an inclusive that embraces a variety of communities, methodologies, and technologies.

Open Access Journals (OAJ) : Many journals content available online, while the majority of their content is accessible only through traditional access paths.

Subject gateways : Subject gateways are sets of Web Pages containing lists of links to resources. Subject gateways access to networked-based resources in a definite subject area.

Electronic Thesis and Dissertation : Digital library of theses and dissertations, which are easily available over the Internet from any university ex. Shodganga.

E-database : An electronic database is a collection of data arranged in a systematic way to make the search easy and fast.

Digital Library : digital library as an organized and focused collection of digital objects, including text, images, video and audio, with the methods of access and retrieval and for the selection, creation, organization, maintenance and sharing of collection.

2. OBJECTIVES OF THE STUDY

Following are the objectives of the study:

- To find out awareness of E- resources among LIS students of BBAU;
- To identify the frequency and purposes of using E-resources;
- To know about different type of E- resources use by the users;
- To find out the basic search strategy for accessing E- resources;
- To find out the satisfaction level of users;
- To find out the advantage and constraints of using E- resources.

3. REVIEW OF LITERATURE

(Kaur, 2012) studied that due to the advancement of information technology libraries gradually shifting towards the electronic libraries with electronic resources. Growth of electronics resources even though slower than what is expected will force the libraries to switch over to more and more electronic resources in future.(Chander, 2012) studied that lack of training among users and proper infrastructure in library is major de-motivating factors for use of electronics journals. (Gautam, Chauhan & Shukla, 2012) described libraries need to manage electronics resources effectively to the optimum utilization by overcoming the issues and challenges. (Patel, 2012) states that libraries need to manage electronics resources effectively to the optimum utilization by overcoming the issues and challenges. (Pandey & Shukla, 2012) examined the majority of academic libraries use internet resources; still most of the students, research scholars, and teacher prefer print journal as well as electronic journal. (Rajan,

Mathew &Jasimudeen, 2012) states that the influence of digital era in the library environment claims the modernization of library resources and services. (Singh, 2012) investigated the technology which help the reader to get the information in various other formats than the traditional means. (Choudhary, 2012) states that the library is considered as the backbone of any higher education and it provides the literature and information through e-resources and services in order to carry out their academic activity, i.e. teaching and research for users.(Sharma & Akhtar, 2012)described the impact of web based e-learning and teaching environment has influenced every facet of library and information services including electronic and multimedia publishing, internet based information services, global networking, web based digital resources etc. (Habiba& Chowdhury, 2012) studied most of the researchers and faculty members want current issues of article, some of them told that they have no need to see the back issues of e- journals.

4. PROFILE OF THE STUDY AREA

The Babasaheb Bhimrao Ambedkar University (BBAU) Lucknow is one of the premier Central Universities in the country. The jurisdiction of this residential University is over the entire state of Uttar Pradesh established on 10th January 1996. This University promotes advanced knowledge by providing instructional and Research facilities for integrated courses in Science and key frontier areas of Technology and other allied disciplines. This university has 6 Schools and 22 departments. There is main Central Library at university campus which is connected to all departments and Schools. A separate Periodical section has recently been set up for students and faculty members. It comprises the collections Books: 8500, Reference Books: 500, Periodicals: 500, Current Periodicals, 40, Indian: 13, Foreign: 27, Light Magazine: 11 etc. Access to online journals is being provided by the Central Library, campus Library and departmental libraries with the assistance from UGC info NET.The Central Library provides access to Springer Link and JCCC through UGC-INFONET consortium and Bibliographical Databases. Library users Access more than 1800 e-journals and Springer, JSTORE and web of science E data bases, J-Gate Custom Content for Consortium (JCCC) through UGC-INFONET Consortium. Library provides *Internet Search Services*, Photo copy facilities, the Reference & Information collection etc. (BabasahebBhim Rao Ambedkar University).

5. RESEARCH METHODOLOGY

The target population of the study was students of library science department in BBAU, Lucknow. For this study 100 questionnaires distributed in Library science Department and using stratified random sampling techniques. Out of the 100 questionnaires, only 76 respondents answered the questionnaire and only 70 questionnaire considered usable for the research. For analysis survey table and chart have drawn. After analysis, the breakdown is given in Data Interpretation.

6. ANALYSIS AND INTERPRETATION OF DATA

The obtained data analyzed using simple statistical method and also through Excel. For analysis survey table and have drawn. Further the analyzed data presented in table, graphs wherever required.

Table 1. Awareness about online Resource

Name of the University		*Responses*	*Percentage*
Babasaheb Bhimrao	Yes	60	85
Ambedkar University	No	10	15
	Total	70	100

The concerned table shows the awareness about

online Resources among the Research Scholars of BBAU Central University. For the study data collected from 70 respondents and found that 85% of researchers are aware about online resources, whereas 15% of researcher is not aware.

Table 2. Online database accessible by the library

Online database	*Percentage*	*Online database*	*Percentage*
Web of science	68	Science direct	No
Science finder scholar	No	EMREALD consortia	No
Social science library	No	BIOSIS	No
DELNET	No		

The table reflects that BBAU library has information resources provided by UGC-Infonet digital library consortium only.

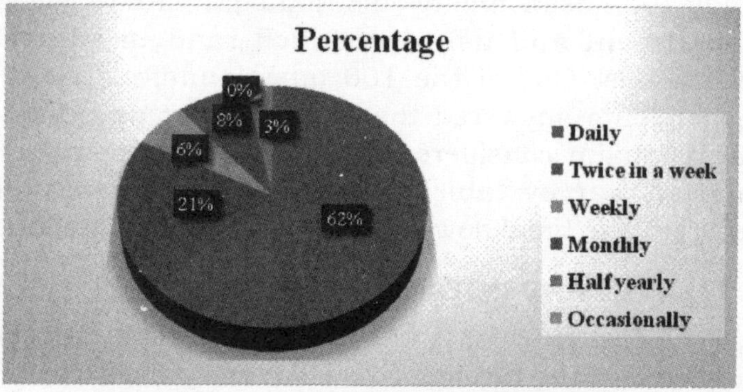

Fig. 1. Frequency of use of online resources

The above table reflects the frequency of use of online resources. Through analysis it is observed that most of the respondents use online resources daily. A total of 37(61%) LIS students/ research scholars use online resources daily and 21% of them is using twice in a week whereas no researchers are using online resources in occasionally.

Table 3. Different purposes of using online information sources

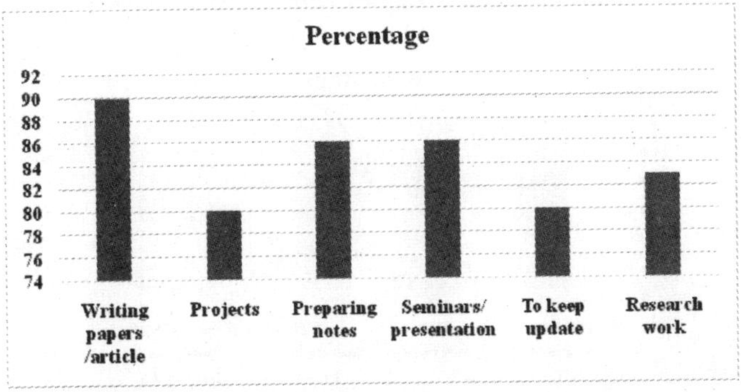

The above table shows the purpose of using online resources among the respondents. It is found that 90% LIS students/ research scholars are using online information resources for writing research article that is highest; 86% respondents are using online information resources for preparing notes and seminars/presentation that is equal and 80% respondents are using for their project works and to keep update their knowledge.

Table 4. Various online resources and services being used

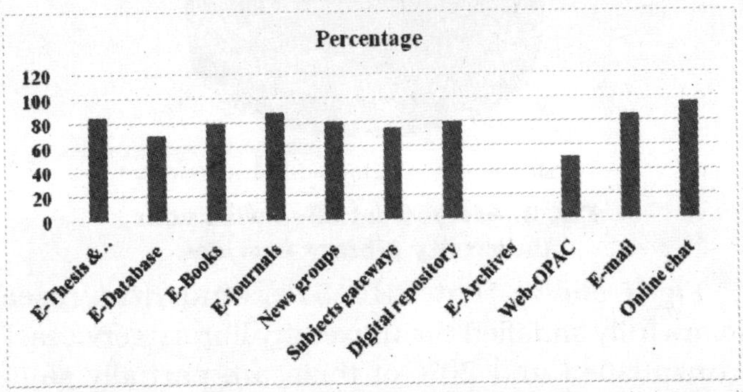

Table 5 highlights the different type of online resources and services being used by the LIS students and research scholars. From the table it is observed that excluding e-archives all the mentioned information resources are being used by the maximum number of users.

Table 5. Types of searching techniques

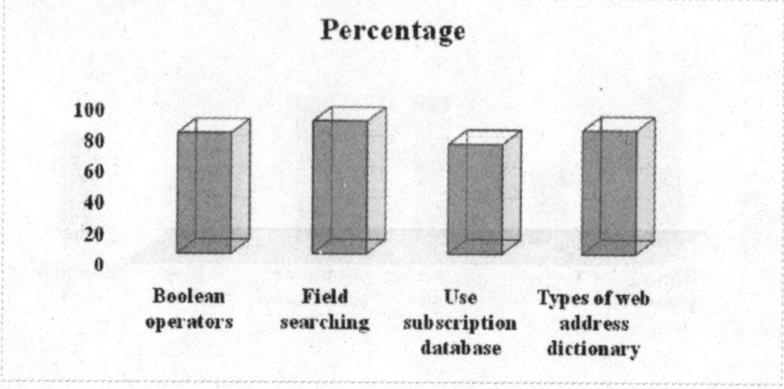

Table 5 show that most of the student's research scholars of BBAU are using various searching techniques for the access online information. 86% respondents using field searches; 80% through types of web address dictionary; 78% of them through Boolean search and remaining 71% are using subscription databases etc.

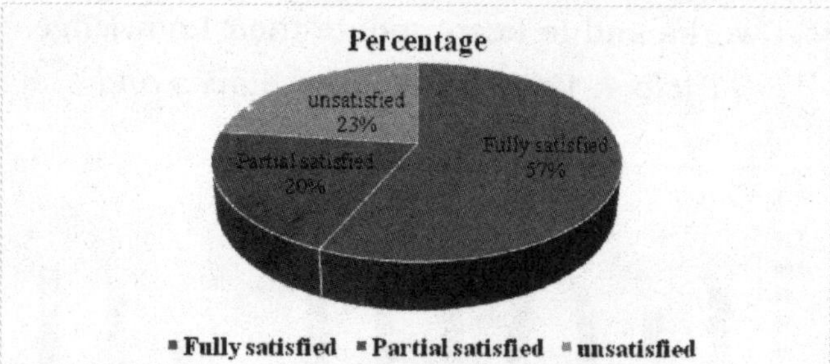

Fig. 2. Are you satisfied with your University Library Services

Fig 2 shows that BHU 57% students/ research scholars fully satisfied the university library services; 23% are unsatisfied and 20% of them are partially satisfied with the university library services.

7. CONCLUSION AND SUGGESTION

In present era E-resources play a vital role for growth

and development of any University as well as higher education with the help of Internet and computer everybody canaccess E- resources anywhere viz. home, school, libraries, during travel etc. E-resources can be change in any format which is available quickly and more than one person can read a text at the same time. E-resources need no place like printed books and accessed at very low price. Many users use electronic resources simultaneously it can solve the problems of missing issues of on line resources. From the above discussion it is found that 85% of researcher is aware about online resources, whereas 15% of researcher is not aware. Further it is analyzed that 90% LIS students/ research scholars are using online information resources for writing research article and most of the respondents use online resources daily. It is also observed that services provided by the library are not satisfactory it is because the central library of BBAU does not have rich collection of online information resources and services; so for library authority should take initiative for the improvement. It is very essential for library to be dynamic and change their outlook to adopt new technologies.

REFERENCES

1. Kaur, S. (2012). *E-resources in modern library . Ranganathan vision on future library*. Lucknow: JBS.
2. Chander, D. (2012). *Use of e-journals among the faculy member punjan university. Ranganathan vision on future library*. Lucknow: JBS.
3. Gautam, N. C. (2012). *Utility & importance of e-resources in library: an over view. Ranganathan vision on future libraries*. Lucknow: JBS.
4. Patel, K. K. (2012). *E-Resources In Modern Libraries. Ranganathyan Vision On Future*. Lucknow: JBS.
5. Pandey, A & Shukla, U. (2012). *E-resources in the modern academic libraries a new era. Ranganathan vision on future libraries*. Lucknow: JBS.
6. Singh, P. (2012). *Importance of e-resources in digital environment: an overview*. Lucknow: JBS

7. Choudhary, D. K. (2012). *Collection development and management of electronic resources in the university library of Bihar: A case study.* Lucknow: JBS.

8. Sharma, K. & Akhtar, S. S. (2012). *E-Resources in academic library: A theoritical concept.* Lucknow: JBS. Retrieved *on December 12, 2014* from http://dx.doi.org/10.3329/el.v23i1.12122.

9. Habiba& Chowdhury, R.(2012). *Emergence of adopting e-resources in modern libraries: A perspective study.* Lucknow: JBS.

10. BBR Ambedkar University, Lucknow, Central Library home page (2014). Retrieved July 11, 2014, *http://www.bbau.ac.in/Central%20Library/Library.aspx.*

Scholarly Communication

17

Citation Management Tools: A Useful Web Gizmo for Managing Academic References

Mahendra K. Sahu
Librarian, GIMS
Gandhi Group of Institutions, Gunupur, Odisha

ABSTRACT

Citation management tools are very important to make the academic task much easier. It allows users to generate citation from the database, while doing research or writing an academic literature. The main objective of the paper is to illustrate about citation and citation management tools. There are varieties of citation management tools are available on the web, according to their nature, it has been divided into four distribution model. In this paper four most important citation tools like, Zotero, Mendeley , Endnote and Bibtex, which will help the researcher and the librarian grapple with the decision which citation management tools will be suitable for their academic assignment has been described.

Keywords : Citation, Citation management tools, Model of CM, Refworks, Zotero, Mendeley

1. INTRODUCTION

Academic writing involves documentation of

resources in the form of bibliographic references such as, references, citations, footnotes, end notes etc. Author, title, publication information and page numbers must authentic and in a consistent format, Generally most of the researchers following commonly used style guide such as APA (American Psychological Association). With the advent of information and Technology, all most all the sector has hugely impacted and academic research is not put away from it. The emergence of web and the increasing of online publishing have given rise to a whole new class of tools, which help the scholars and students to access the information easily. Citation management tools are a set of computer programming available on the web, allow users to create a database of citations while doing their academic assignment, and automatically export notes and bibliographies in the right format, correctly punctuated, abbreviated, alphabetized, etc., as per the rules of the style.

Most of the citation management tools can switch formatting between the major styles without any further editing for the user and those citations can be again useful for other assignments, without duplicative data entry. Better citation managers are the capacity to import citations from bibliographic databases and library catalogs into the citation manager without keying of data whatsoever. Generally it produce two kinds of process of importing citation form the information source and preserving it into the citation manager, such as ProQuest, Science Direct and Ebrary, and it can be directly exported to one of the major citation management tool such as Refworks or Endnote. There are varieties of citation management tools are available, which makes difficult to select which tool is better. In this paper, the author emphasized on citation management tools and selected three tools such as, EndNote, Zotero and Mendeley, which is most use full tool for the scientific community.

2. WHAT IS CITATION?

A citation is a reference to the source of information utilized as a part of specific research. Whenever browse the library information for articles or any other purposes, a list of bibliographic information will be shown, is a list of citations. It clearly recognizes the source, in which the full-content of the thing is to be found. A citation gives adequate data to recognize the creator and identify the thing easily. The cited information is quite standard, but the array of citation may change depending upon the kind of thing being referred and the style of manual are utilizing it includes: author, title of books, articles, journals etc, information about publication and online resources.

3. WHY TO CITE?

The citation is an essential part of scholarly literature. It recognizes intellectual links throughout scholarly literature, it can be helpful not only when writing but also when conducting research. It offers credit to the first author by citing sources of other people's work without plagiarizing. There are some other reasons it includes as follows:

- It helps the person to locate the information easily, and also helpful them to recognize the original sources
- It acknowledges the amount of research work done by a researcher
- It provides outside support to one's ideas, which strengthens the research work.
- It helps to find out the desired information of the user on his/her particular subject area.
- It helps to avoid plagiarism
- It helps the user to track down the sources used by citing them accurately in the paper by means of footnotes, bibliography and reference list.

4. CITATION MANAGEMENT TOOLS

Citation management tools are a set of application tools for organizing bibliography citations and references. It normally consists of databases on which electronic literature can be stored, and then extract bibliography reference and citation from the database in different format i.e. APA, MLA and Chicago etc. It helps the users to expedite research work in most organized and effective manner. Generally the modern citation management tools are incorporated with word processors, therefore a reference list within the correct format is continuously generates as a piece of writing is formed. It has also a facility for importing the details of publication from bibliographic.

Important Function of Citation Management Tools

Whenever a scholar or a student writing first research paper on a particular field or preparing an article for a seminar / conferences, most of the resources they obtained from online. Since the existing of library catalogues online, they trying to set up efficient and logical method for preserving those resources like: copying and pasting to word, bookmarking the relevant site, saving URLs through email and printing hard copies for annotation etc. and this process is very cumbersome. The advent of citation tool enables students / scholars make their research easier than the past. Now a days citation management tools become very popular and most of the academic students /scholar used this tools to preserve, organize and generate citation for their research and academic assignment (Gilmour, 2011). It provides different functions as given below

- Importing Citations and references from Bibliographic frame work and websites.
- Collects metadata form PDF files
- It provides Annotation of citations.

- It helps to interchange data with other CM products through standard metadata formats i.e RIS, Bib Tex etc.
- It generates formatted citations in different style.
- It facilitate in text citation to collaborate with word processor.

Model of Citation Management Tools

The citation management tool is normally a set of applications tools designed to import and export the bibliographic references. The model of the tools not standardized and often changes in various qualities. Therefore the distribution model of the tools is divided into four categories i.e. Desktop based, Web based, Browser based and Hybrid based (Willman, 2012).

Desktop Based : It is installed on the personal computer, expecting that there will be nothing happens with the hardware, the system stays unaltered on that machine until either overhauled or erased. This model worked for quite a long time and conveys with it various preferences and weaknesses. To start with, the user is in control of a program that is shown on her machine and is not dependent on a web. It has powerful features, for example, the capacity to search, select databases from its interface, sync with cell phones, or associate with resources through an institution intermediary server. It may run only six dependent on a specific operating system, information is stored locally and remains under the control of the user. It may be susceptible to loss the information in case of accidental deletion, misplaced USB drives or hardware problems. This model has worked for a considerable length of time and conveys with it various preferences and impediments. e. g. Bookends (http://www.sonnysoftware.com/), Papers http://www.mekentosj.com/papers), JabRef (http://jabref.sourceforge.net) runs according to the traditional model of computing, with both proprietary and free options available.

Web based tools : It refers to any program that is accessed over a network connection through HTTP, instead of existing in a device's memory. It often runs inside a Web program. Additionally, these tools also may be client-based, where a little piece of the program is downloaded to a Clint's desktop, however the processing is carried out over the Internet to an external server. Some, for example, Refworks and Easybib, offer portable enhanced version. The information is preserved in the cloud and shielded from PCs. The adaptability of cloud computing, however, is both the best resource and accountability as the failure of an internet connection brings to an end to work.

Browser based tools : It is an open source application tool supplies online functionality as well as the ability to work without an internet connection. It supplies an inconspicuous information, aim to manage references from the spot where users perform the majority of their research. It can interface with a number of mobile applications on both iOS and Android mobile platforms. Data is stored locally and can be synced with the server for back-u and read only access. However, there are two main disadvantages connected with this tool.First, stable versions are tied to the Firefox browser, distancing the individuals those who use other non-supported browsers. Second, data is tied to a particular browser instance, meaning that in a lab environment, where multiple users may access the same browsers daily, it is difficult to separate and ensure confidentiality of data. The example of the model is Zotero (Zotero 3.0 Beta *http://www.zotero.org/blog/announcing-zotero-3-0-beta-release/*)

Hybrid tools : it comprise of a desktop customer that can interface with a web-based tools, allowing both online and offline access to work. The information can be stored locally and in the cloud. Mobile devices are frequently supported by this tool. Most of the tools are proprietary in nature, with its support for both the safari and Chrome browsers, adds an open-source component to the field and warrants special attention towards further development. These tools attempt to offer point-of-need assistance in this case, however, during the writing process instead of the search process. Both Microsoft Office and Open Office offer databases to store and manage citations as well as support with bibliography creation. Microsoft Office 2007 and 2010 offer support for MLA, APA, and Chicago citation styles; Microsoft Office 2010 Service Pack 1 for Windows includes an increased range of citation styles, like, APA 6th edition, MLA 7th edition, Harvard-Anglia 2008, and IEEE 2006. OpenOffice permits users to generate bibliographies in any citation style by editing the entry's structure through a user interface. Finally, with including of citation generator into large database aggregators, provides users the option to cut and paste a bibliography format according to their own citation style i. e. EBSCO, Gale, ProQuest etc.

5. CHOOSING A CITATION MANAGEMENT TOOL

Selecting a reference management tool will depend on the needs and workflow of the user as each tool has its particular strengths and weaknesses(Sahu, 2014). There are a few tips to choose right Citation management tools as follows:

- Consult with the people your own discipline or department to see what citation tools currently they are using. If there is one tool that is a clear winner, go with the same.
- Go through briefly at the user interface and analysis the tool to see which one make suitable for you.
- Go through the details features offered by different tools to see which tools well- suited your needs and which are compatible with your operating system and software.

If a scholar / students work from multiple computers and locations, it is suggested to go with a web-based tool such as RefWorks or Zotero. Any one share a research paper detections with others, Mendeley allows for social sharing and discovering of research. This may be of specific interest to interdisciplinary scholars. If someone wants to do research with free online web and want to save the web site for review then Zotero is the right tools for them. It allows users to snapshots of web pages and can extract the related citation for website.

5.1. RefWorks

It is a web based citation management tools developed in 2001 by a business unit of ProQuest. It is a license based tools helps uses to generate personal databases and utilize them for a variety of research activities. Citations can be generated expedite from both text and online database. It can be used to organize, preserve and annotate the electronic resource very rapidity and smoothly. Users can automatically insert references from their database into their papers and generate formatted citation in a fraction of a second.

Features of Refworks

- It organizes and creates a personal database online
- Generates citations and in seconds
- Import citation from different databases, i. e. EBSCO, PubMed etc.
- Providing alerting services
- It automatically creates author, descriptor and periodical indexes

5.2. Zotero

It is both web and desktop based citation management tools, offers users to collect, organize, cite. Share and collaborate research work. Zoterois the only research tool that automatically senses content in your web browser, allowing you to add it to your personal library with a single click. Whether you're searching for a preprint on arXiv.org, a journal article from JSTOR, a news story from the *New York Times*, or a book from your university library catalog, Zotero has covered you with support for thousands of sites. It collects all your research in a single, searchable interface. You can add PDFs, images, audio and video files, snapshots of web pages, and really anything else. Zotero automatically indexes the full-text content of your library, enabling you to find exactly what you're looking for with just a few click.

Feature of Zotero

- Data can be exported to other documents in various format.
- It leverage the concept of tagging
- It organizes user generated information including snapshots images etc.
- It annotate and collaboration with the internet archives
- Automatically extract certain types of metadata i.e. URL. Date time accessed, title form common online archives.
- Tag and sort records and perform advanced searches.
- View records in personal collection when offline.
- Cite records in any language

5.3. Mendeley

It is both desktop and web based citation management tools, provides user to manage and sharing research papers, discovering research data and collaborating online. It combines Mendeley Desktop, a PDF and *reference management application* (available for Windows; OS X and Linux) with Mendeley Web, an online *social* network for researchers. It requires the user to store all basic citation data on its servers storing copies of documents is at the user's discretion. It provides the user with 2 *GB* of free web storage space, which is upgradeable at a cost. It is available either as a premium payable version or a basic version that is free but requires registration.

Features Mendeley

- It generates Citation automatically
- It collaborates easily with other researchers online
- It imports papers and other document from external websites (e.g. Pubmed, Google Scholar, Arxiv) easily through browser bookmark let.
- Allow user Back-up and synchronization across multiple computers and with a private online account
- It discovers relevant papers based on what you're reading
- It allows to access your papers from anywhere online
- Usage-based readership statistics about papers, authors and publications. Read papers on the go, with Smart Phone.

6. CHALLENGES FOR CITATION MANAGEMENT TOOLS

- Web based citation tools are based on the assumption that users will always have access to the Internet. However, failure of the internet or other means, when access will not be possible. Users will have to remember to download backup copies of important citations for use offline.
- Some of the citation tools have a complex in nature and it is very difficult to understand their basic. It requires dedicated significant time to learn even the fundamental.
- Web based citation tools are not integrated with existing library digital resources or online

collections. It creates complicated workflow, thus it requires adding citations to the digital resources or online collection.

- Most of the CM tools generate citations easily for research materials, but user needs to add citation content from other sources manually.
- An institution may be reluctant to change the existing platform to a new platform, for which it already have invested causing to support , import / export citation, and training issues.
- Sometime faculties also hesitant to change to a new platform due to the challenges of importing/ exporting their existing citations, changes in their scholarly process.
- Students may be tempted to use the "cut & paste" approach for gathering research materials from the Internet. By picking and choosing quotes from content as opposed to reading and summarizing entire articles, students may lack a more complete understanding of the material.

7. CONCLUSION

Managing citation for research work or writing a paper for seminar / conference is one of the most complicated processes for scholar / students. The boredom of arranging citations focused around a variety of citation styles has made the citation manager an essential tool for researchers at all levels. The availability of different citation management tools makes it difficult to select the right one. However, there are various citation tools are available for generating citation. In this paper, it is selected, Refworks, Mendeley, and Zotero, which are more extraordinary and established among the academic community. Both Zotero and Mendeley are award-winning CM tools, whereas RefWorks has the advantage of user based CM tool. However, none of these tools are continuously generates exact citation without any difficulty. Managing citation from any one of them produce even a few problems, it may be for the user or system fault.

Mendeley is the most user-friendly and comprehensive CM tools, which allow users to build a library of articles and sources, annotate them by highlighting content or including notes anywhere on a page. It also works as an academic social network, and allow accessing an extensive library of importing resources for the most recent article in the field. Zotero is a portable web interface extracts metadata from various file formats like its opponent. Refworks is a commercial CM tool, which includes the convenient feature. Like it create the citation very easily from other bibliographic tools.

REFERENCES

1. Harlow, H. F. (1983). Fundamentals for preparing psychology journal articles. *Journal of Comparative and Physiological Psychology, 55*, 893-896.
2. Beel, J. (2014). Comprehensive comparison of reference managers: Mendeley vs. Zotero vs. Docear. Retrieved December 4, 2014 from http:// www.docear.org/2014/01/ 15/comprehensive-comparison-ofreference-managers-mendeley-vs-zotero-vs-docear/.
3. Butros, A. (2015). Managing information: evaluating and selecting Citation management sofrtware, a look at endnote,Refworks, mendeley and zotero. Retrieved January 4, 2015 from *darchive.mbl.edu/bitstream/handle/.../Butros-Taylor_iamslic2010.pdf?.*
4. Embi, Mohamed Amin. (2012). Web 2.0 Research tools: a Quick guide, Centre for Academic Advancement
5. Fraser, W. D. (2014). Reference Management with Open Source Tools. *Aviation, Space, and Environmental Medicine, 85*(7), 766-768. doi: 10.3357/asem.4049.
6. Marino, W. (2012). Fore-cite- Tactics for Evaluating Citation Management Tool. *DigitalCommons@EMU*, 1-24.
7. Noguchi, S. A. (2009). Case Study of Web-Based Citation Management Tools With Japanese. *Journal of East Asian*

Libraries, 147, 09.

8. Reiswig, J. (2010). Mendeley. Journal of the Medical Library Association. 98, 193-194. DOI= http://dx.doi.org/10.3163%2F1536—5050.98.2.021

9. Ron Gilmour and Laura Cobus-Kuo. (2011). Reference Management Software: a Comparative Analysis of Four Products, Issues in Science and Technology Librarianship, 66. DOI: 10.5062/F4Z60KZF

10. Sahu, M.. K. (2014). Research2.0: a use full web platform for academic research. In *National Conference On Academic Librarianship In Digital Era*,1, 55-67.

11. Zhang, Y. (2012). Comparison of select reference management tools. *Med Ref Serv Q*, 31(1), 45-60. doi: 10.1080/02763869.2012.641841.

12. Mendeley. Retrieved January 4, 2015, from http://www.mendeley.com/en/1/1/

13. Reference management software. Retrieved January 4, 2015, from http://en.wikipedia.org/wiki/Reference_management_software.

14. Zotero. Retrieved January 4, 2015, from https://www.zotero.org/.

15. Wikipedia (2011), Comparison of reference management software - Wikipedia, the free encyclopedia, Retrieved January 3, 2015, from http://en.wikipedia.org/wiki/Comparison_of_reference_management_software

16. Wikipedia. Retrieved January 4, 2015 from https://en.wikipedia.org/wiki/Reference_management_software.

17. (n.d.). Retrieved January 3, 2015, from http://www.ais.up.ac.za/vet/infomania/infomania16/refworks16.htm

18

Mendeley, Refworks and ".CSV" the File Format: A Comparative Analysis of Citation Management Tools

Kshirod Das
Senior Technical Assistant BPCL,
National Institute of Technology Rourkela, Odisha - 769008, India

R. K. Mahapatra
Principal. CLIS, SMIT, Ankushpur, Ganjam,
Odisha – 761100, India.

ABSTRACT

The use of citation management tools for recording of bibliographic citations is now insidious among researcher. This study compares the results between Mendeley, RefWorks and .CSV file format. The results were drawn, that Mendeley has imported more fields from SCOPUS then RefWorks and .CSV file format. The analysis also shows that, using these tools are more helpful then manual system for citing accurate information.

Keywords : Citation Management, Citation Imports, Reference Management Software, Bibliographic Management Software, Analysis

1. INTRODUCTION

Citation Management Tool is a mechanism for scholars and authors to use for recording of bibliographic citations (references). Scholars often called these tools as 'Reference Management Software, Bibliographic Management Software' or 'Citation Management Software'. These packages, like EndNote, RefWorks, Mendely, Zotero, BibTex saves lots of time and is become very popular among researcher and authors.

A website is defined "citation management tools" enable researchers to capture bibliographic information about research materials, create bibliographies, add footnotes, and manage research collections.

As per Telstar "a Reference Management Software" enables an author to build a library of references by entering the details of each reference in a structured format. They usually support mechanisms for organizing sets of references by tagging or use of folders, and will generate references, citations or bibliographies in a range of referencing styles.

"Reference Management Software" is used by researchers in academics to manage the bibliographic citations they encounter in their research. With these tools, scholars keep track of the scientific literature they read, and to facilitate the editing of the scientific papers they write. Several different software packages exist, with sometimes different features and purposes.

A website licensed under creative common, has mentioned "a reference manager is the software you use to handle references and full-text documents, and citations while writing. References can be handled manually as well, but the reference manager allows for greater flexibility and efficiency.

2. AN ESSENTIAL RESEARCH TOOL

Citation management software makes mining and

using information resources easier and more effective, helping you to as stated by the Columbia University Library:

- Capture bibliographic and full-text information as you explore
- Organize, evaluate, annotate, and search within your collection
- Cite and list those resources in a wide range of bibliographic styles
- Access that information on your desktop or online
- Synchronize your data across multiple machines and share your research with others.

3. AIMS AND OBJECTIVES

This article aims to compare and analyze two methods of export citation information i. e. direct export to Mendely & Ref Works and export of citation to a file format (.CSV). The study also aims to see which export method and software can produce more accurate and systematic information for the research scholar. The pertinent aim and objectives are as follows:

- To know, which software provides more accurate information about citation, and references?
- To identify, which software is ease for research scholars?
- To see, the similarities for the fields of citation management tools.

4. REVIEW OF LETERATURE

This section aims to present the earlier studies in the same area. Many of these cited literatures are discussed with the available features and benefits of citation management software, few have compared those tools and few of them compared the search interface and search results of reference management software. Basak, in the year 2014 have presented the comparison of imported fields from RefWorks and Zotero from Google Scholar. The result shows that RefWorks can import more information from Google Scholar for researchers (Basak, 2014). A study by Hensley has reflected the role of the librarian in choosing, promoting, and teaching citation management software. For this she examines four of the most popular citation managers from the perspective of both the patron and the librarian. More than just reviewing features, she provides best practices for the instruction and support of these important research tools (Hensley, 2011).

A study have compared the internal search interfaces and its results between academic databases versus EndNote. Their result shows mixed search reliability, depending on the database and type of search performed (Fitzgibbons, &Meert, 2010). Maniro, has explored a general set of criteria, which can be used by librarians and information professionals for the evaluation of citation management tools. He has raised some of the key questions that can assist information professionals in the evaluation process (Maniro, 2012).

Another study have focused not only the popular products like EndNote, EndNote Web, and RefWorks but also examine free tools Mendeley and Zotero. They demonstrated the main features, pros and cons by comparing those products, and also discussed their experience while using these products (Maniro, 2012). A research result shows, the best practices for supporting, recommending, and teaching tools for the many aspects of citation management (Childress, 2011).

So far no such work has been done on comparing the import result between RefWorks, Mendeley and import using the file format "(.CSV)".

5. CITATION MANAGEMENT TOOLS: A REVIEW

Marino, has quoted, the term citation management tool is often applied to the gamut of software applications specifically designed either to store and manage a user's citations or generate her bibliography (Marino, 2012). These tools, however, are by no means homogenous and often differ in a number of qualities such as their distribution model i.e. if they are desktop-based, web-based, etc. and whether they are free or proprietary in nature. Citation management software falls into one of four distribution models:

- Desktop-based
- Web-based
- Browser-based
- Hybrid.

Each distribution model can be further divided into proprietary and open-source material. A detailed and comprehensive list is given on the Wikipedia page "Comparison of reference management software", where very detailed information about each such tool is given.

5.1. RefWorks

RefWorks is a web-based tool for reference management by ProQuest. RefWorks supports hundreds of online databases and output styles covering a broad range of subject areas. RefWorks collaborates with some of the world's most prestigious online information service providers including ProQuest, BioOne, EBSCO, Elsevier, HighWire, H.W. Wilson, ISI, OCLC, Ovid and Serial Solutions (RefWorks).

Jennings, in the year 2003 written in a website, the RefWorks is a "fully functioning, general use bibliographic management program that stores, organizes, and formats data" and also creates full-text citations in addition to footnote formatting" (Jennings, 2003). An article study has stated that RefWorks is web-based and compatible on all platforms. Most database vendors have adapted their interface to export references relatively easily into RefWorks. Users can also import references from library catalogs, other citation managers, RSS feeds and web sites. RefWorks can be customized to suit your organization by adding a link resolver. Since RefWorks added the attachment feature, researchers can upload a variety of file types for up to a limit of 100 MB and the administrator can increase this limit later up to 5GB (Hensley, 2011).

5.2. Mendeley

Mendeley is a free reference manager and academic social network that can help you organize your research, collaborate with others online, and discover the latest research. (Francese, 2012) stated that, Mendeley combines both a desktop and a web-based application that is compatible across platforms. There is a "Cite this document" feature that allows users to copy and paste a citation for a single item using the major citation styles. (Childress, 2011) quoted, the most valuable advancement Mendeley boasts is comprehensive PDF management. (Hensley, 2011) in her paper discussed that, Mendeley Dashboard takes academic collaboration to a new level by leveraging the users of Mendeley to watch research trends. Research groups, which can be made public or private, have the ability to collaboratively annotate and share notes. As for cite as you write, Mendeley generally works a little different than other software programs, it inserts formatted citations by dragging and dropping into any text editor including Google Docs, LaTeX, blogs and e-mails. There is also a Microsoft Word plug-in. Other features include: link resolver capability, iPhone and iPad applications, generation of overall Mendeley and individual statistics, synchronization with Zotero and CiteULike, as well as a simple, yet research changing feature, the ability to mark papers as read or unread.

5.3. Comma Separated Values (.CSV) File Format

Comma-separated values (.CSV) alternatively called as character-separated values. Files are stored in tabular form (i.e. numbers and text). A .CSV file may consists of any number of records, separated by line breaks; each record consists of fields, separated by some other character or string, most commonly a comma or tab, usually all records have an identical sequence of fields (Wikipedia).

One can export up to 1,000 items to Mendeley and up to 2,000 items to any of the other export options. Export is possible up to 20,000 records in citations only format to a comma-separated (.CSV) file. In .CSV fil format these characters do not display correctly in Excel unless you save the file and then use Excel's data import functionality to view the file (Exporting results from Scopus).

6. METHODOLOGY

For this study, I decided to consider bibliographic database 'SCOPUS', because of availability of access with NIT Rourkela. SCOPUS offers integrated export functionality with Mendeley and RefWorks, Or else to choose a file format like RIS format (EndNote, Reference Manager), CSV (Excel), BibTex and Text (ASCII in HTML). Finally this study decided to consider both the integrated export function i.e. RefWorks, Mendeley and a file format called .CSV (which exports data into excel format) from 'SCOPUS'.

The keywords used to import information (citation fields) from the SCOPUS database are based on the recent research areas of the NIT Rourkela are *"Degradation of FRP Composites"*. For importing of citation fields I was downloaded and installed both RefWorks and Mendeley software in the laptop PC with its default customization. (.CSV), the file format was imported & saved in laptop PC.

The information presented here are the outcome of the export process offered from the available reference manager or file type.

7. DATA ANALYSIS

Below table clearly reflects, that both software and .CSV format are similarly capable of importing first 7 fields (i.e. Author, Title, Year, Journal Name, Vol. no., Issue no., Pages), from SCOPUS database. But we can see importing capacity is not similar in some cases. Neither software nor .CSV file format could able to import *Publisher & ISSN No.* fields.

Table 1. Import results from Scopus Database

Sl. No.	*Fields*	*RefWorks*	*Mendeley*	*File format (.CSV)*
1	Author	1	1	1
2	Title	1	1	1
3	Year	1	1	1
4	Journal Name	1	1	1
5	Volume No.	1	1	1
6	Issue No.	1	1	1
7	Pages	1	1	1
8	Publisher	0	0	0
9	ISSN No.	0	0	0
10	URL	1	1	0
11	DOI	0	1	1
12	Author Keywords	0	1	0
13	Abstract	0	1	0
14	Database / Data Source	1	0	1

1 = Fields imported from SCOPUS

0 = Fields not imported from SCOPUS

Result also shows many differences between three citation management tools like, .CSV file format is not able to import *URL* filed, RefWorks is not able to import *DOI* field. Similarly *Author keyword & Abstract* fields are imported by Mendeley software only. At the same time Mendeley is failed to import *Data Source* field. An interesting difference is .CSV file format uses *EID (Electronic Identifier),* instead of DOI.

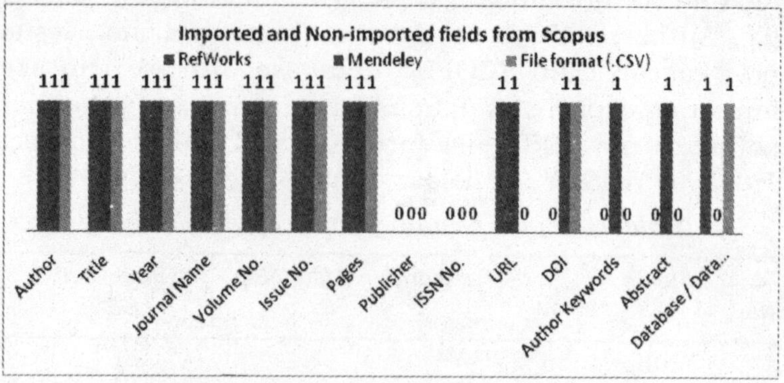

Fig. 1. Comparative analysis of RefWorks, Mendeley and .CSV file format

Figure 1 appears the graphical presentation imported and non-imported fields using RefWorks, Mendeley and .CSV file format.

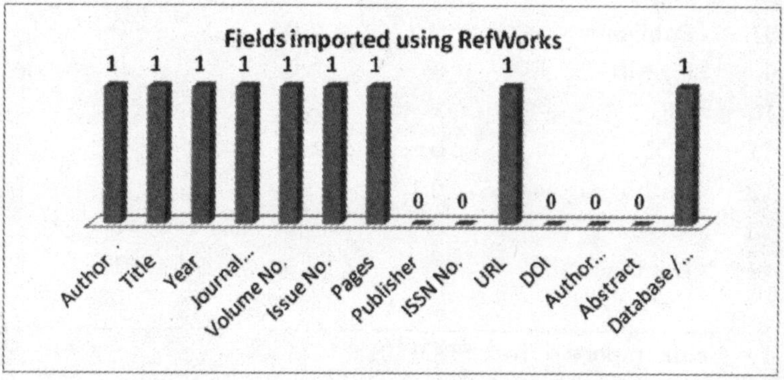

Fig. 2. Imported fields using RefWorks (Citation Management Tool)

Figure 2 shows the Citation Management Tool (RefWorks) imported all fields except few fields from SCOPUS such as *Publisher, ISSN No., DOI, Author Keywords, and Abstract.*

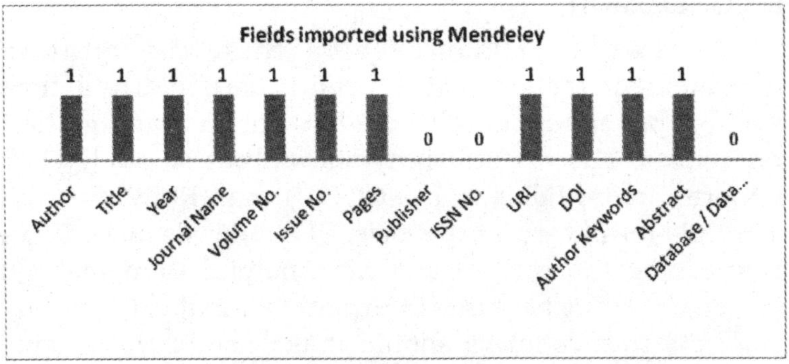

Fig. 3. Imported fields using Mendeley (Citation Management Tool)

Figure 3 shows the Citation Management Tool (Mendeley) has imported all the fields except 3 (three) from SCOPUS i.e. *Publisher, ISSN No. and Database / Data Source.*

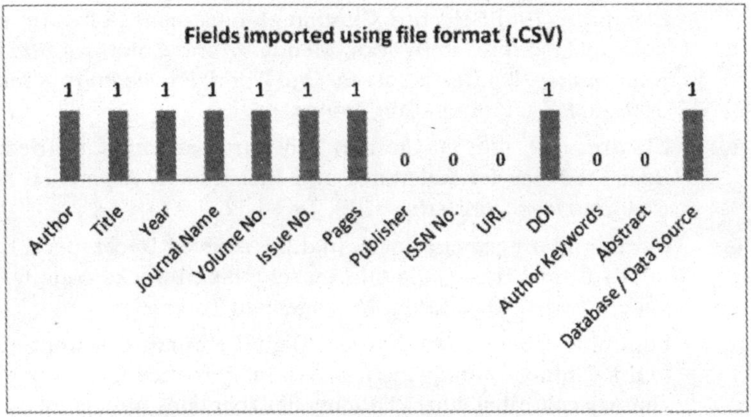

Fig. 4. Imported fields using file format .CSV (Citation Management Tool)

Figure 4 shows the import result from SCOPUS using .CSV file format. This tool has also didn't import several fields such as *Publisher, ISSN No., URL, Author Keywords and Abstract.*

8. CONCLUSION

This study has revealed that, the citation management tools are very useful, particularly a time saving tool for research scholars for managing their references. The result clearly shows that Mendeley has imported more fields from SCOPUS than RefWorks and .CSV file format with little ease. The analysis also shows that, using these tools are more helpful then manual system for citing accurate information. Finally, this study suggests that scholars should make use of these tools for managing citations.

REFERENCES

1. Basak, S. K. (2014). Reference Management Software: Comparative Analysis of RefWorks and Zotero. *International Journal of Computer, Information, Systems and Control Engineering*, 8(11), 1622–1625.
2. Butros, A., & Taylor, S. (2010). Managing Information: Evaluating and Selecting Citation Management Software, a Look at EndNote, RefWorks, Mendeley and Zotero. *Netting Knowledge: Two Hemispheres/One World: Proceedings of the 36th IAMSLIC Annual Conference.*
3. Childress, D. (2011). Citation Tools in Academic Libraries: Best Practices for Reference and Instruction. *Reference & User Services Quarterly, 51*(2), 143-152.
4. Citation Management Tools. (n.d.). Retrieved December 11, 2014, from https://digitalresearchtools.pbworks.com/w/page/17801648/Citation Management Tools.
5. Columbia University Libraries. Digital Humanities Center. (n.d.). Citation Management Software. Retrieved from http://library.columbia.edu/locations/dhc/citation-management-software.html
6. Comparison of reference management software. (n.d.). *Wikipedia.*
7. Exporting results from Scopus. (n.d.). Retrieved December 30, 2014, from http://help.scopus.com/Content/h_export.htm
8. Fitzgibbons, M., &Meert, D. (2010). Are Bibliographic Management Software Search Interfaces Reliable?: A

Comparison between Search Results Obtained Using Database Interfaces and the EndNote Online Search Function. *Journal of Academic Librarianship, 36*(2), 144-150.

9. Francese, E. (2012). Reference Management Software as Digital Libraries: A survey at the University of Torino. *Advances on Information Processing and Management, 1*, 293-296 Retrieved from http://hdl.handle.net/10760/16975\nhttp://hdl.handle.net/10642/1274

10. Hensley, M. K. (2011). Citation management software: features and futures. (ACCIDENTAL TECHNOLOGIST). *Reference & User Services Quarterly, 50*(3), 204-208. Retrieved from http://uoc.summon.serialssolutions.com/caES/search?spellcheck=true&utf8=?&s.q=Citation+management+software:+features+and+futures.

11. Jennings, A. F. (2003). RefWorks and Easybib.com: A comparison of the basic features of two electronic citation formatting products. *The Charleston Advisor, 5*(1), 18–21.

12. Marino, W. (2012). Fore-cite: tactics for evaluating citation management tools. *Reference Services Review, 40*(2), 295–310.

13. Reference Manager. (n.d.). Retrieved December 11, 2014, from http://www.phdontrack.net/review-and-discover/reference-managers/.

14. RefWorks. (n.d.). Retrieved from http://en.wikipedia.org/wiki/RefWorks.

15. Telstar. (n.d.). N. Retrieved November 28, 2014, from http://www.open.ac.uk/blogs/telstar/remit-toc/remit-what-is-reference-management/2-2-reference-management-software/.

19

DRM in Digital Era: An Overview

Malatee Padhan
Asian Worker Development Institute,
Bastia Memorial Trust, Sec-6, RKL
Roji Barik
Biju Patnaik Central Library, NIT, Rourkela

ABSTRACT

Digital right Management (DRM) is emerging as a formidable challenge and essential for DRM system to provide interoperable services. The digital revolution inspired the development of DRM to prevent us from using a copyrighted digital work beyond the degree to which the copyright owner wishes to allow us to use it, the purpose of this article is summarized the different DRM technologies and its impact on libraries.

Keywords : IPR, DRM, DRM Techniques, DRM and Library

1. INTRODUCTION

Due to the revolutionary development of ICT, the world moves from traditional to the digital environment, where the information is made available to anyone and anywhere at least cost. The internet is a worldwide network which interconnected millions of people around the globe and making the information sharing so easy. Now it has become a global duplicating system, where the digital content can be copied, altered and distributed to a large number of end users with ease for low cost over the network without losing quality. Now it arises so many questions on protection of intellectual property of creators, producers and distributors.

1.1. Intellectual Property

Intellectual property is deals with the creation of human intellect which belongs to the original creator. It is a cluster of legally recognized right associated with innovation and creativity, the work of mind of human being, as against physical products, land and other tangible resources (Chaudhari, n.d.). A creator's innovative works and strategic efforts to intellectual thought content which in terns have a crucial value in economy. It is recognized as a personal property of the creator that can be sold and traded like other property. Intellectual property is broadly divided into two types.

- Industrial property (patent, industrial design, tread marks)
- Artistic and literary property (copy right- music, literature, symbol)

Intellectual property right is a right legally granted to an individual or organization on their intellectual output such as invention, literary and artistic work, patent, trademark, industrial design, symbol, name, image etc. which aims at to protect the creation form the unauthorized use of property. But in case of electronic media, DRM is used to protection of intellectual property of creator.

1.2. DRM : The concept

DRM is the acronym for Digital Rights Management. In literarily we can described it in three aspects as

Digital : concerned with digital resources available in cyberspace, such as database, websites, e-resources

Rights : deals with legally granted power to the copy right holder to protect the digital work

Management : concerned with mechanism to control or prevent copying the intellectual output

DRM is nothing but a digital content creator's weapon to protect their intellectual properties. It is set of tools designed to control the access and protect digital content (encryption), control specific operations on the content (play, print, copy, save) and to limit the number of times a particular operation may be exercised on the content (e.g. view three times) (Mallik, & Singh, 2004).The term "digital rights management" refers to procedures and systems that individuals or organizations use to track copyright permission status, access parameters, and other qualities of a digital object that govern its access or use (Copyright Resources Project, n.d.).DRM has two parts:

- Management
- Enforcement

Management deals with how to manage the digital right and Enforcement is based on encryption and key management, by ensuring that the digital content is only used for purposes agreed by the right holder (IEEE New Technology Connections - Future Directions. (n.d.).

1.3. Characteristics of DRM

A DRM system has following Characteristics. Such as-

- Metadata
- Security features and copyright protection
- Personalization
- Granularity
- Interoperability
- Ease of use
- Payment system

2. FUNCTIONAL ARCHITECTUR OF DRM

There is no any standard architecture of Digital Rights Management; different vendors are given different DRM architecture. Overall DRM architecture is best suited to building of digital rights enable system, such as Functional architecture and Informational architecture.

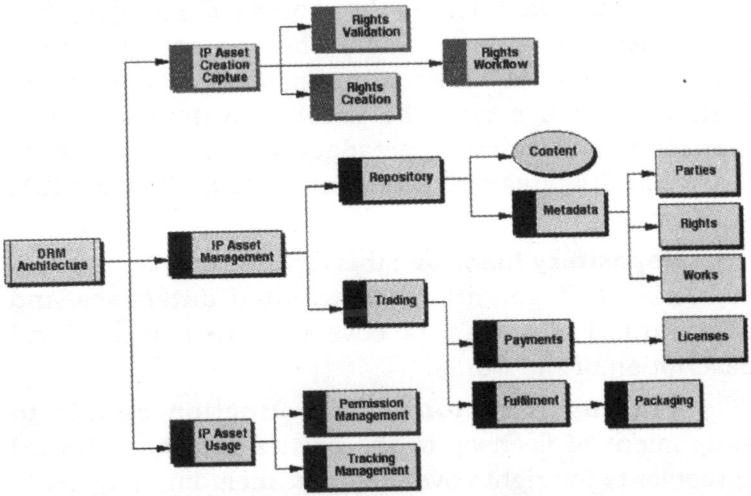

Fig. 1. Functional Architecture of DRM

The functional architecture of DRM is based on three important modules.

2.1. Content Creation & Capture

It deals with the creation and capture of content, which can be easily traded. This modules gives more emphasis on asserting digital right when a new document is created for first time (or reused and extended with appropriate rights to do so) by various content creators/ providers. It supports:

Rights validation : when a new content is created from existing content, it ensure that the rights are validated and approved to their owner or not.

Rights creation : after a content creation, the rights

are assigned to a new content which specify the right owner allow uses permission.

Rights workflow : the series of workflow or step by step process is required to publish the content. Such as review the content, approval o right.

2.2. Content Management

This module refers to the process of managing and enablement the trade of content which accept the content from the creators and use as an input for an asset management system. The trading system needs to manage the descriptive metadata and rights metadata (e.g., parties, usages, payments, etc.). This module supports

Repository function : this function enable to access or retrieval of potentially distributed databases and metadata. The metadata covers parties, rights and description of the works.

Trading functions : this function enable to assignment of licenses to the parties who have traded agreements for rights over content, including payments from licensees to rights holders (e.g., royalty payments). In some cases, the content may need to go through fulfilment operations to satisfy the license agreement. For example, the content may be encrypted/ protected or packaged for a particular type of desktop Usage environment.

2.3. Content Usage

This module refers to the process of usage of content after it has been traded. It supports restriction over the traded content in specific desktop system or software. It module supports:

Permissions management : the system must enforce the rights associated with the content in the usage environment. For example, if the user only has the rights to view the document, then printing will not be allowed.

Tracking management : it enable to monitoring the usage of the content where such tracking is part of the agreed to license conditions. For example, the user has a license to play a video ten time

3. DRM TECHNIQUES

There are several technical perspectives which are used to secure the content; such as-

3.1. Encryption

It is a process that encodes the message or information in such a way that can be read only by the authorized user. The authorized users can decrypt the message with the key provided by the owner to recipients. (Wiki). DRM uses encryption technology to lock the content which needs a secret key (a particular phrase or string of numbers), that we usually known as password. Only the password holder can unlock the content and read it.

3.2. Public/private keys

It is also an encryption system that uses a pair of keys. Those keys are usually known as public and private key. Each key can used to encrypt or decrypt the content. If one of the key is used to encrypt the content then other one is used to decrypt it. The public key is "made available to everyone via a publicly accessible repository or directory. On the other hand the private key must remain confidential to its respective owner. Because key pair is mathematically related, whatever is encrypted with a public key may only be encrypted by its corresponding private key and vice versa" (PublicKey and Private Keys, n.d.).

3.3. Digital certificate

A digital certificate is an electronic passport that allows a person, computer or organization to exchange private information securely over the internet using the

Public Keys Infrastructure (PKI). It may also be referred to as a public key certificate (Digital certificate, n.d.). It is a link between a person & his virtual identity. It is an electronic document to which used to prove the ownership of public key. Digital certificate gives information about the public keys, its owner identity and digital signature of the person or organization, that has verified the certificate's contents are correct. The digital signatures are issued by the certificate authorities that offer guarantees that the public key belong to the person whose name is in the certificate. The best example is e-mail message transmission. When sending an e-mail message, it is protected by encryption with a recipient public key. There is no any other way or key to decode the message. Only the recipient's private keys can decrypt the encrypted message, the confidentially the e-mail content can be secured.

3.4. Digital watermarking

It is embedded information. It is a technology that hides the information related to digital signal (an image, song and video) within the signal itself which provide evidence of its authentication. It cannot visible by human eyes in image or ear in audio content. It is a copy right stamp into the image, sound and video and it is practically maintain by host media. The watermark is maintained in all formats before they are allowed into the content chain. Only the knowledge of a secret key allows extracting the watermark from the original image.

3.5. Access control

An access control system maintains a user's access to access the content, and it is access through some kind of password protection. DRM uses to access control system to protect the intellectual property of copy right holder. Only an authorized user can access the copyrighted materials.

3.6. Secure communications protocols

Secure Sockets Layer and Transport Layer Security are cryptographic protocols that provide secure communications on the internet. IP security, shortly IPsec is a standard for securing internet protocol (IP) communications by encrypting and authenticating all IP packets.

3.7. Fingerprinting

"It is an important method to protect the digital media is to fingerprint each copy with the purchaser's information. If the purchaser makes illegitimate copies, they will contain his name" (Arsenova, n.d.). It's an extension of watermarking. It is a content-based identification technology which can be visible and invisible. "Digital fingerprinting is a technology which enables content owners exercise grater control on their copyrighted content by effective identification, tracking and monitoring across distribution channel (broadcast, radio, live, web etc..) while opening additional monetization avenue by exploiting extend value of digital assets (Concept Series: What is Digital Fingerprinting?, n.d.).

3.8. Right specification language

Right specification language deals with a technology or mechanism which describes the author or publisher rights. This data dictionary of rights terms gives a standard vocabulary to describe the DRM and other relevant issues.

3.9. Trust infrastructure

The term "trust infrastructure" refers to the technologies that support transport, opening, displaying and disposing the package. In current era, to support the market, DRM has to provide secure package containing content and accompanying metadata. DRM support to transport this secure package from author or content provider to consumer or end user.

3.10. Hashing

Hashing is the transformation of a string of characters into a usually shorter fixed-length value or key that represents the original string (Hashing, n.d.). DRM uses hashing techniques to protect digital content. In one-way hash function a hash value or simple value is called as message digest, is a number generated from a string of text. It takes digital content of any length as input and produced an output message is called message digest. "Hashes play a vital role in security systems where they are used to ensure that transmitted messages have not been tempered with. The sender generated a hash of the message, encrypts it, and sends it with the message itself. The recipient then decrypts both the message and the hash, produces another hash from the received message and compares the two hashes. If they are same there is a very high probability that the message was transmitted intact.

4. DRM & LIBRARIES

As we know that library is the light house of intellectual property which is not only meant for education and research but also it has direct impact on economic growth, literacy and quality of life of people. Now it has shifted from traditional environment to digital media by enhancing the way of accessing the content with innovative services with in minimum cost and span of time. It mostly leads to copyright infringement and revenue losses to content owners. For the security of digital data DRM is essential as because through this large amount of new content can be made available safely and in trusted environment.By embedding controls within the product, providers can prevent the public from use that is non-infringing under copyright law as well as enforce restrictions that extend far beyond those specific rights enumerated in the Copyright Act (or other laws). Thus, DRM changes the fundamental relationship between the creators, publishers, and users, to the detriment of creators, users, and the institutions that serve them (Chaudhari, n.d.).

Copyright terms : DRM may be used to prevent copying of works beyond the terms of their copyrights, or may be used to impose copy protection for works otherwise in the public domain, or works that have been licensed for less restricted general uses.

Preservation and archiving : DRM may be used to limit librarian's ability to preserve or archive a work, e.g., by preventing a work from being moved from more perishable to more permanent storage media.

Artistic creation : It has long been understood that the creation of new artistic works may require the excerpting or transformation of older ones; DRM may be used in ways that prevent such excerpting or transformation from happening.

Historiography : Historical research fundamentally depends on being able to access and quote older documents and other kinds of works. DRM can be implemented in ways that make historiography far more difficult, if not impossible, in many contexts.

Fair use : The ability of anyone to make unlicensed use of the protected works of other within limits established by law and precedent — can be curtailed by broad implementation of DRM.

5. CONCLUSION

It is so fundamental to all things in the world that is the most important obstacle to overcome in a game of survival of the fittest. In this sense, the changing era of 21st century has brought a great change in the field of library due to advent in Information & Communication Technology. So now library has to create a balance between the digital revolution & techno savvy users group. The adoption of DRM technology is most necessary if libraries are not to be lost in a world of omnipresent information. DRM provides a framework or a set of technologies and tools for the management of digital content. It could be valuable for tool for both content creators and user.

REFERENCES

1. ALA (2012). Digital Rights Management, ALA DCWG Tip Sheet, Retrieved January 11, 2015, from http://connect.ala.org/files/94226/DRM%20Library%20Education%20Tip %20Sheet_DEFINITIVE_7_11_12.pdf
2. Arsenova, Emilija (n.d.) Technical Aspects of Digital Rights Management, Retrieved January 16, 2015 from http://www.hit.bme.hu/~jakab/edu/litr/DRM/old/Techn_Asp_of_DRM.pdf
3. Boucqueau, Jean-Marc (2006). Digital Rights Management. IEEE, Retrieved Retrieved January 11, 2015 from http://www.ieee.org/about/technologies/emerging/digital_rights.pdf
4. Chaudhari, S. K. (n.d.), Digital Rights Management –a Technological Measure for Copyright Protection and its Possible Impacts on Libraries, Modernization of Libraries: A Challenge in Digital Era, Retrieved January 11, 2015 from http://eprints.rclis.org/13110/1/Digital_Rights_Management- Impact_on_Libraries.pdf
5. Concept Series: What is Digital Fingerprinting? (n.d.). Retrieved January 15, 2015, from http://www.mediaentertainmentinfo.com/2013/06/3-concept-series-what-is-digital-fingerprinting.html
6. Copyright Resources Project. (n.d.). Retrieved January 14, 2015, from http://www.bampfa.berkeley.edu/copyright_project/copyritetoolbox/Toolbox_DigitalRights.php
7. Coyle, Karen(2003).The Technology of Rights: Digital Rights Management, Retrieved January 15, 2015 from http://www.kcoyle.net/drm_basics.pdf
8. Digital certificate. (n.d.). Retrieved January 12, 2015, fromhttp://searchsecurity.techtarget.com/definition/digital-certificate

9. DorteBohner, (2008), Digital rights description as part of digital rights management: a challenge for libraries, *Library Hi Tech*, 26(4), 598 – 605 Retrieved January 11, 2015 from http://dx.doi.org/10.1108/07378830810920923

10. Ghatak, P., Tripathi, R. C. &Chakravarti, A. K. (2004). Journal of Intellectual Property Rights, 9(4), 313-331. Retrieved January 11, 2015 from http://nopr.niscair.res.in/bitstream/123456789/4878/1/JIPR%209%284%29%20313-331.pdf

11. Godwin, M. (2004).Digital Rights Management: A Guide for librarian. ALA, 1-44. A Retrieved January 12, 2015 from http://www.cs.yale.edu/homes/jf/Godwin-Libraries.pdf

12. Harinarayana, N. S., Somu, C. S. & Sunil, N. V. (2009). Digital rights management in digital libraries: An introduction to technology, effects and the available open source tools. In *CALIBER 2009, Feb-25-26,* 455-462. Retrieved January 12, 2015, From http://www.inflibnet.ac.in/caliber2009/CaliberPDF/57.pdf

13. Hashing. (n.d.). Retrieved January 14, 2015, from http://searchsqlserver.techtarget.com/definition/hashing

14. Ian Kerr Jane, Bailey (2004). The implications of digital rights management for privacy and freedom of expression, *Journal of Information, Communication and Ethics in Society*, 2(2), 85–95, Retrieved January 12, 2015 fromhttp://dx.doi.org/10.1108/14779960480000245

15. Iannella, R. (2001). Digital Rights Management (DRM) Architectures, D-Lib Magazine 7(6), Retrieved January 12, 2015 fromhttp://www.dlib.org/dlib/june01/iannella/06iannella.html

16. IEEE New Technology Connections - Future Directions. (n.d.). Retrieved January 22, 2015, fromhttp://www.ieee.org/go/emergingtech

17. Mallik, M. & Singh, S. (2004) Digital Rights Management and Libraries. In *PLANNER,* 242-245. Retrieved January 12, 2015 from http://ir.inflibnet.ac.in/bitstream/1944/450/1/04Planner_30.pdf

18. PublicKey and Private Keys. (n.d.). Retrieved January 12, 2015, fromhttps://www.comodo.com/resources/small-business/digital-certificates2.php

19. Subramanya, R. & Yi, B. K. (2006). Digital Management. IEEE Potential, 31-34. Retrieved January 12, 2015 from

http://www.ieee.org/about/technologies/emerging/digital_rights.pdf

20. Zhang, Xiao (2011). A Survey of Digital Rights Management Technologies http://www.cse.wustl.edu/~jain/cse571-11/ftp/drm/index.html

20

Citations Management in Scholarly Communication with Mendeley to Avoid Plagiarism

Arpita Basu

Assistant Librarian, Narula Institute of Technology, Kolkata, West Bengal

Joydip Chandra

Librarian, Barrackpore Rastraguru Surendranath College, Kolkata, West Bengal

ABSTRACT

The present society is based on knowledge economy. It's our right to free access of knowledge but protection of intellectual property rights (IPR) acts sometimes create hindrances to free flow of knowledge and information. Protection of IPR is essential for the economic aspects of knowledge property. Infringement of IPR by the academicians may be treated as plagiarism. To avoid plagiarism it's important to acknowledge the creator(s) as well as the source where it is available. For acknowledging, the knowledge of citation styles is required. Present advancement of information and communication technologies, emerged a number of free and fee based software for managing the citations that are helpful to cite references in a hassle freeway. Mendeley, one of the free such software is become most useful for this purpose. Installation, salient features and application of Mendeley is discussed.

Keywords : IPR, Copyright, Plagiarism, Citation Tools, Mendeley

1. INTRODUCTION

In the present Knowledge society, technology and knowledge are the main two ingredients of development. Every society has its own knowledge assets (UNESCO, 2005). It is necessary to work towards connecting the different forms of knowledge that already possess and new forms of that are emerging. Knowledge is typically non-excludable in that it is not possible to prevent others from applying new knowledge even without the authorization of its creator. According to Universal Availability of Publications (Hussain, 1984) and Right to Information, we have rights to use information irrespective of its form except classified information (BIT Pilani, 2007). Again human rights and the inclusive participatory character they inherited from the Enlightenment, the importance of basic rights translates into the particular emphasis on (UNO, 1948):

- Freedom of opinion and expression as well as freedom of information, media pluralism and academic freedom; and,
- The right "freely to participate in the cultural life of the community, to enjoy the arts and to share in scientific advancement and its benefits"

But on a contrary, the right of creator of the information in whatever of its nature is protected through Intellectual Property Rights (IPR) laws. The argument in favor of IPRs is that, without such protection, competitive market systems fail to provide private agents to invest in generation of the new ideas and technologies. Thus knowledge society emphasizes the efforts to create innovative labour forces, and efforts to secure intellectual property rights over innovations (European Foundation for the Improvement of Living and Working Conditions, 2009).

2. INTELLECTUAL PROPERTY RIGHTS (IPR)

Intellectual property (World Intellectual Property Organization, 2004) refers to creations of the mind: inventions; literary and artistic works; and symbols, names and images used in commerce. Intellectual property is divided into two categories:

Industrial Property : It includes patents for inventions, trademarks, industrial designs and geographical indications.

Copyright : It covers literary works (such as novels, poems and plays), films, music, artistic works and architectural design.

Intellectual property, very broadly, means the legal rights which result from intellectual activity in the industrial, scientific, literary and artistic fields (World Intellectual Property Organization, 2008). Intellectual property rights are like any other property right. They allow creators, or owners, of patents, trademarks or copyrighted works to benefit from their own work or investment in a creation.

Article 27 of Universal Declaration of Human Rights (UNO, 1948) describes IPR as:

- Everyone has the right to freely participate in the cultural life of the community, to enjoy the arts and to share in scientific advancement and its benefits.
- Everyone has the right to the protection of the moral and material interests resulting from any scientific, literary or artistic production of which he is the author.

The World Intellectual Property Organization (WIPO), established in 1970, is an international organization dedicated to helping ensure that the rights of creators and owners of intellectual property are protected worldwide, and that inventors and authors are therefore recognized and rewarded for their ingenuity.

3. PLAGIARISM

Scholarly publishing is a key factor for any person in academia. It is the creation, transformation, dissemination and preservation of knowledge related to teaching, research and scholarly endeavors. Scholarly communication is the system through which research and other scholarly writings are created, evaluated for quality, disseminated to the scholarly community, and preserved for future use. This system includes both formal means of communication, such as publication in peer-reviewed journals, and informal channels, such as electronic listservs (ACRL Scholarly Communications Committee, 2003). Among the many scholarly communications issues include author rights. Plagiarism (Bella, 2014) is a type of infringement of copy right laws. It is the use of others' published and unpublished ideas or words (or other intellectual property) without attribution or permission, and presenting them as new and original rather than derived from an existing source.

The intent and effect of plagiarism is to mislead the reader as to the contributions of the plagiarizer. This applies whether the ideas or words are taken from abstracts, research grant applications, Institutional Review Board applications, or unpublished or published manuscripts in any publication format. Plagiarism is scientific misconduct and should be addressed as such (Bella, 2014):

- Ignorance
- Cheating in self-defense
- Lack of perceived punishment
- Many researchers have poor time management and planning skills
- Some researchers do not believe editors actually read research papers

A flowchart can better explain the plagiarism (Indiana University; School of Education, 2014):

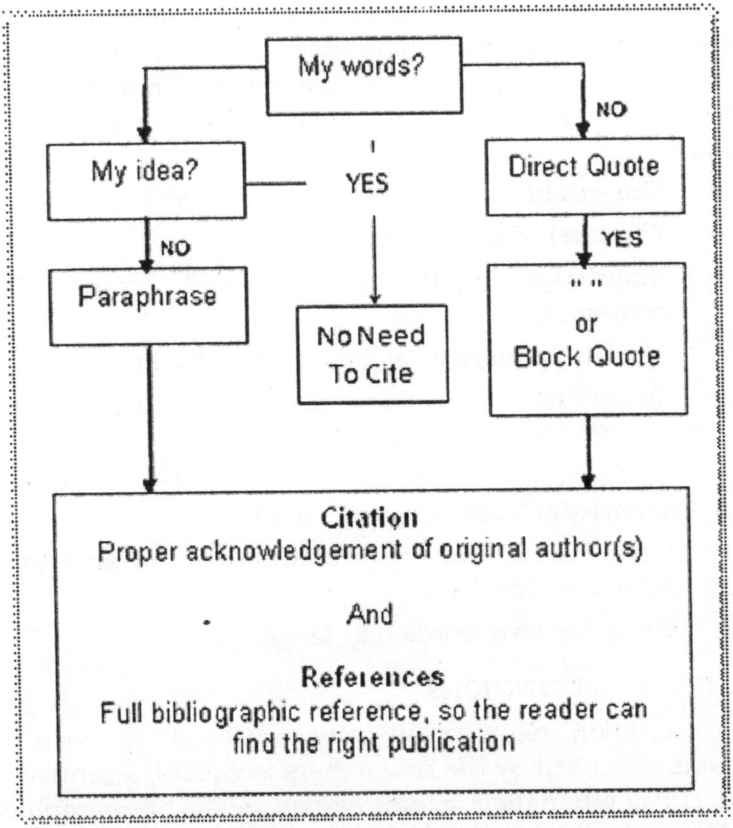

Fig. 1. Flowchart to recognize plagiarism

4. AVOIDING PLAGIARISM

The researcher / author must not only learn how to avoid plagiarism, but also why should avoid it. The main consequences of plagiarism are penalties that can range from warnings to various forms of legal sanctions. While consensus on how, when and the way to apply such sanctions is nearly non-existent, the consensus in applying sanctions is definitely absolute. Plagiarism is viewed as an extremely negative attitude, even when performed in a very slight extent. In order to establish and apply penalties against plagiarism, it is first necessary to define what is considered plagiarism from a technical standpoint. the characterization of plagiarism should include the analysis and documentation of how this was detected and analyzed, taking into account (Berlinck, 2011):

- The extent to which it was committed;
- The level of convicted;
- Knowledge of institutional rules and norms by the convicted;
- The disciplinary rules adopted by the institution.

To minimize or avoiding plagiarism, the points to be considered are (Hensley, 2011):

- Understand the difference between "common knowledge" and "original" ideas
- Give credit, mark direct quotations, and use reference citations
- Use your own words and ideas.

5. TOOLS FOR CITATIONS

Citation management software (Basak, 2014) is a tool that is used by the researchers (scholars, scientists, etc.) to maintain their records and utilize the bibliographic citation. Again, it may be described as a tool (Childress, 2011) that may be any resource, program or service and supports citation management, or, the understanding, gathering, organization, and use of citations in research and information literacy. So it is programs that allow researchers to store, organize output and share bibliographic citations.

Reference management software reduces the workload burden for the researchers to edit, proofread, and avoid formatting errors. Most of these tools are cloud-based Software as a Service products (University of Southern California, 2013). Data is stored online and users can access and add to their citations using a standard web browser, mobile device, or desktop software.

Citations can be entered manually, created from web site content, or created automatically from content provided by the platform vendor.

The application of citation tools can be better understood with help of the following diagrams. The diagrams are influenced with the illustrations (Open citations corpus import process, 2013):

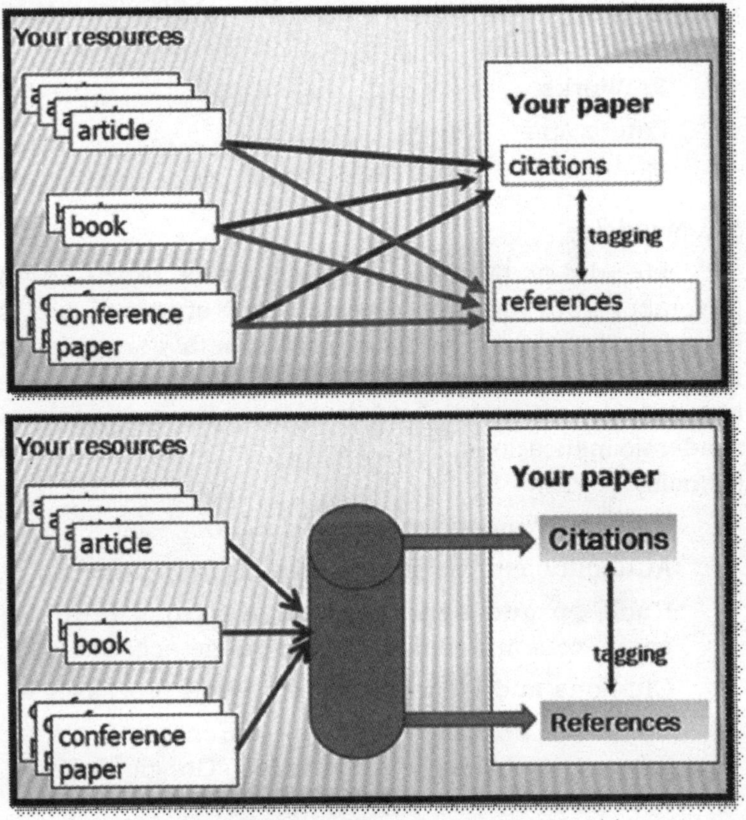

Fig. 2. How citation tools work

Actually when a researcher starts his/her paper s/he has some resources with the help of which s/he will write the paper. The steps involves to cite these resources s/he has to cite the resources according to some standard style manual, and collect the bibliographic information and compile detail bibliographic references. With the help of a citation management tool, the users have only to upload the resources into the database of the tool and the rest including the preferred form of citation will do by the tool itself.

Although there are many tools currently available, here focus is pointed on those that are widely used by academicians (University of Southern California, 2013):

- EndNote
- RefWorks
- Zotero and
- Mendeley

5.1. Mendeley

Mendeley (Mendeley, 2009) was founded in November 2007 by three German PhD students and is based in London. The first public beta version was released in August 2008. The team comprises researchers, graduates, and developers from a variety of academic institutions. The basic features of Mendeley are (Hensley, 2011):

- Runs on Windows, Mac and Linux.
- Automatic extraction of metadata from papers.
- Back-up and synchronization across multiple computers and with a private online account.
- Citations and bibliographies in Word processor
- Import of documents and research papers from external websites (e.g., PubMed, Google Scholar, Arxiv)
- BibTeX export/file sync
- Phone app
- Share references
- Manage PDFs

Mendeley (Curran, 2011) combines both a desktop

and a web-based application that is compatible across platforms. Mendeley is also fairly intuitive to learn and features drag and drop technology. The most valuable advancement Mendeley boasts is comprehensive PDF management. Mendeley Dashboard takes academic collaboration to a new level by leveraging the users of Mendeley to watch research trends. Research groups, which can be made public or private, have the ability to collaboratively annotate and share notes. Mendeley generally works a little different than other software programs, it inserts formatted citations by dragging and dropping into any text editor including Google Docs, LaTeX, blogs and e-mails.

The development of Mendeley is a clear indication of the future direction research tools. Citation management is going beyond generating bibliographies and citations (Hensley, 2011).

A comparative statement of the citation tool (University of Southern California, 2013) shows that show that Mendeley reference management software looks as a useful tool (Basak, 2014) for electronic reference management for researchers. This study will also help to researchers about the reference management software tool that is very essential in terms of citation and referencing.

5.2. Working of Mendeley

5.2.1. Create collections

To create collection with Mendeley, there are broadly two methods i.e.

1. Download files or papers from search engines and these are uploaded into Mendeley by clicking the Add Document button on the far left of the toolbar. Mendeley will then attempt to detect the document details (bibliographic data).
2. Alternatively library catalogues, databases having

linkage with Mendeley can directly upload the documents along with the bibliographic details to Mendeley database.

3. Any documents whose details Mendeley is uncertain about will be added to the Needs Review collection for manual verification.

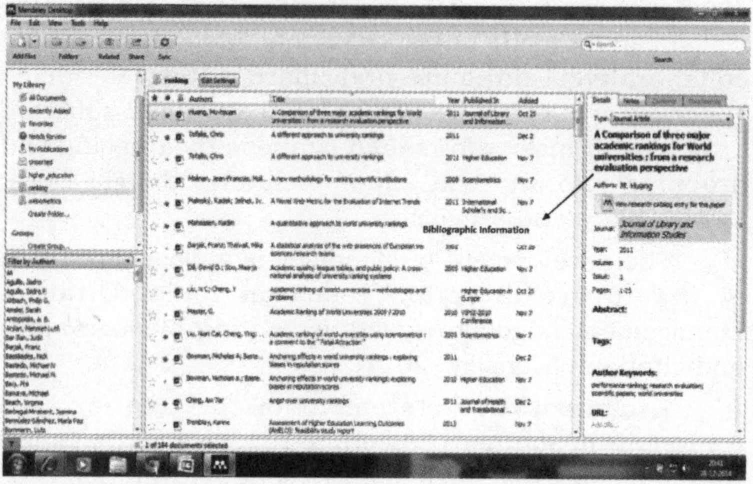

Fig. 3. Create collection in Mendeley

The commercial or open databases support direct uploading of bibliographic information to Mendeley are (Mendeley, 2009):

- ACM Portal
- Amazon
- APS
- APA PsycNET
- arXiv
- CiteseerX
- CiteULike
- Copac
- EBSCO
- Google BookSearch

- Google Scholar
- IACR ePrints
- IEEE Xplore
- IngentaConnect
- ISI Web of Knowledge
- JSTOR
- NASA ADS
- Wiley
- PubMed
- RePEc
- ScienceDirect
- SpringerLink
- Wikipedia
- WorldCat
- Zetoc

5.2.2. Organize Collection

Web importer & Word Plug-in

When the documents are uploaded in Mendeley, user can cite and reference them within Word and OpenOffice with ease. The Mendeley Word & OpenOffice plug-in integrates Mendeley into these word processors.

Cite documents

Currently the Word plug-in is only available for Windows. Mac support is expecting soon. When to create a paper and author want to cite a document from Mendeley Library the user may follow the following screenshot:

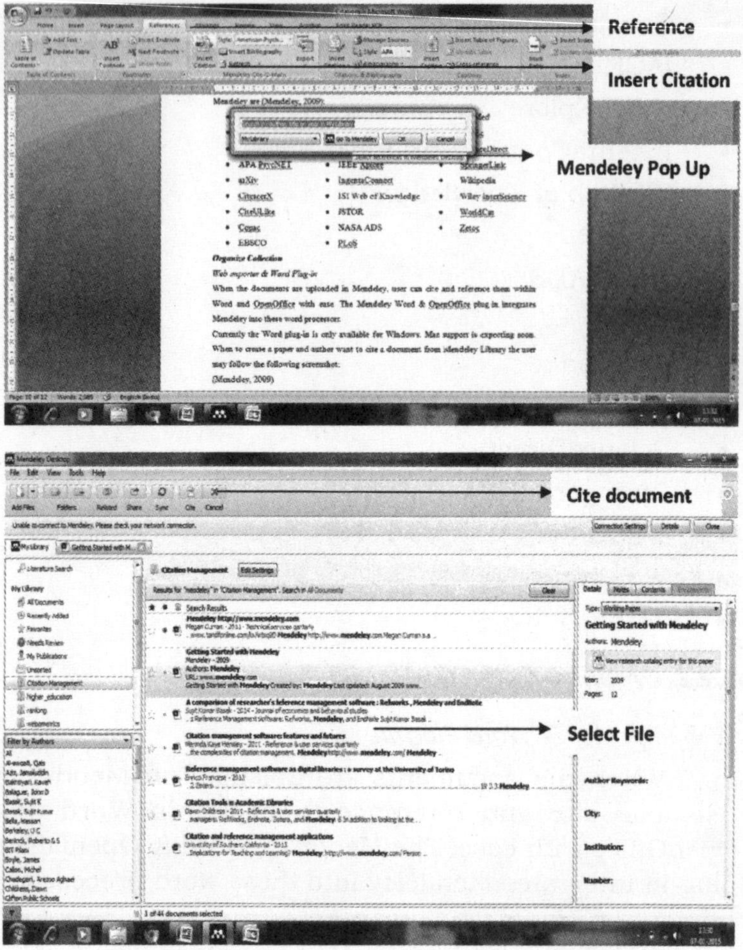

Fig. 4. Citation procedure with Mendeley

Create Bibliography

After citing the documents in the paper/article it is required to create bibliography at the end of the paper/article to describe the details bibliographic information of the cited documents. The snapshot below shows the process of creation of bibliography with the help of Mendeley:

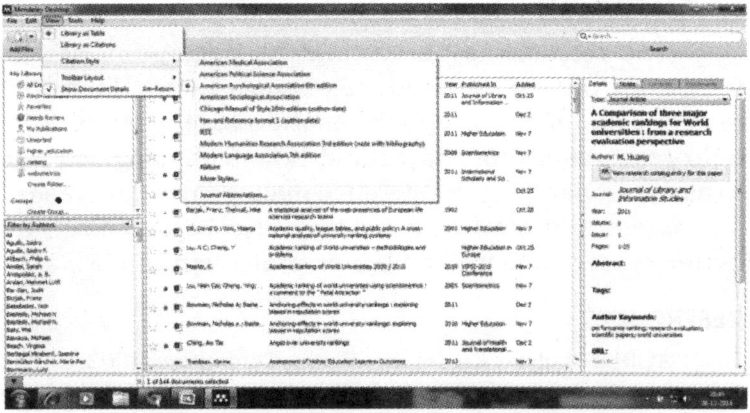

Fig. 5. Inbuilt citation patterns in Mendeley

Mendeley supports the style manuals as suggested by American Medical Association, American Political Science Association, American Psychological Association American Sociological Association, Chicago manual, Harvard Reference Format, IEEE, Modern Humanities Research Association, Modern Language Association, Nature and more. An example is cited here following APA style manual:

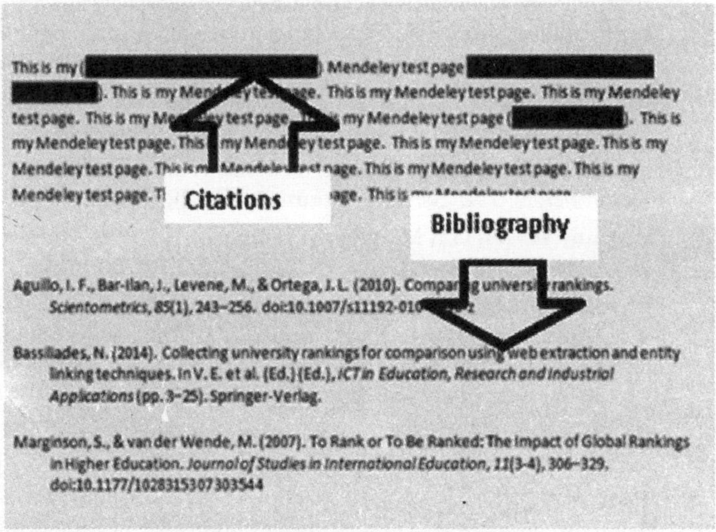

Fig. 6. Output from Mendeley

6. CONCLUSION

The role of the library and its perception are an important part of the study, as shown by the literature review. One of the purposes of the present study is to help researchers to understand how technology can do to assist researchers in reference management. Increased awareness and staff training may also be organized for better research as well as better protection of IPR.

REFERENCES

1. ACRL Scholarly Communications, Committee (2003, June). Principles and strategies for the reform of scholarly communication. Retrieved on December 24, 2014, from *http://www.ala.org/acrl/publications/whitepapers/principlesstrategies*
2. Basak, S. K. (2014). Reference management software/ : comparative analysis of RefWorks and Zotero. *International Journal of Computer, Information, Systems and Control Engineering,* 8(11), 1682–1685.
3. Bella, H. (2014). Plagiarism. *Saudi Journal of Medicine and Medical Sciences,* 2(2), 127 – 29. Retrieved on December 24, 2014, from http://www.sjmms.net/
4. Berlinck, R. G. S. (2011). The academic plagiarism and its punishments - a review. Brazilian Journal of Pharmacognosy, 21(3), 365–372. doi:10.1590/S0102-695X2011005000099
5. BIT Pilani (2007). A manual on Intellectual Property Rights (1st ed.). Pilani: BIT Pilani.
6. Childress, D. (2011). Citation Tools in Academic Libraries. *Reference & User Services Quarterly,* 51(2), 53–62.
7. Curran, M. (2011). Mendeley. *Technical Services Qarterly,* 28(4), 454 – 56. doi:10.1080/07317131.2011.598069
8. European Foundation for the Improvement of Living and Working Conditions. (2009). Handbook of knowledge society foresight. Dublin: the Foundation. Retrieved on December 21, 2014, from *www.eurofound.eu.int*
9. Hensley, M. K. (2011). Citation management software: features and futures. *Reference & User Services Quarterly,* 50(3), 204–208.
10. Hussain, S. (1984). Universal availability of publications:

problems and prospects. *Annals of Library Science and Documentation*, 31, 38–43.

Indiana University; School of Education. (2014). Overview: How to Recognize Plagiarism. Retrieved January 5, 2015, from https://www.indiana.edu/~istd/shouldDo.html

11. Mendeley. (2009). Getting Started with Mendeley. Retrieved on December 20, 2014, from www.mendeley.com
12. Open citations corpus import process. (2013). Retrieved January 5, 2015, from https://opencitations.wordpress.com/2013/03/06/open-citations-corpus-import-process/
13. UNESCO. (2005). Towards Knowledge Societies. Paris: UNESCO.
14. University of Southern California. (2013). Citation and reference management applications. California: the University.
15. UNO. (1948). Universal Declaration of Human Rights. Retrieved on December 26, 2014, from https://unp.un.org/rights.aspx
16. World Intellectual Property Organization. (2004). What is Intellectual Property? Geneva: WIPO.
17. World Intellectual Property Organization. (2008). Intellectual property handbook (2nd ed.). Geneva: WIPO.

21

Factors of Academic Plagiarism in the Information Era: Issues and Challenges

Jayashree Majhi
Library Professional Trainee, BPCL, NITR

Prameeta Sharma
Library Professional Trainee, BPCL, NITR

ABSTRACT

At present in the age of information explosion the readily available e-sources has many positive aspects but at the same time it has some negative aspects also. It has created an environment where someone else's ideas, thoughts, processes, works etc., is being used to produce the same commodity with new packing and labels, without giving credit or acknowledging the works. Plagiarism has risen in the academic world tremendously. Practice of plagiarism by the students in the colleges, universities is common but, it has resulted in arising challenges for the information producer as well as for the facilitators. This paper basically deals with the different types of plagiarism among students in the academics. It also explores the factors behind them. Free and commercial anti-plagiarism software's have also been given. The issues and challenges associated with plagiarism have been discussed along with what can be the role of LIS professionals in reducing plagiarism in the information era.

Keywords: Plagiarism, Citation, Software, Information, Academic Plagiarism

1. INTRODUCTION

In the present modern day, we have Google, WWW, Social Networking Sites and many different applications to help us to quench our thirst for knowledge. As it is well known that we require information in the same way as we require the other basic necessities of life, i.e., food, clothing and shelter. To earn our bread, we are engaged in different types of professions and businesses. But in the core of all the activities what so ever done, to earn the livelihood lie the, term "ethics", i.e., the right way or a code of conduct. The ethics states that we must know what is right and what is wrong and we must follow the right path at all cost.

In the teaching and learning process, writing assignments, and doing research at higher level is mandatory. It requires certain skills and methods and above all, thorough subject knowledge. In the process of research, generating new ideas and inventions are the basics of any research study. Along with these what are important are hard work, proper guidance and stipulated time. But the scenario of the academics is quite different. In the absence of knowledge, improper guidance and time constraint, students fall prey to copying and pasting, which is actually leading them to a wrong direction in their long term career. The unacknowledged patch work has resulted in the discovery of a new term in the field of writing i.e., "Plagiarism". In the darkness of incorrect and less knowledge, plagiarizers are stealing the intellectual property, in contrast to the other thieves, who steal physical property. The patch work which is going on, in the academic world to finish off the course is actually a cheating, a fraud, not only to the author whose work or idea has been copied but also to one self. In reality they are finishing off their whole career.

2. ORIGIN OF PLAGIARISM

Plagiarism comes from the Latin word plagiarius,

which means kidnapping, or plundering. The English word 'plagiary' firstly surfaced in 1601 in Ben Johnson's, 'The Poetaster', means a literary thief who wrongfully takes another's words or ideas. (Wikipedia)

3. DEFINITIONS

"Plagiarism is the practice of taking someone else's work or ideas and passing them off as one's own."

—New Oxford American Dictionary

"Plagiarism means to steal and pass off (the ideas or words of another) as one's own. To use (another's production) without crediting the source."

—Merriam–Webster Dictionary

IEEE defines plagiarism as "the use of someone else's prior ideas, processes, results, or words without explicitly acknowledging the original author and source".

Plagiarism may take various forms. The most serious form of plagiarism is "to obtain and submit as your own paper written by someone else." (*Visser, Haidegger & Papanikolopoulos, 2012*)

4. TYPES OF PLAGIARISM

There are different types of plagiarism and all are serious violations of academic honesty. The general types of plagiarism are as follows:-

4.1. Direct Plagiarism

Direct plagiarism is the word- for- word transcription of a section of someone else's work without attribution and without quotation marks. The deliberate plagiarism of someone else's work is unethical academically dishonesty and ground for disciplinary actions, including expulsion.

4.2. Self-Plagiarism

Self-plagiarism occurs when a student submits his/ her own previous work, or mixes part of previous works, without permission from all professors involved.

4.3. Mosaic Plagiarism

Mosaic plagiarism occurs when a student borrow phrases from a source without using quotation marks or find synonyms for author's language, while keeping the same general structure and meaning of the original. It is also called patch writing.

4.4. Accidental Plagiarism

Accidental plagiarism occurs when a person neglects to site their sources or misquotes their sources or unintentionally paraphrases a source by using similar words, group of word and sentence structure without attribution. (Bowdoin).

According to (WriteCheck, 2014) there are various types of plagiarism such as:

Clone : Submitting another's work, word for word as one's own.

Ctrl+C : Contains significance portion of text from a single source without alterations

Find-Replace : Changing key word and phrases but retaining the essential content of the source.

Remix : Paraphrases from multiple sources made to fit together.

Recycle : Borrows generously from the writer's previous work without citation.

Hybrid : Combines perfectly cited sources with copied passages without citation.

Mashup : Mixed copied material from multiple sources.

404 Error : Include citation to non-existent or inaccurate information about the sources.

Aggregator : Includes proper citation to sources but the paper contains almost no original work.

Re-Tweet : Includes proper citation, but relies too closely on the text's original wording and/or structure.

5. FACTORS BEHIND PLAGIARISING

The various basic factors that are responsible for academic plagiarism are:

- Unfair means and lazy mentality of students and people.
- Language and content problem faced by the students.
- Lack of understanding the importance of citations and references.
- Lack of linguistic mechanics to successfully integrate sources within their academic writing.
- Lack of motivation among students.
- Lack of aspiration for higher grades.
- Lack of desire for a better product.
- Lack of adequate and stringent laws of copyright.
- The delay and hassles in the implementation of such regulation.
- Cultural background is a major factor (one of the problem but not a sole problem).
- Lack luster attitude on the part of authorities.

6. DETECTION OF PLAGIARISM

Basically in the academic world writing assignments, research papers, theses, dissertation, etc., is the part and partial of education/learning. But the increasing activity of patch and copy and paste work, in academics has actually necessitated its prevention. The methods of detection of plagiarism are:-

6.1. Manual Detection

Done manually by human beings. It is suitable for lecturers and teachers, while checking student's assignments, theses, dissertations, research papers etc. But it is not so effective and useful. It is impractical for large number of documents. It is not economical and requires a lot of effort and wastage of time. Therefore, it is not successful in the internet era.

6.2. Automatic Detection (Computer Assisted Detection)

There are many free and commercial types of software are used in automatic plagiarism detection. Every software has its own unique features and work differently. Some check originality andsome detect correct grammar in documents. (Ali, Abdulla & Sel 2011)

Free Softwares	*Commercial Softwares*
Viper	Turnitin
DupliChecker	iThenticate
Copyscape	Writecheck
Plagiarism Detect	Plagscan

7. CONSEQUENCES OF PLAGIARISM

According to iThenticate (http://www.ithenticate.com/resources/6-consequences-of-plagiarism)

The consequences of plagiarism can be personal, professional, ethical and legal. With different plagiarism detection software's so readily available and in use, plagiarists are being caught at an alarming rate. Different types of plagiarists include- academics, professionals, students, journalists, authors and others. The basic consequences of academic plagiarism are:

- Plagiarism can get students expelled from their courses of study.
- Plagiarism can result in destroying works.
- Plagiarism can result in expulsion from academic institution.
- Plagiarism can result in legal action.
- Plagiarism destroys the chances of developing

critical, creative and independent thinking.

- Plagiarism decreases the chances to develop skills in students.
- Plagiarism leads to receiving a reduced grade in studies.
- Plagiarism can lead to failing in the assignments.
- Plagiarism can lead re-doing the assignments.
- Finally, the student-teacher relationship is damaged and students lose the trust of their teachers.

8. HOW TO AVOID PLAGIARISM

Some of the important points that can be useful in avoiding academic plagiarism are:

- To minimize plagiarism it is needed from the part of educationists like teachers, lecturers, professors etc., and facilitators like LIS professional to work together and create such an environment where the basics of writing a paper for an assignment or a research is taught.
- By teaching how to quote the source properly?
- By paraphrasing the source properly.
- Educating the skills of referencing and citation by conducting training programmed.
- Also, generate in student the necessary skills required for critical analysis and building an argument.
- By different free and commercial plagiarism detection software we can, avoid it.
- And, above all the emphasis should be on the total involvement of the students and generating interest rather than giving punishment or penalties.

9. ISSUES AND CHALLENGES

The greatest challenge today in some of the academic institutions, like universities, colleges and schools is the detection and prevention from rising plagiarism. The various issues and challenges are as follows:-

- Detecting cheater is of course an important issues but the greatest challenge is to prevent it from doing so.
- Intentional plagiarism is also a matter of great concern and important issues.
- Unintentional plagiarism in the darkness of proper guidance about citation and references is also an issue.
- Creating awareness and educating the student about what constitutes plagiarism and the penalties for it also due an issue.
- Generating an understanding of creating something new and unique of their own by the students is one the major issue at academic level.
- Cultural issues like religious beliefs, customs and assumptions, all of which are product of our societal upbringing. These are not sole problem but also significant part of plagiarism.
- Linguistics problem is also an issue, but it is not count as major issues.

10. ROLE OF LIBRARY AND LIS PROFESSIONALS TO OVERCOME ISSUES AND CHALLENGES

The number of emerging cases of plagiarism arising every now and them for the last couple of decade has necessitated our interference. Although we have been the hub of knowledge since ancient time but still the easy availability of electronic resources has ignited plagiarism. Therefore we LIS professionals have a very major role to play i.e., to conserve and preserve the intellectual assets. It is obvious that plagiarism can be prevented but with sincere efforts and continuous awareness. The LIS professional's role can be:

- To develop web pages, guides, instructions for proper citation and referencing.
- To educate the user and faculty through library users training program.
- To provide plagiarism checking services to its users.
- To discuss about the problem of plagiarism with the user from time to time.
- Generating awareness by conducting seminars and conferences can be a good way to combat the plagiarism.

11. CONCLUSION

The growth of plagiarism among the students and in the learning Centre's i.e., academics is a matter of great concern. Today in the reign of internet we have been graced with easy accessibility to enhance, increase and multiply our knowledge. But, still we indulge our shelves in the cobweb of plagiarism. Although we know the dire consequences but we are unable to refrain our shelves from it. Therefore, how we can refrain and restrict from practicing plagiarism? Is a great challenge. We librarians being the proactive facilitators of information need to universally acknowledge the problem of plagiarisms along with the teachers, instructors and information producers. Specifically we need to take some solid steps in explaining, illustrating and promoting good writing practices and dedicated writing modules. Above all what is most important is creating self-consciousness against the practices of plagiarism among the future generation.

REFERENCES

1. Ali, A., Abdulla, H., &Sel, V. (2011). *Overview and comparison of plagiarism detection tools. Ostrava, Poruba: Czech Republic* Retrieved from http://ceur-ws.org/Vol-706/poster22.pdf
2. Aziz, J., Hashim, F., &Razak N. A. (2012). *Anecdotes of plagiarism: some pedagogical issues and Considerations, 8(10), Canadian Center of Science and Education* Retrieved

from http://ccsenet.org/journal/index.php/ass/article/view/19319/12782

3. Bowdoin (n.d). *The common types of plagiarism: Bowdoin College Brunswick* Retrieved from http://www.bowdoin.edu/studentaffairs/academic-honesty/common-types.shtml

4. Koovakkai, D. (2011). Diagnosing plague: tools and techniques for detecting plagiarism. Ahmadabad :In *INFLIBNET Centre* Retrieved from http://ir.inflibnet.ac.in/bitstream/1944/1629/1/37.pdf

5. More, T., &Shelar, V. (2011). *Plagiarism and copyright violation: a need of information literacy framework towards ethical use of information. Goa: Goa University* Retrieved from http://ir.inflibnet.ac.in/bitstream/1944/1640/1/48.pdf

6. Sharma, B. (2007). *Plagiarism among university students: intentional or accidental?* Retrieved from http://www.academia.edu/962450/Plagiarism_among_University_Students_Intentional_or_Accidental

7. Vij, R., Soni, N., &Makhdumi, G. (2009). *Encouraging academic honesty through anti-plagiarism software,* In *CALIBER 2009.* Retrieved from http://www.inflibnet.ac.in/caliber2009/CaliberPDF/55.pdf

8. Visser, L., Haidegger, T., & Papanikolopoulos, N. (2012). *Pitfalls of publications: on the sensitive issue of plagiarism,* 19(4), 85-87. Doi: 10.1109. Rourkela, NIT: IEEE Retrieved from http://ieeexplore.ieee.org/stamp/stamp.jsp? arnumber =6377466

9. WriteCheck. (2014). *Types of plagiarism.* Retrieved from http://www.plagiarism.org/plagiarism-101/types-of-plagiarism/

22

Open Access Online E-Resources in Library and Information Science

Kundan Jha
Assistant Librarian, Hon'ble Judges Library
High Court of Chhattisgarh, Bilaspur, 495220

Tejaswini Gupta
Research Scholar (M. Phil) DLIS,
Dr. C. V. Raman University, Bilaspur, 495113

Nidhi Gupta
Assistant Professor, DLIS, Dr. C. V. Raman University,
Bilaspur, 495113

ABSTRACT

This paper mainly describes about various aspects of E-Resources, its purpose, need, features and benefit of E-Resources. This paper also emphasizes on some of the open access E-resources in library and information science. Ten open access online e-resources in library and information science are analyzed.

Keywords : E-resources, Open Access Resource, Open Access E-resources in LIS, Library and Information Science, Electronic Information.

1. INTRODUCTION

Open access online information source can be accessed on internet without paying any subscription charges to the publishers and the user does not need to have any membership in the organization. User can access and download required information available on these source in their computer and can use for their academic, research and educational purposes. Since emergence of the web in 1990s, there has been a continuous increase in the volume of open access E-resources, these resources have been providing a scope for researcher and author in various disciplines. Library and Information science is no exception to this. Libraries have witnessed that print medium are increasingly giving way to the electronic form of material.

Use of information technology has marked a tremendous impact over all function and services created by the traditional library and information professional. Information source in a given discipline are referred to as "Literature" that includes all definitive sources of information. WWW is the best alternative medium to searches for scholarly literature and to use web resources to support their research productivity. Recent past have witnessed a considerable growth in digital information resources like the traditional library system is transforming itself into hybrid information system having a mix of digital and traditional paper resource.

The hi-tech development in science and technology coupled with information technology has led to the drastic change in the library and information product and services. The user community is becoming more familiar with the new medium over time and has started to actively bid for alternative form of access. Technology improvement in the communication network paired with the decreasing cost of hardware creates greater incentives for innovation. Several traditional journals are now being publishes both on the web and in print. Online subscription of e-resources is becoming very popular now a day (Chauhan & Mahapatra, 2013).

2. OBJECTIVE OF THIS STUDY

The main objective of study aims:

- To consolidate the Information on e-resources.
- To find out the facilities provided by e-resources to their users.
- To know the purpose, need, features and benefit of e-resources.
- To know the e-resources of information
- To know some webpage in open access online e-resources in LIS.
- To know the open access online e-resources in LIS.

3. METHODOLOGY

For data collection methodology, the main source of data collection are various observations which are from primary (journal and conference paper) and secondary source (Books and Handbook) of information and different type of search engine such us Met crawler, Google, Yahoo, MSN, 123, and other type of search engine.

4. ELECTRONIC RESOURCES

An electronic resources is defined as a resource which requires computer access or any electronic product that delivers a collection of data, be it text referring to full text data bases, electronic journals, image collection, other multimedia products and numerical, graphical or time based, as a commercially available title that has been published with an aim to market. E-resources are basically distributed of information in any electronic form such as CD-ROM, floppy disk, magnetic disk or magnetic tape or across a computer network like E-journals, E-books, and E-magazine etc.

AACR2 Rule 9.0A1 states "electronic resources consist of data (information representing numbers, text, graphics, images, maps, moving images, music, sounds, etc.), programs (instruction, etc., that process data for use), or combination of data and programs "

5. PURPOSE OF ELECTRONIC RESOURCES

The main purpose of e-resources is

- Providing current and latest information.
- Updating information for project and research work.
- Saving the time of information user/seeker and information professional /Staff.
- Solving the space problem in libraries and information center.
- Easy to use, storage and disseminate.

6. NEED OF ELECTRONIC RESOURCES

The main purpose of e-resources is to provide current and latest information to the information seeker/ user. We need e-resources so that-

- E-resources can be downloaded instantly.
- User can read an e-resource any time and any places.
- Due to portability one place to other places.
- Font size and font name can be changed suitably.
- Physically disabled users can hear audible Electronic resources.
- E-resources do not require bindery and repair.
- E-resources save human resources and manpower for shelving and rectification of information.

7. FEATURES OF ELECTRONIC RESOURCES

The main features of e-resources is following:

- Text can be searched, except when represented in the form of images.
- Hundreds or thousands may be carried together on one device. Approximately 500 average e-books can be stored on one CD.

- Type size, name and type face may be adjusted.
- E-resources can be used with text-to-speech software.
- Distributed at low cost.
- Distributed instantly, allowing readers to begin reading at once, without the need to visit a bookstore.
- No risk of damage, vandalism, etc. on the pages.

8. BENEFITS OF ELECTRONIC RESOURCES

Accessibility and Availability : Rapid advances in ICT have resulted the researchers being able to access information resource from all over the world.

Cost Effective : The cost of electronic journal is decreased because of eradication of paper printing, postage etc.

Better Storage and Retrieval : Digitally available information has eradicated the problem like- binding, shelving, storage, maintenance etc. and gives opportunity for better retrieval.

Time Saving : The time is saved in terms of digitally submission of research work to the publisher, the same is the same for peer review, selected rejected or return to authors for necessary amendments in electronic form and finally by providing the electronic access to the libraries.

Excellent Searching Techniques : The user can search the information by using and, or, not, between, up to, after etc. phrases. The publisher provide hyperlink to connect the related work.

Multi-user Access : This is a wonderful gift of electronic publication that by subscribing the electronic journals, books, databases etc. many users can access the same material at the same time from different places connected through intranet/internet.

9. ELECTRONIC RESOURCES OF THE INFORMATION

E-resources of the information are also called types of e-resources:-

- E-database
- E-book
- E-magazines
- Newsletter and other e-resources
- E-thesis and dissertation
- Electronic news paper
- E-reference books
- CD-ROM
- E-journals

10. STRUCTURE OF OPEN ACCESS ONLINE ELECTRONIC RESOURCES IN LIBRARY AND INFORMATION SCIENCE

See Table 1 on next page.

11 FINDINGS

- It gives a wide area of searching information.
- This facility is available easily anywhere and anytime.
- This can be access by many numbers of peoples at one time.
- The Journal of the Rutgers University Libraries has provided LIS open access e-resources of 77 years from 1937-2014.
- New Knowledge Environments has least number of LIS open access e-resources of only one year 2009.
- There are twenty LIS open access e-resources websites which provide up-to-date information.
- There are two LIS open access e-resources website which have not added any information after 2009, two LIS open access e-resources website which have not added any information after 2012 and one LIS

Table 1. E-resources in Library and Information Science

Sl. No.	*Title*	*Uniform Resource Locator (URL)*	*Archive*	*Free Full text*
01	Digital Library of Archives	http://scholar.lib.vt.edu/ejournals/VALib/	Vol. 30 No. 01, 1984 To Vol. 60 No 02, 2014	1984-2014
02	Webology	http://www.webology.org/	Vol. 01 No.02, 2004 To Vol. 11 No. 01, 2014	2004-2014
03	The Journal of the Rutgers University Libraries	http://jrul.libraries.rutgers.edu/index.php/jrul/index	Vol. 01 No.01, 1937 To Vol. 65, 2012	1937-2012
04	South African Journal of Information Management	http://www.sajim.co.za/index.php	Vol. 01 No.01, 1999 To Vol. 16 No. 01, 2014	1999-2014
05	Practical Academic Librarianship: The International Journal of the SLA Academic Division	https://journals.tdl.org/pal/index.php/pal/index	Vol. 01 No.01, 2011 To Vol. 04 No. 01, 2014	2011- 2014
06	Partnership: the Canadian Journal of Library and Information	https://journal.lib.uoguelph.ca/index.php/perj/#.U9tiz1fXihp	Vol. 01 No.01, 2006 To Vol. 09 No. 01, 2014	2006- 2014

	Practice and Research			
07	North Carolina Libraries	http://www.ncl.ecu.edu/index.php/NCL	Vol. 60 No.03, 2002 To Vol. 71 No. 02, 2013	2002- 2013
08	New Knowledge Environments	http://journals.uvic.ca/index.php/INKE	Vol. 01 No.01, 2009 To Vol. 01 No.01, 2009	2009- 2009
09	Library and Information Science Research e-Journal	http://libres-ejournal.info/	Vol. 06 No.01, 1996 To Vol. 23 No.02, 2013	1996- 2013
10	Library Philosophy and Practice (e-journal)	http://digitalcommons.unl.edu/libphilprac/	Vol. 01 No.01, 2005 To Vol. 01 No.01, 2014	2005- 2014
11	Library and Information Research	http://www.lirgjournal.org.uk/lir/ojs/index.php/lir	Vol. 17 No.59, 1993 To Vol. 38 No.117, 2014	1993- 2014
12	LIBER Quarterly	http://liber.library.uu.nl/index.php/lq	Vol. 09 No.02, 1999 To Vol. 23 No.04, 2014	1999- 2014
13	Journal of the Medical Library Association	http://www.ncbi.nlm.nih.gov/pmc/journals/93/latest/	Vol. 90 No.01, 2002 To Vol. 102 No.03, 2014	2002 – 2014

14	Journal of the Canadian Health Libraries Association	http://pubs.chla-absc.ca/journal/jchla	Vol. 25 No.01, 2004 To Vol. 35 No.01, 2014	2004- 2014
15	E-JASL: The Electronic Journal of Academic and Special Librarianship	http://southernlibrarianship.icaap.org/index.html	Vol. 01 No.01, 1999 To Vol. 10 No.03, 2009	1999- 2009
16	Journal of Medical Internet Research	http://www.jmir.org/	Vol. 01, 1999 To Vol. 16, 2014	1999- 2014
17	Journal of Library Innovation	http://www.libraryinnovation.org/	Vol. 01 No.01, 2010 To Vol. 15 No.01, 2014	2010- 2014
18	Journal of Information Literacy	http://ojs.lboro.ac.uk/ojs/index.php/JIL/index	Vol. 01 No.01, 2007 To Vol. 08 No.01, 2014	2007-2014
19	Journal of Information and Organizational Sciences	http://jios.foi.hr/index.php/jios	Vol. 30 No.01, 2006 To Vol. 38 No.01, 2014	2006-2014
20	Journal of Health Informatics in Developing Countries [JHIDC]	http://www.jhidc.org/index.php/jhidc/index	Vol. 01 No.01, 2007 To Vol. 08 No.02, 2014	2007-2014
21	Journal of Digital Information	https://journals.tdl.org/jodi/index.php/jodi	Vol. 07 No.01, 1997 To Vol. 13 No.01, 2012	1997-2012

22	Information Technology and Libraries	http://ejournals.bc.edu/ojs/index.php/ital/index	Vol. 01 No.01, 1968 To Vol. 33 No.02, 2014	1968-2014
23	Information Research	http://www.informationr.net/ir/	Vol. 01 No.01, 1995 To Vol. 19 No.02, 2014	1995-2014
24	Evidence Based Library and Information Practice	http://ejournals.library.ualberta.ca/index.php/EBLIP	Vol. 01 No.01, 2006 To Vol. 09 No.02, 2014	2006-2014
25	The Electronic Journal of Knowledge Management (EJKM)	http://www.ejkm.com/main.html	Vol. 01 No.01, 2003 To Vol. 12 No.02, 2014	2003-2014

open access e-resources website which have not added any information after 2013.

- The Journal of the Rutgers University Libraries and Information Technology and Libraries has most number of information available.

12. CONCLUSION

From the above data we can conclude that open access online E-resource in library and information science is a major tool for searching information. If it is utilized effectively, then it will be very much helpful for different types of users for using and disseminating information as well as knowledge.

REFERENCES

1. Mahapatra, R. K., & Panda, K. C. (2001). Information needs of working journalists in Orissa. *IASLIC Bulletin*, 46(2), 105-110.
2. Ramaiah, C. K. (2013). Electronic Resource Management in Libraries. New Delhi: Allied Publishers Pvt. Ltd.
3. Velmurugan, V. S. (2013). E-Resoueces. *e-Library Science Research Journal*, 1(12), 01-04.
4. Singh, J. (2015). Libraries: Traditional to Modernization. Solapur: Laxmi Book Publication.
5. (n.d.). Retrieved January 7, 2015, from http://www.sajim.co.za/index.php
6. DigitalCommons@University of Nebraska - Lincoln. (n.d.). Retrieved January 8, 2015, from http://digitalcommons.unl.edu/libphilprac/
7. Editorials. (n.d.). Retrieved January 8, 2015, from http://www.ncbi.nlm.nih.gov/pmc/journals/93/latest/
8. E-JASL. (n.d.). Retrieved January 8, 2015, from http://southernlibrarianship.icaap.org/index.html
9. Electronic Journals. (n.d.). Retrieved January 7, 2015, from http://scholar.lib.vt.edu/ejournals/VALib/
10. Evidence Based Library and Information Practice. (n.d.). Retrieved January 8, 2015, from http://ejournals.library.ualberta.ca/index.php/EBLIP

11. Information Research: An international electronic journal. Information science, Information management, Information systems, Information retrieval, Digital libraries, Information seeking behaviour, Information seeking behavior, World Wide Web, WWW. (n.d.). Retrieved January 8, 2015, from http://www.informationr.net/ir/
12. Information Technology and Libraries. (n.d.). Retrieved January 8, 2015, from http://ejournals.bc.edu/ojs/index.php/ital/index
13. JMIR-Journal of Medical Internet Research. (n.d.). Retrieved January 8, 2015, from http://www.jmir.org/
14. Journal of Digital Information. (n.d.). Retrieved January 8, 2015, from https://journals.tdl.org/jodi/index.php/jodi
15. Journal of Health Informatics in Developing Countries. (n.d.). Retrieved January 8, 2015, from http://www.jhidc.org/index.php/jhidc/index
16. Journal of Information and Organizational Sciences. (n.d.). Retrieved January 8, 2015, from http://jios.foi.hr/index.php/jios
17. Journal of Information Literacy. (n.d.). Retrieved January 8, 2015, from http://ojs.lboro.ac.uk/ojs/index.php/JIL/index
18. Journal of Library Innovation. (n.d.). Retrieved January 8, 2015, from http://www.libraryinnovation.org/
19. LIBER Quarterly. (n.d.). Retrieved January 8, 2015, from http://liber.library.uu.nl/index.php/lq
20. LIBRES e-journal | ISSN 1058-6768. (n.d.). Retrieved January 8, 2015, from http://libres-ejournal.info/
21. New Knowledge Environments. (n.d.). Retrieved January 7, 2015, from http://journals.uvic.ca/index.php/INKE
22. North Carolina Libraries. (n.d.). Retrieved January 7, 2015, from http://www.ncl.ecu.edu/index.php/NCL
23. Partnership: The Canadian Journal of Library and Information Practice and Research. (n.d.). Retrieved January 7, 2015, from https://journal.lib.uoguelph.ca/index.php/perj/#.U9tiz1fXihp
24. Practical Academic Librarianship: The International Journal of the SLA Academic Division. (n.d.). Retrieved January 7, 2015, from https://journals.tdl.org/pal/index.php/pal/index

25. The Journal of the Rutgers University Libraries. (n.d.). Retrieved January 7, 2015, from http://jrul.libraries.rutgers.edu/index.php/jrul/index

26. Webology. (n.d.). Retrieved January 7, 2015, from http://www.webology.org

27. EJKM - Journal home. (n.d.). Retrieved January 8, 2015, from http://www.ejkm.com/main.html

28. Library and Information Research. (n.d.). Retrieved January 8, 2015, from http://www.lirgjournal.org.uk/lir/ojs/index.php/lir

23

Relevance & Role of Librarians in Age of Web 2.0

A K Sharma

Librarian, Assam University, SILCHAR-788 011

ABSTRACT

After the advent of computer and specially internet, people started talking that the librarian will totally be facing the destiny of dinosaurs.The article discusses the role and relevance of librarians and libraries in the era of Web 2.0. How the librarians proved their relevance in the era of Web 2.0 and survived on the tune of Darwin's theory of Survival of Fittest. With the advent of full text journals and e-books on the net, and in the era of powerful search engines like Google, Yahoo- the existence of librarians seems to be in danger. In the era of powerful search engines and ICT can the existence of the librarians be justified? How the role of librarians has changed in the present scenario. The number of active users visiting the library is decreasing day by day and the library users are expecting every piece of information on their desktop. The article discusses how the librarians can fit themselves in the changing environment.

1. INTRODUCTION

We are living in a society of Information Communication Tools (ICT) where the information is reaching at the users' desktop in a fraction of seconds. The society is highly influenced by information and communication all around and finally it has laid its impact on the libraries. Change in communication tools has changed the flow of information drastically. The biggest problems of today's librarians' are decreasing footfalls, low patience level of the SMS generation users and finally follow ability of the data. The role of librarian has totally transformed from the custodian of information to information providers to the right user at right time. Although framed in 1931, Five laws of Dr. SR Ranganathan have not lost their relevance in the era of internet and ever changing ICT tools and technology when the technology is changing at a very fast pace. With the advent of latest ICT tools and gadgets, librarians/ Information Professionals are facing challenges as the today's clientele is more technology oriented and they need the information immediately on their desktop/ palmtop or smart phones or whatever mode/device of communication they are using.

Our response to the technology is haphazard and as a result not only the men and material, but also the most important aspect, the information, has to be made available at the beck and call of the user requiring the same at an appropriate time. If such information remains uncontrolled, unmanaged and unsystematic, it will lead to an inadequate and defective knowledge creation process. The new ICT has changed the scenario of the library completely. The traditional approaches have become obsolete and the new paradigms of library services have changed the physical getup of the libraries as well as the mental setup of the library users. The libraries of today are no more libraries, they have transformed into knowledge centers and the Librarians of today have become knowledge managers. The libraries has made a total shift from collection of books to collection of useful information containing useful material in print as well as electronic media. Consequently the librarians are also adopting new tools and techniques to respond to their users' information queries in a much faster way.

The tools and technologies are getting obsolete at a very faster rate than it used to be in earlier time. Any ICT tool/technology which seems to be advances today will become obsolete tomorrow. Change is at a very faster pace, days have passed when the librarians used to talk about the phenomenon like Information Explosion. Advent of World Wide Web(www)/internet has made information available on the desktop of the users. The fast development in the internet technology from one generation to another has changed the ways of information dissemination. Then the question of survival of library professional and librarians arises. How the librarian can adapt themselves with the changing environment of fast growing internet & web 2.0 tools or Library 2.0.

2. THE CHANGE PHENOMENON

Change is a regular phenomenon of nature. In society also, we have seen lot of changes in every sphere of life including library and its services. Invention is the mother of necessity and wherever, there is a necessity, new invention takes place and replace the older one. In the world of librarians, there is drastic change in the tools and technologies of library. In the changing environment, the expectations from the librarian have also changed. The role of a librarian has been changed from the custodian of history to the gatekeepers of the future. The focus of the librarianship has shifted from the conventional service providers to knowledge manager. Variety of form and format of information, diverse channels to disseminate the right information at right time, increased users' expectations contributed positively in bringing about a wave of change. Analysis, synthesis, packaging and repackaging of information have started finding places to cope with the continuing information stress. (Maurice, 1998) in a recent paper identified some key areas of research and discussion in the field of information. He identified internet as one of the key areas covering several topics and such as: bibliographic control, quality control, implications of style and format, implications for libraries, individualization of information access, and so on.

In 1997 the Board of Editors of the journal *Library and Information Science Research* (Burke, 1997) was asked to submit a short list of areas they felt would be or should be the focus of the Library and Information Science [LIS] research into the next millennium. The response of each individual is, in some or other, related to information retrieval research, such as-

i. Internet and www (Information retrieval aspect);
ii. Search engines and algorithms;
iii. Bibliographic control of the internet;
iv. User interface, including common user interface, natural language interface, etc.
v. User needs/requirements analysis;
vi. Information seeking behavior of users and the cognitive approach;
vii. Digital libraries;
viii. Summarization and representation of information;
ix. Visual information;
x. Intelligent information retrieval including intelligent agents.

Change is an inevitable requirement for the survival of the libraries and librarianship in today's dynamic knowledge economy. The advent of ICT and internet revolutionized the form and format of the information resources along with its retrieval and dissemination. The change not only brought with the various opportunities of information management, but also resulted in challenges to convert lots of information into knowledge. Information overload is not a function of the volume of information and the tools we have to assimilate that information into knowledge (Foley, n.d.).

Information retrieval can be broadly categorized into the following research areas[4]-

- Search engines
- Retrieval evaluation
- Reliability of information on the web;
- User interface
- User studies
- Organization of information on the web
- Vocabulary control
- Search output from the web
- Intelligent search engines; and
- Web *Vs* traditional databases (online and CD-ROM)

As (John, 2004) clarifies that in today, researchers and authors have a wide variety of means with which to communicate their research findings, from traditional publishers (both commercial and society-based) as well as through many other means, including preprint servers, institutional depositories, content aggregators, and syndicators, among others. These publishing vehicles are further organized by frequently overlapping services, such as secondary databases, web portals, search engines, online vendors, local system providers, institutional library vendors, and so forth. Additionally, the user is confronted with what may be a bewildering array of services to choose among for accessing this material, again including local web services and portals, online and/or local system services, database services, primary publishing search services, and knowledge management systems. Finally, the recent new development of 'author pays'-based journals - known as 'Open Access' - adds still another alternative for authors in our modern information supply chain.

3. ROLES OF INFORMATION AND KNOWLEDGE PROFESSIONALS IN NEW PERSPECTIVE

Knowledge Management (KM) is the future, although many of the roads to be travelled have yet to be built. While the librarianship is practices by the librarians, KM is practiced by the knowledge communities, both internally within the organization and between the organizations, and in the wider public communities. There are roles for knowledge experts or professionals in promoting and facilitating effective KM, but the paradigm shift from librarianship to KM is one of scale and perspective. KM is integrated into effective organizations, communities and societies, and these success of KM depends on the contribution of all of the members of the knowledge community. In a study done by (The Advisory Board Company, 2011) on Key Strategic Insights for Libraries, the usage statistics for library in the internet age was not very promising. In the study there was a comparison made between the search strategies of students and faculty i.e. from where the students and faculty start their search on any topic. Among the students 83% are dependent upon search engines, 7% on wikipedia, 2% on social networking sites, 1% on emails, 1% on email subscriptions, 1% on databases and the dependency of library website was 0%. Similarly in case of faculty. 47% were using specific electronic research resources, 32% were using a general search engine, 18% were using online library catalogue and 4% visited the library building physically for the consultation of resources available in the library.

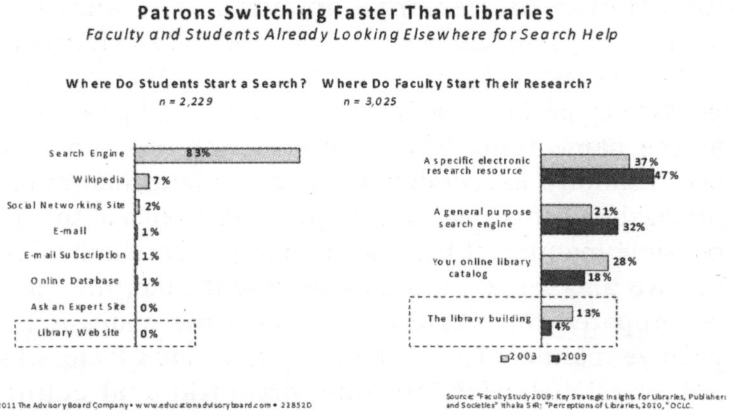

Fig. 1. Changing pattern of users

Taking (Carillo's, 2002) model as a point of departure it is possible to conceive three main roles for the knowledge professionals:

i. Managing knowledge repositories
ii. Facilitating knowledge flow and communication; and
iii. Leveraging value generation capacity

The advent of internet/world wide web brought with it many opportunities and challenges for the information professionals. The initial insecurity from the internet has been replaced by the enthusiasm and motivation to exploit the potential. The most dramatic change is the transformation of traditional librarians to information professionals. Informational Professional is a new brand for the librarians or perhaps a whole new job profile with different implications and expectations. The information professionals manages information resources and services with the deployment of technology. Competence to work with search engines, e-resources, digitization, etc. is to be taken for granted as it directly mirrors the implications of the internet revolution.

The proliferation of information and communication technologies, wide variety of information sources, techniques, tools and skills to manage them has left information professionals in lurch. The answer to successfully manage these technologies is to continuously and consistently learn and master them, which could best be done by performing the role of learner and practitioner at the same time. Changing economy has increased organization's expectations, which demand information professionals to update and exploit their skills in the best possible manner. If the information professionals are to survive and thrive in today's turbulent time, they must be prepared to initiate and manage the changes in a positive manner. The importance of various factors like individual behavior, attitude, organizational culture, Information Technology applications, knowledge and information sharing, are now required now more than ever.

When working in a knowledge environment, the information professionals have three primary roles and responsibilities (Sharma, 2005).

i. To provide information, products and services that continually and consistently match the requirements of the organization,

ii. To educate the information users to ensure that they can access and use the information, products and services effectively to maximize the quality and consistency of the organizational knowledge; and

iii. To facilitate the sharing and transfer of knowledge.

New roles demand not only the core skills of librarianships and information management, but some of the following set of attitudes, skills and values as well:

- Knowledge management skills
- Marketing aptitude
- Continuous learning
- Interpersonal effectiveness
- Human resource management

- Ability to work in cross-functional teams
- Problem solving abilities
- High performance standards
- Analytical thinking
- Sprit of team work
- Multi-tasking
- Process orientation
- Positive approach
- Identifying perspective clientele
- Designing customized content management solution to manage the challenges triggered by the internet
- Managing changes
- Professional networking
- Innovation

(John, 2004) in his article on Battle between mindshare emphasizes the importance and attitude of librarian as compared to other information seekers. In a survey for his lecture, librarians and scientists were asked to name the top scientific and medical search resources that they use or are aware of. The difference is startling. Librarians named Science Direct, ISI Web of Science, and Medline, while scientists named Google, Yahoo, and PubMed (librarians also named PubMed). Here the role of librarian becomes very specific in any organization as an information provider. He is the person who is directing his users to right information at the right point of time. The search engines like google are giving thousands of link on a single click but what about the relevance and currency factor? A librarian is right person who understand the information needs of his users better than any search engine and he can provide the right information to the right user by his year's long experience amongst the users as any machine can do. Only librarian can judge the relevance of tools like Discovery tools, etc.

In addition to the above, a number of research activities can be noticed through the published literature which may not be directly related to the internet or www, but whose results can be extended to this environment to get better information retrieval results. It has also been revealed that the lack of comprehensive coverage, the inability to distinguish between popular material and the serious research material and serious research works, lack of controlled vocabulary, and moreover a casual approach of the web page designer often make the web database more difficult to search. Another problem relates to the response rate: because many of the search engines are located in North America and internet traffic is increasing rapidly, at times the response rate may be frustratingly low.

Several researchers are trying to tackle the problem of electronic access and retrieval. They are trying to come up with a common user interface and a metadata set to users know what is available and also let them easily access and retrieve the information irrespective of the software and hardware variation. The traditional approach to access the use of remote information is changing fast, and traditional online information providers are quickly adapting to the web technology. The research studies mentioned above also indicates that the user studies have always remained critical area and a user oriented approach to design, development and evaluation of information system is becoming more and more important in the digital library environment.

The subject approach of information, which has traditionally been controlled by the library and information professionals with the help of classification, cataloguing and vocabulary control tools, is an important area of research in the internet environment. Intelligent search agents can do something good, but they try to tackle the problem from the retrieval side because they are trained by a user in using a number of keywords or phrases for searching and filtering of information, whereas they have no control over the way various websites are selected and indexed by the various search engines. One should always try to address the problem at the input stage by taking appropriate measures for cataloguing, classification and vocabulary control of information that is mounted on the web.

One possible way to overcome this problem could be a classy approach, where, ideally speaking, all information available on the web would be classified in some standard way, and search and retrieval could be based on that classification approach. There are many other areas that need attention and warrant serious research, such as text/information summarization/ repackaging, natural language user interface design for the internet and so on. Nevertheless, as many researchers argue, information professionals with their rich experience in organization and searching of information, as well as identifying user's needs, should work in hand with the software professionals in organizing the so-called anarchy of the internet. It is the experience and expertise of the information professional that can make the hits searched by the search engine- less, accurate and precise.

4. TOWARDS A LEARNING ORGANIZATION AND LIBRARY 2.0

Persistent learning and sharing have become mandatory in today's knowledge era. Sharing of knowledge and group learning to empower employees is now finding place in almost every organization. With the need built awareness of knowledge sharing, came the various means and methods to do the same. Communication, Information Technology and people's cooperation & coordination is needed in achieving a learning organization. Application of ICT plays an important role in collecting, organizing, sharing, managing and distributing of information. An open, transparent and accountable organizational culture is being adopted to facilitate flow of lessons learnt. Various formal and informal means of communications like discussions, meeting, in-house seminars, message boards, etc. have become the day to day culture of an organization.

For information professionals, learning and sharing of workplace is essential because of the diversification of roles to be played in the knowledge environment. Anticipating users' information needs, updating oneself with the latest tools and technologies to provide information services effectively and efficiently, working towards the organizational goal by continuously keeping abreast the organization's business perspective, grooming personal competencies, and innovating new ways to perform the same jobs can go a long way in fostering a successful learning environment for the individual and the whole team. Librarian can introduce some push off services by pushing notifications keep the users up-to-date with the latest news and developments through Library 2.0/Library 3.0 Tools and Techniques-Instant Messaging (IM), RSS Feeds, Streaming Media, Podcasting, SMS Enquiry Service, Blogs, Wikis, Social Networking, Tagging, Social Bookmarking Services, Mashups, AJAX, API or Library Tool Bars. Based on the budgetary resources and manpower, they can suggest for in-house services as well as cloud based services- where the technical expertise is lacking. In today's world a librarian is missing something if the SMS inter phase of services of the library is missing i.e. library should provide SMS based services like catalogue, circulation, transaction, etc. While replying the queries of the users some instant messaging services must be used i.e. Instant Messaging (IM), RSS Feeds, Streaming Media, Podcasting, SMS Enquiry Service, Blogs, Wikis, Social Networking, Tagging, Social Bookmarking Services, Mashups, AJAX, API or Library Tool Bars. In order to evaluate the library services, the librarian must organise users speak and Users meet very frequently. To give value addition to the library services, a constant feedback from the Friends of Library must be obtained.

5. CONCLUSION

The value of information and its conversion into knowledge cannot be underrated, along with its management to make optimum utilization for the benefit of the society. The aim and objectives of are therefore, to tame the entire ocean of information and knowledge for a utility-oriented approach. Therefore, it is first necessary to understand the dynamics of the changing pattern of the job environment, the quality of the library used by, the patrons, professional approach of management towards the libraries, etc. and second, to continuous and consistent learning and mastering new tools and techniques for information and knowledge management.

REFERENCES

1. Line, Maurice B. (1998). An information world apart: the Royal Scientific Information Conference of 1948 in the light of 1998. *Journal of Documentation* 54(3), 284-292.
2. Burke, M., Chang, M. D., Charles H., Hernon, P., Marchionini, G., Nicholls, P., et al. (1997). Editorial: a research agenda beyond 2000. *Library and Information Science Research,* 19(3), 209- 216.
3. Foley, John (n.d.). Managing information: Infoglut. New tools can help tame an ocean of data. Retrieved October 30, 1995 from http://www.informationweek.com/551/51mtinf.htm
4. Chowdhury, G. G. (1999). The internet and information retrieval research: a brief review. *Journal of Documentation* 55(2), 209-225.
5. John, J. (2004). The Battle for Mindshare: A battle beyond access and retrieval. *In 2004 Miles Conrad Memorial Lecture, 46th NFAIS Annual Conference.*
6. Key strategies insight for libraries, publishers and societies: Perceptions of libraries. (2011). Retrieved n.d. from www.educationadvisoryboard.com

7. Carillo, F. J. (2002). Capital System: implications for a global knowledge agenda. *Journal of Knowledge Management.* 5(1), 68-75.
8. Sharma, M. (2005). Changing role of information professionals in knowledge era. In: Digital information resources and network in India. In R. Cilana (Ed.), *Essays in honour of Professor Jagindar Singh Ramdev on his 75th Birthday* (pp. 135-137). New Delhi: UBSPD.
9. Henczel, S. (2004). Supporting the KM environment: The roles, responsibilities, and rights of information professionals: Constructive thoughts on knowledge management. *Information Outlook.*

Emerging Technologies and Trends

24

Management of Journals through Koha Open Source Software: An Overview

Asheesh Kamal
Assistant Librarian, School of Planning and Architecture, Andhra Pradesh

ABSTRACT

In the era of open communication and knowledge sharing, the role of libraries has been increased manifolds. New technologies and applications have added advantages for the libraries to meet their large community of users' demands. This paper mainly emphasis on journal management system in "Koha" – open source library management software. While studying the importance of print and electronic journals management in the library, Koha is one of the widely used library management software and source code availably openly and it provides many options for user customization and advantages for journal management and information search and retrieval.

Keywords : journal, Koha LMS, Cataloguing Modules, Open Source Software, Serial Modules

1. INTRODUCTION

In the era of open communication and knowledge sharing, library and information centers have increased greater responsibilities to serve a large community of users (students, researchers, faculty and staff) .Access to journals in the library is ever-increasing task; the librarians must look into it widely and intelligently to fix. New concepts and applications have not only attracted libraries but also users to do their routine academic and research assignments using open source library management system. Indeed, libraries have been largely faced difficulty in managing subscribed print journal and e-journals. Libraries have been also used various kind of library management software to encounter the problems arise in the serial control module.

Koha is one of the powerful open source library management tool that deal basic to high-end customization to manage, search and retrieve serials and its missing issues management etc.

2. WHAT IS KOHA SOFTWARE?

Koha was created in 199 by Katipo Communications for the Horowhenua Library Trust in New Zealand, and the first installation went live in January 2000. Koha is web-based Integrated Library Software; the name comes from a Maori term for a gift or donation, with a SQL database (MySQL preferred) backend with cataloguing data stored in MARC and accessible via Z39.50 or SRU. The user interface is configurable and adaptable, which has been translated into many languages.

Features of the Koha

- Easy, interface for user & librarians
- RSS feeds & Web 2.0 services
- Make Union catalog facility
- Customizable search
- Circulation (check-in, check-out, renewal and reservation) management
- Complete Acquisitions module– manage library budget- pricing information (Vender & Currency Conversion), new book entry

- Serial Module for Periodicals (Print-Electronic), Magazines and Journals
- Report generation for administrative acceptations
- Book index list, and Online Public Access Catalogue(OPAC) for users

3. WHAT IS CATALOUGING AND CLASSIFIYNG ITEMS IN THE KOHA?

Shelving Locations : Shelving locations are the broadest way to classify item in Koha? Journal, Periodicals or Magazines?

Item types : Item types are used to determine circulation rules and regulations.

Like : Books, Journals and all electronic documents.

Circulation & Holding : Circulation & Holding are set by each separate library.

Collection Codes and Call Numbers : Collection Codes and Call Numbers are also used to further classify an item.

Shelving Location Codes : Shelving Location Codes are set by each individual library.

An image showing a visual Overview of journal might be cataloged in Koha Software:

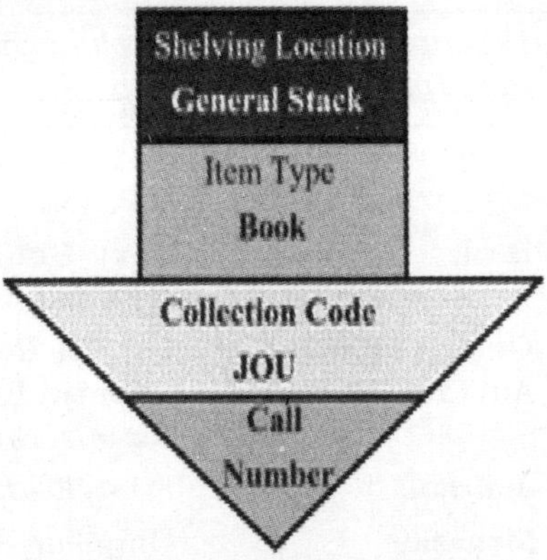

Fig. 1. Visual overview of journal

Table 1. Collection Code Menu: what display in the Koha Software

Collection Codes	*Collection Description*	*Notes*
BIOGRAPHY	BIOGRAPHY	
BOARDBK	BOARDBK	
BOOKONDIGT	BOOK ON DIGITAL	
DISPLAY	ON DISPLAY	
DVD	DVD	
GENEALOGY	GENEALOGY	
GRAPHIC	GRAPHIC NOVEL	
INSPRATION	INSPIRATIONAL	
JOU	JOURNAL	Print/E-Journals
MAGAZINE	MAGAZINE	
MUSIC	MUSIC CD	
NEW	NEW	
ON-ORDER	ON-ORDER (JUST NEW)	
PAPERBACK	PAPERBACK	
EASY	IMAGEBOOK	
WALKIN	WALK-IN COLLECTION	
XXX	(UNCLASSIFIED)	

Table 2. Koha item Type Code & item Type Description is showing on Koha Item Type Menu bar

Code-Koha Item Type	*Description-Koha Item Type*	*Explanation of Koha Item Type*
Audiobook	Audiobook	All E-formats: Cassette, CD, MP3, MP4 And MPG
Book	Book	Text Book-monographs Formats
ILL	Onloan From Another Library	For Use Connected Library: Interlibrary Loan Resources (Book)
JOU	Journal	Print/E-journals
Periodical	Magazine	Only For Reading Purpose in Library

Media	Media Formats	Video-non Fature; Education And Research Related Software; Cdrom; MP3 Audio Resource (Lectures, Conference, Languge Learning, Etc.).
Microformat	Microfilm and Microfiche	Micro Fiche/Film, Machine Readable Formats
Onorder	Onorder (print in Publication)	Forthcoming Book (Title), Print In Publication
Reference	Reference Material	In-library Use Only
XXX	(Unclassified)	No Item Type Defined

4. WHAT IS CATALOGUING MODEL IN KOHA?

Cataloguing module are most important part for any integrated library management software, it is directory of library collections. The Library collections (Journal, Book etc.) are automated than reader will get right information at exact time because the user's requirement will need collection catalog or assistance about library collection. In this Section we discus about Koha cataloging Module, MARC tags, and working condition of Koha Cataloging Module. Table 3 shows the cataloguing Module in Koha.

Table 3. Cataloguing module functions

1	Catalogue administration
2	Retro-conversion
3	Full cataloguing
4	Import catalogue records from internet
5	Modify catalogue records
6	Search catalogue functionality
7	Abstracts
8	Change copy status
12	Bar code generation

Cataloguing Module is the knowledge based mirror image of any Academic library; it can reveal the share of the library with bibliographic details of an item/Title. Table 4 shows the cataloguing module administration in Koha contains MARC bibliographic framework:

Table 4. Cataloguing Administration contains MARC bibliographic framework

1. Bibliographic Records
   - Adding Records
   - Editing Records
   - Duplicating Records
   - Merging Records
2. Item Records
   - Adding Items
   - Editing Items
   - Moving Items
   - Item Specific Circulation History
3. Authorities
   - Adding Authorities
   - Searching Authorities
   - Editing Authorities
4. Cataloging Guides
   - Bibliographic Record Cataloging Cheat Sheet
   - Item/Holdings Record Cataloging Guide
   - Handling On Order Items and Holds

Before start of journal cataloging in Koha some basic setups need to be configured. Most importantly to make sure that your frameworks are all create and defined the way you want.Once in the cataloging module you will not be able to add or remove fields and subfields so your frameworks must be ready before you start cataloging.

Follow some basic setups of cataloging module:

4.1. MARC Bibliographic Frameworks

Think of frame works as templates for creating new bibliographic records. Koha comes with some predefined frameworks that can be edited or deleted, and librarians can create their own frameworks for content specific to their libraries. (Koha Community, 2013).

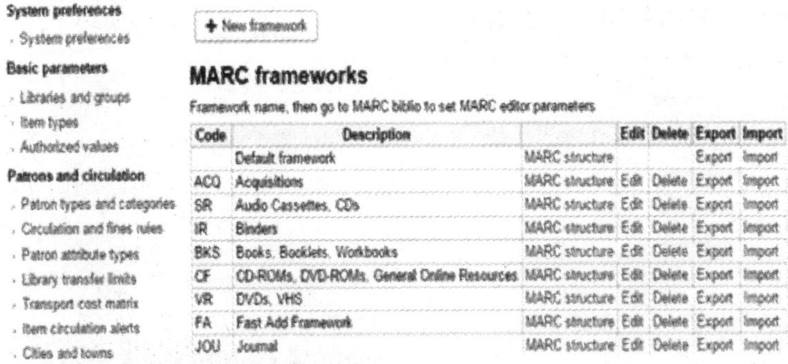

Fig. 2. MARC Bibliographic Framework for journal

4.2. Add a new FRAMEWORK '→ Click 'New Framework'

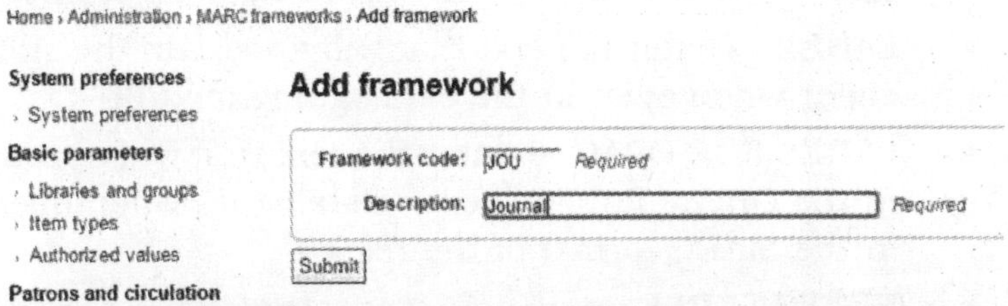

Fig. 3. MARC Bibliographic New Framework for journal

4.3. Add subfields to FRAMEWORKS

If you want add a field to a Framework, please Click 'NEW TAG' button at the top of the Framework window

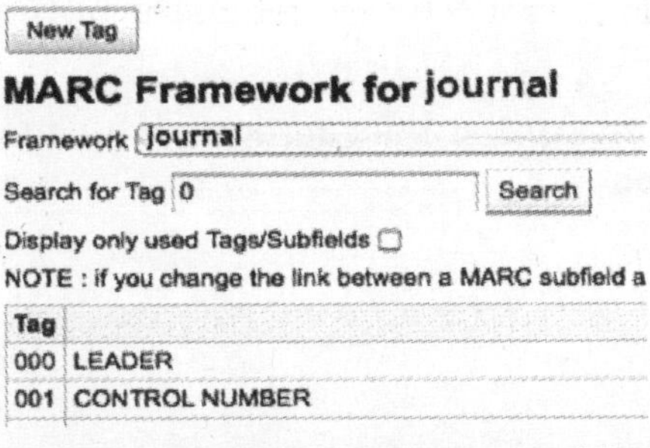

Fig. 4. MARC subfield Tag for Journal framework, see details table no.7

This will be display up a blank window from for entry in MARC field data, see details bellow

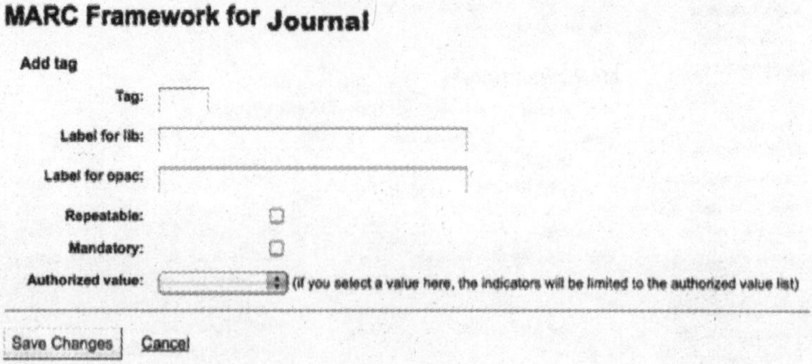

Fig. 5. MARC field data for creation new tag

Please enter the information about new tag:

- TAG → enter a MARC field MARC field tag number
- LABEL → enter the text that will appear in the staff client when open in the cataloguing module
- LABEL FOR OPAC → enter the text that will appear in the Online Public Access Catalogue- when open in the MARC format of the record
- REPEATABLE → if you want this field can be repeated, please check the box
- MANDATORY →if you want this field can be mandatory, please check the
- AUTHORIZED VALUE → if you select a value here, the indicators will be limited to the authorized value list

If you put-up the information about new tag, click 'Save Changes'.

4.4. To create framework for Journal

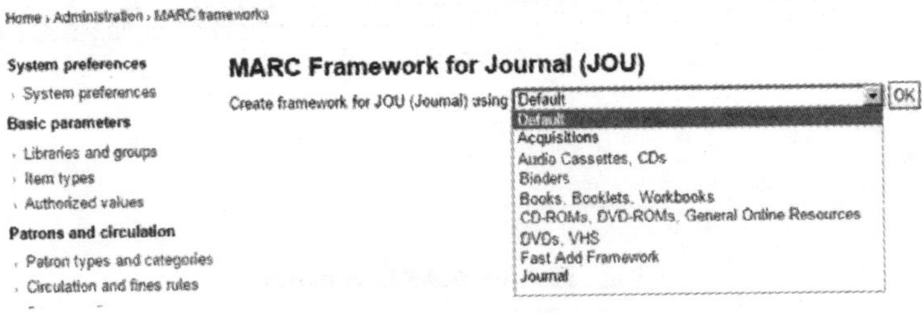

Fig. 6. MARC framework for journal

4.5. To Create MARC Structure for Journal

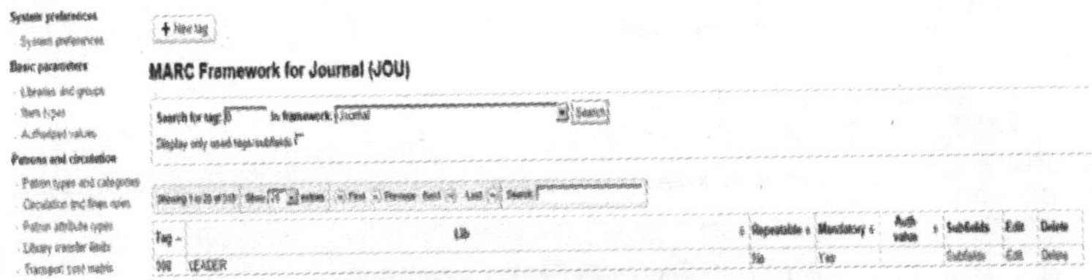

Fig. 7. MARC structure for journal

4.6. Bibliographic Records → Add to the Records

Records can be added to Koha via Z39.50 or original copy → Click 'New Record'.

Fig. 8. Add bibliographic records

If Choose the framework you would like to base your record off. Once you've opened a blank framework window or imported a record via Z39.50 you will be presented with the form to continue cataloguing.

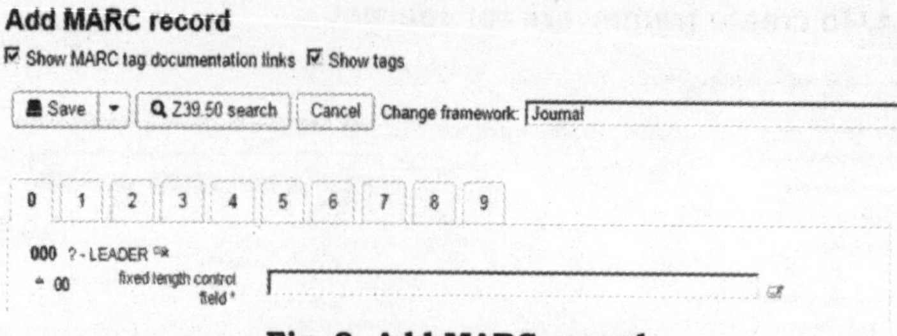

Fig. 9. Add MARC record

If you are importing a record via Z39.50, click the SAVE' button at the top, and check duplicate records

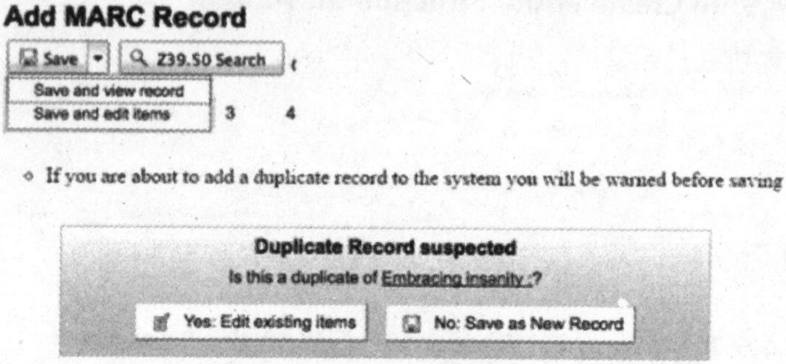

Fig. 10. Adding Z39.5

4.7. Some Cataloguing tools available in Koha LMS to customize on Library Catalogs

Table 5. Cataloguing tools

Features	*Descriptions*
Delete- Batch items	Easy to delete unwanted batch items
Modify- Batch items	Easy to modify items in the frame of batch
Data Export	All type data export: bibliographic, holding, new arrivals, & authority records items
Label creator	Label creation for print form barcode through Catalogue Module
Sudden Spine label creator	Enter a barcode to generate a print form spine label
Modify-MARC template	Modify and managing to MARC

	records during data entry to new records import via Z39.50
Bibliographic details import via Z39.50	Modify and managing to MARC records during data import via Z39.50
Step-MARC record managing	Several customizable benefits for librarian to managed staged MARC records
Upload own institute logo/image	Easy process to upload institute logo/ images for display OPAC

Important: Same step follow for e-resources of cataloguing in Koha LMS.

5. WHAT IS OPEN SOURCE SOFTWARE?

Open Source Software (OSS) is computer technology based software deal with its source code customizable made available with a license in which the copyright holder provides the rights to study, change and distribute the software to anyone and for any purpose. Open source software is often development and often compared to (technically defined) user-generated content or (legally defined) open content movements (Vrtis, 2008).

6. ROLE OF OSS TO JOURNAL MANAGEMENT IN KOHA SOFTWARE?

Koha Library Management Software provides Serial module administration is more functional in sub category to help the library staff/ clients. Serial parameters are ideal in the Koha software with all significance of journals/ periodicals and magazines. Koha OSS has additional flexibility to add new subscriptions,ordering subscriptions, processing of bill/invoices, payment structure, cancelling or re-ordering, Receiving of loose issues, sending reminders to publishers for unsupplied issues and renewal of subscription is possible in Koha OSS. It is found from the study that serial module management is better than other integrated library management software's. So, I will try to how to manage print-journal and e-journals in Koha library management software environment. My paper is to solve "how to manage of journals/e-resource in cataloguing model on Koha software and how to convert back volume on Database".

Serial Module Functions

Table 6. Serial module functions

1	Administration
2	Configuration
3	Serial subscription details
4	Add acquisition record
5	Approval of serial
6	Ordering
7	Subscription/ maintenance
8	Receive loose issues
9	Reminders
10	Renew subscriptions
11	Binding management

6.1. How to Management of journals in Koha software?

Follow below steps for the management of Journal:

Table 7. Steps for the management of Journal

Items/steps	*Details*
Acquisitions module	Go to the Acquisitions module
New Vender	Create New Vender list
Serials module	Go to the Serials module
New Subscriptions	Create New Subscriptions for journals
Biblio	Go to the Biblio tab
Create Biblio	Create Biblio for journals
Cataloguing module	Go to the Cataloguing module
Change Framework	Create & Change Framework for journal
Journal	Go to the Journal item marc framework

Bibliographic Detail	Add to the Bibliographic Details for journal
022	ISSN
044	Cataloguing Source: Original Cataloguing Source
245	Name of Journal
260	(a) Place of Publication → (b) Name of Publisher → (c) Publication Year
440	Series → (a) Volume → (b) Number of Part → (c) Name of Part
Subscriptions Detail	Again go to Subscriptions Detail
Library	Add Library Name
Location	Add library Location
Number of Issue to display Staff	Number of Issue to display Staff
Number of Issue to Display on OPAC	Number of Issue to Display on OPAC
First Issue Publication Date	First Issue Publication Date of journal
Frequency	journal Frequency
Number Pattern	journal Number Pattern
Subscription Start Date	journal Subscription Start Date from vender
Subscription Length	journal Subscription Length for journal
Search Title	Go to the Search tab
Journal Title	Search Journal Title for: 1. Receive → 2. Arrived → 3, Continue→
Cataloguing module	Go to the Cataloguing module:
Serials	Go to the serials module: 1. Edit journal Volume → 2.edit journal Name → 3. edit journal Issue
Items/steps	Details
Acquisitions module	Go to the Acquisitions module

Note: if received total issue of year 2014

- Convert to Back volume
- Total number of issue to display on OPAC
- first copy and Last Issue of Journal
- Go to the Cataloguing Modules and edit items for Journal with Barcode
- Go to the Public Note and edit VOLUME, ISSUE Number and Name of Issue

Implementation of Journal Management at Central University of Bihar (CUB) Central Library, Patna:

In practical journal management is one of the major factors in the Koha library management software to plan, process and organize journals. The journal management in Koha has been implemented in the Central Library at CUB-Patna Campus as follows:

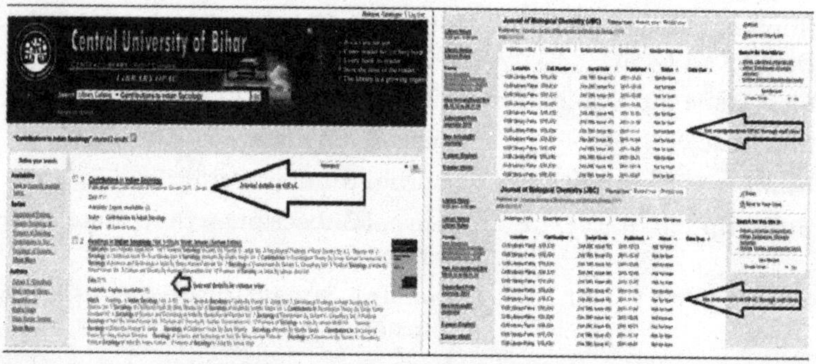

Fig. 11. Print Screen of OPAC image from Central University of Bihar, Patna Campus Website.

7. CONCLUSION

In the academic library setup, journal management is the process of delivering and serving its users in exact time at a quicker mode to save the reader's time. The Koha is one of the best web enabled open source software for library automation. The analysis of Journals through Koha Serial module, Koha has built on open source era and it is easy to install and apply. The study report search modules of cataloguing and serials control of Koha has its own design and architecture. Both modules are connected each other. Koha more enhanced features which are important for selecting cataloguing administration module for journal management. As a result, Koha serial module is advanced and new features for catalogue management e-resource management, back volume periodicals management based on library needs.

REFERENCES

1. Koha Community, Koha 3.2.3 Library Software. (2013). Retrieved October 18, 2013, from http://Koha-community.org.
2. St. Laurent, & Andrew, M. (2008). Understanding Open Source and Free Software Licensing, Sebastopol: *O'Reilly Media.*
3. Verts, William T. (2008). Open source software, *World Book Online Reference Center.* Retrieved October 18, 2014, from http://en.wikipedia.org/wiki/Open_source_software.
4. Ramareddy, C. S. Venkata (2014). Comparative study of free/open source integrated library Management systems with reference to Koha, Newgenlib and e-granthalay.*e-Library Science Research Journal,*1(12).Retrieved *From* http://www.lsrj.in/UploadedArticles/171.pdf.
5. *CUB Patna* Website (2014) Retrieved October 18, 2014, from http://www.cub.ac.in.

25

Mobile Technology in Libraries for Discovering E-Resources and Services

Alekha Karadia
Library Trainee, Biju Patnaik Central Library, NIT Rourkela
Arabinda Kumar Seth
Jr. Librarian, The Prameya, Summa Real Media (P) Ltd., Bhubaneswar
Dibya Kishor Pradhan
Asst. Librarian, Biju Patnaik Central Library, NIT Rourkela

ABSTRACT

The advancement of mobile technology provides portable, instantaneous access to the world of information, across boundaries of subject, discipline and industry. Present-day libraries are not behind those technologies, they are adopting mobile technology in their services to deal with the increasing demand for electronic resources and ongoing acquisition and archiving of digital contents. The application of mobile technology is helped to the library users to link the physical and virtual collection offered by the library, which enhance the user experience. This paper tried to outline the application of mobile technology in discovering & identifying e-resources with the practical application of QR code, and specifically studied the successful case in Central Library of NIT Rourkela.

Keywords : Mobile technology, QR Code, Digital Libraries, E-Resources Management.

1. INTRODUCTION

The use of information communication technology and particularly mobile technology has increased significantly over the last twenty years. According to the Internet and Mobile Association of India (IAMAI) and IMRB International the mobile internet users in India are expected to reach 213 million by June this year on the back of growing smart phone penetration (The Hindu, 2015). Simultaneously the libraries are proactively adapting these mobile technologies to fulfil the reader's need & expectations. In today's mobile environment, mobile devices are changing the way of information delivery and access. Now a day's an increasing number of libraries provide services and content through mobile devices. With the help of mobile technology the QR Codes as a tool of identification and discovery is now highly attractive to the users. QR Codes in the library help to link the user to the physical and virtual collections of the library. It enhances the user experience and expands the reach to the diverse collections and changed the role of librarians radically.

2. MOBILE TECHNOLOGY AND LIBRARY SERVICES

Recent advancement in mobile tools and techniques provide handy, instantaneous access to information across boundaries of subject and discipline (Thomas, 2010). Libraries are also engaged to adopting the advance technologies to provide their resources and services and the ongoing acquisition and archiving of digital content (Thomas, 2011). Now a day when one thinks of advance mobile technologies, the first device that comes to mind has to be the cell phone or the Smartphone, and libraries are tried to provide their services through the Smartphone (*Kosturski*, 2011). The primary consideration of library to provide mobile services is mobile-based website. Many library resource providers, such as Westlaw, EBSCO, Science Direct, and Ref Works, have mobile apps or mobile sites that can offer to more wired users.

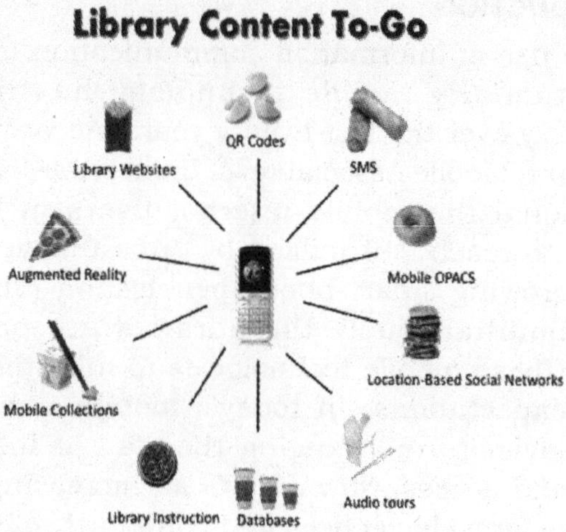

Fig. 1. Library Services over Mobile
Source **: http://www.slideshare.net/ellyssa/mobile-tech-in-libraries**

Some of the mobile applications for libraries are such as:

1. SMS Service : For the library & its user the SMS services can be useful to the following:

- Send SMS to collect books;
- Send reminder on overdue, fines etc.;
- Acknowledgment about issue, renewal & return;
- Alert on recent & new arrivals of documents;
- Informing library events, etc.

2. Audio Tour : Libraries can provide an audio tour of a library, which will be very helpful to visually impaired people.

3. Mobile Collections : User can download documents from the library websites to their mobile devices (e. g. images, videos, audio books, eBooks, streaming music, etc.)

4. Augmented Reality : User can augment reality

(event) which becomes more prevalent in textbooks and other print materials.

5. Library Websites : Library website can be browsed through mobile.

6. Library Instructions : Library instructions can be followed via mobile which guides the user to the different locations of the library and facilitates self-help.

7. LBSN : (Location Based Services Network) provide content that is dynamically customized according to the user's location. Here, the physical location consists of the instant location of an individual at a given time stamp and the location, history that an individual has accumulated during certain period.

8. Databases : Libraries have developed mobile websites and apps which are gateways to subscription content and libraries' databases from off campus.

9. OPAC : Library OPAC can be browsed through mobile.

10. New Title Preview : Mobile gadgets can be used to disseminate the information about preview of new titles.

11. Research, consultation and instruction : It is just like customer care service, researchers may have an interaction with the library staff to get the consultation and get suggestions via mobile phones.

12. Access Electronic Information Sources : Libraries can offer Wi-Fi facility to access electronic information resources through mobile devices.

13. Journal Finder : 'Journal Finder' a mobile app provides access to e-journal, magazine, and newspaper content as well as links to titles held in print (Talmale, 2012).

3. MOBILE APPS FOR LIBRARY E-RESOURCES

Following are the e-resource and applications which services are developed and enabled over mobile platforms:

Table 1. Mobile apps for library

E-resources	*App Name*	*Platform*	*Authentication Process*	*App URL*
ACS Journals	ACS Mobile	Apple, Android	Full-text access when connected using Concordia's WIFI.	http://pubs.acs.org/page/tools/acsmobile/index.html
Science Direct	SciVerse Science-Direct	Apple, Android	Register for an Elsevier account in the Science Direct website and need installation.	http://www.info.sciverse.com/sciversemobile-applications/overview
Scopus	SciVerse Scopus Alerts	Apple, Android	Register for an Elsevier account in the Scopus Database.	http://www.info.sciverse.com/sciversemobile-applications/overview

Source: Mobile Apps for Library E-Resources (2012) (http://library.concordia.ab.ca/files/2012/11/moble_apps)

Following are the Mobile Websites for Library E-Resources:

Table 2. Mobile websites for library

Database	*Additional Information*	*URL*
EBSCO HOST	Devices automatically go to mobile site	http://ezproxy.aec.talonline.ca/login?url=http://search.ebscohost.com/login.aspx?authtype=ip, uid&profile=mobsmart
Oxford Journals	Devices automatically go to mobile site	http://www.oxfordjournals.org/mobile/
Royal Society of Chemistry Journals	Devices automatically go to mobile site	http://pubs.rsc.org/en/Journals?key=Title&value= Current

Source : (http://library.concordia.ab.ca/files/2012/11/moble_apps)

4. QR CODE

Abbreviated from Quick Response Code is a machine-readable code consisting of an array of black and white squares, commonly used for storing URLs and other information for reading by the camera on a Smartphone.QR code reader application on is to be installed on mobile phone to able to take a picture of the code which will automatically link to the web page (http://en.wikipedia.org/wiki/QR_code).

According to Talmale (2012) three things are needed to successfully decode a QR code:

- Smartphone, Desktop (with a camera);
- QR code Scanning Software; and
- Internet Connection

There are lot of QR code reader and QR code scanners software available (ib. id), such as:

Table 3. QR Code software

Generator		*Reader*	
Phone	*Desktop*	*Phone*	*Desktop*
QR Stuff	Quick Mark	ScanLife	Quick Mark
Kaywa	ZXing Decoder	BeeTagg	ZXing Decoder
		ReadLaser	

4.1. Application of QR code Technology in Libraries

Mobile technology has transformed the world of education and libraries are fully engaged in the process of adapting the new technologies. QR Codes in Library help to link the user to the physical and virtual collections offered by the library. It enhances user experience and expands to reach the collections.

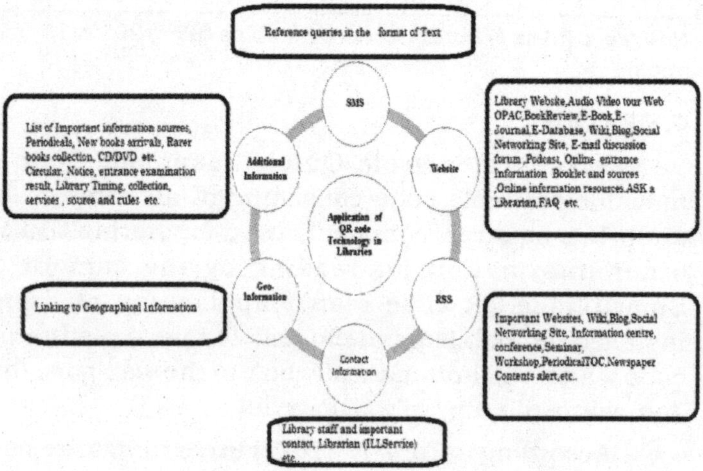

Fig. 2. Library Services over QR Code

***Source* : (Talmale, 2012)**

4.2. Advantages of QR Code in Libraries

QR codes offer a wide variety of useful applications for libraries and libraries find ways to reach those users. According to (Hampton, et. al., 2011) the advantages of QR code in libraries are:

- QR Code technology provides anytime and anywhere link to E-Resources;
- Deliver extra value to your users;
- User can scan QR code which allows them to store the information for future reference;
- Allow to collect contact information;
- Allow to interact with users;
- Inexpensive and quick to set up;
- Allow to track user awareness and engagement;
- QR code offer the expansion of existing library based services through the mobile technology.

4.3. QR Codes Challenges & Issues

Following are the challenges for QR codes in libraries (Hampton et. al., 2011; Thomas, 2012; Talmale, 2012)

- Poor implementation of QR Codes;
- Need for education and promotion;
- Excessive use;
- Everyone not use internet enable device;
- Lack of user awareness and education;
- Every user does not have a smart phone;
- Low budgets, confrontation priorities, skills and perception, insufficient skills on site in libraries;
- Lack of standards for mobile content.

5. ROLE OF LIBRARY PROFESSIONALS TO IMPLIMENT QR CODE IN LIBRARIES

Library professionals should passionately attempt to attract new users and link to E-resources. They can take initiatives to offer the value added library services to users by using QR code for text messaging reference services and notifies, mobile library websites, automatically linkage to website, newsletter, forms, user education video link, free e-resources website etc

(Talmale, 2012). Mobile friendly online catalogs led the way to scholarly guides, digital collections, linking to proprietary databases, virtual library services to meet immediate and emerging needs of smart phone users (Thomas, 2010).

6. USE OF MOBILE TECHNOLOGY IN LIBRARIES: A CASE OF CENTRAL LIBRARY AT NIT ROURKELA

Biju Patnaik Central Library has been modernized to provide computerized services to NITR academic community. The BPCL is automated with integrated library software package called Libsys –LSmart and modernized with latest Radio Frequency Identification (RFID) based automation system that facilitates self-check-in, self-check-out and automatic security system and also BPCL has developed an android application to access library updates through any smartphone which supports android OS. Through this application one can get the detail about e-books, e-thesis, OPAC, E-Rources and other general information available with BPCL. The application can be downloaded at *http://library.nitrkl.ac.in/android.apk*. This technology offers fastest, easiest, most efficient way to track, locate and manage library materials.

6.1. SMS Alert Service

BPCL also provide SMS text messages for the customers (users of a library) know of the availability of any particular book by sending SMS. The SMS facility used as a medium for the communication of reference queries in BPCL. It is a form of virtual reference service. The text messaging technology used for referral services, to guide the users to the source of information. For announcing an event taking place in the library. Its helps to reach out to the users to make them aware of such local functions, which otherwise has to be sent via email.

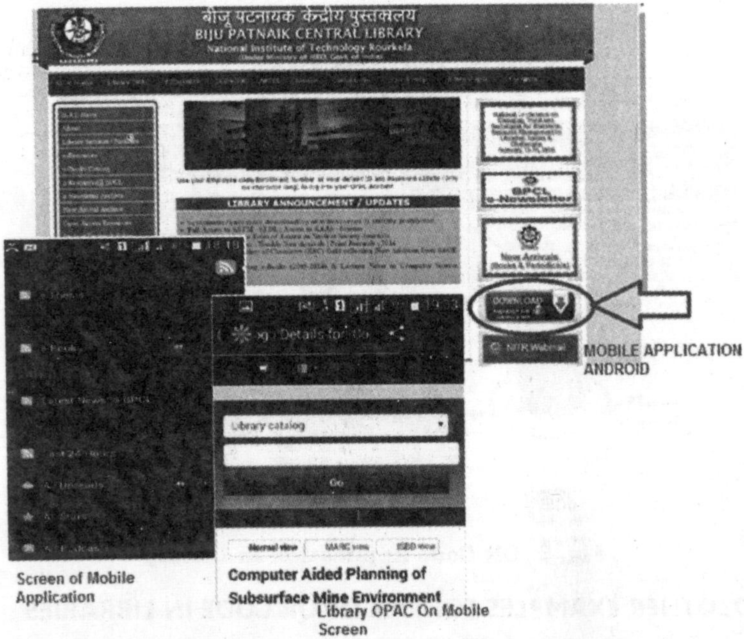

Fig. 3. Android Application in Central Library

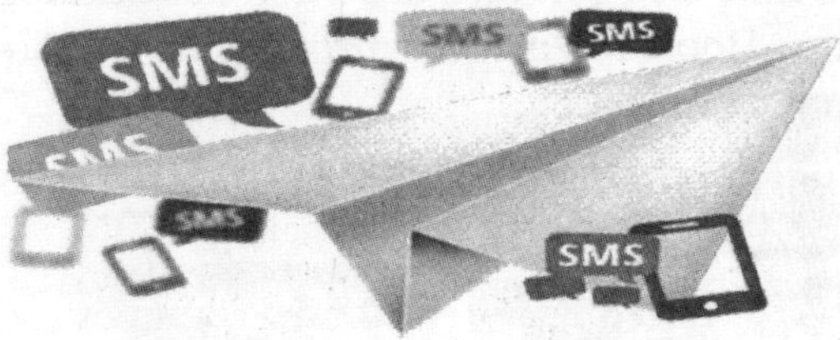

Fig. 4. SMS alert service

6.2. QR Code in Library

BPCL also use QR codes for various library activities and events such as:

- User Education Program,
- Library e-Newsletter,
- Web site,
- Poster, Flyers, Broachers etc.

Fig. 5. QR Code Application in Library

7. OTHER EXAMPLES FOR USE OF QR CODE IN LIBRARIES

Other examples of the use of QR code in various library activities and services are such as: Catalogs, Book for contents, Book for author profile, Journal web site link, Library tutorials etc.

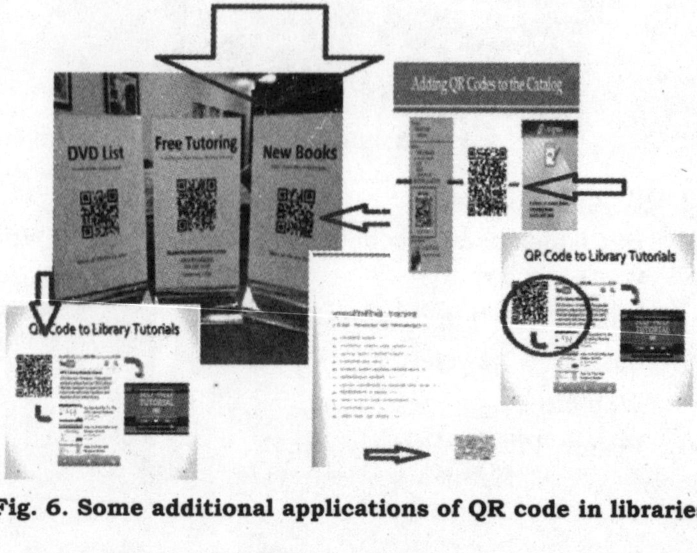

Fig. 6. Some additional applications of QR code in libraries

8. CONCLUSION

With the advent of new technology present day libraries have come far away from the traditional methods of accession, organization, preservation and dissemination of information. Mobile technology and QR code can help the patrons in a more innovative and convenient way. QR codes & mobile technology are effective use in library services. The library professionals have been playing very vital role in providing and prompt library services to maximum users. The Central Library of NITR has successfully implemented mobile applications and QR codes in providing library resources and services.

REFEERENCES

1 Blowers, H. (2009). *QR tags & concept leadership.* Retrieved on January 02, 2015 from http://www.librarybytes.com

2 Dheeraj S. N. (2014).Using mobile technologies in libraries and information centers.*Library Hi Tech News,* 31(5), 14 – 16. Retrieved from http://www.emeraldinsight.com/doi/pdfplus/10.1108/LHTN-05-2014-0034

3 Hampton, D., Peach, A. & Rawlins, B. (2011). Reaching mobile users with qrcodes. kentucky libraries. 75(2), 6-10. Retrieved from http://www.usc.edu/libraries/services/mobile

4 *Kate, K. & Frank, F. (2011). Using Mobile Technologies in the Academic Library. Retrieved from* http://www.infotoday.com/cilmag/jul11/Kosturski_Skornia.shtml

5 *Lakhina,* T. (2011). QR codes to be the digital trend of the future in India. Retrieved on January 02, 2015 fromhttp://www.indiasocial.in/qr-codes-to-be-the-digital-trend-of-the-future-in-india/

6 Mckiernan, G. (2009). JIS/MLA: An introduction to QR codes. Retrieved on Dec 26, 2014 from http://mobile-libraries.blogspot.com/2009/08/introduction-to-mobile-web.html

7 M-Libraries.(2012) Retrieved on January 02, 2015 from *http://Libsuccess.org/index.php?title=M-Libraries*

8 *Mobile apps for library e-resources* (n. d). Retrieved on

January 02,2015 library.concordia.ab.ca/files/2012/11/moble_apps.pdf

9 Mobile Apps for Library E-Resources library (2012). Retrieved from http://concordia.ab.ca/files/2012/11/moble_apps.pdf

10 mobiThink. (2013). Mobile subscribers Worldwide. Retrieved from http://mobithinking.com/mobile-marketing-tools/latest-mobile-stats/a#subscribers

11 Talmale, M. S. (2012). *Use of QR codes in library and information science (lisc) practices.* Retrieved on Dec 27, 2014 www.inflibnet.ac.in/caliber2013/ppt/a1_4.ppt

12 The Hindu. (2015). India to have 213 m mobile internet users. Retrieved from *http://www.thehindu.com/sci-tech/technology/gadgets/mobile-internet-users-to-reach-213-million-by-june-2015/article6785327.ece*>

13 Thomas, L. C. (2010). Service standards for the mobile/social library. *Journal of web librarianship*, 4, 449-451.

14 Thomas, L .C (2011). Libraries, Librarians and Mobile Services. Retrieved on January 02, 2015 https://www.asis.org/Bulletin/Oct-11/OctNov11_Thomas.pdf

Challenges & Issues Related to ERM

26

Knowledge and Access of ICT on Information Among the Students of Management Study Colleges in Chennai, Tamil Nadu, India

A. Saleem
SG. Librarian, Aalim Muhammed Salegh Group of Educational Institution, Chennai, TN

Shabana Tabusum. S. Z
Librarian, MEASI Institute of Management, Chennai 600 014, TN

M. Sadik Batcha
Prof. & Head , Dept. Library & Information Science, Periyar University, SALEM, Tamil Nadu

ABSTRACT

The term 'ICT knowledge' refers to the ability to use ICT tools and internet to access, manage, integrate, evaluate, create and communicate information in order to function in a knowledge society. Institutions of higher education are responsible for preparing well-informed. skilled and globally competent workforce. There is need to sensitize them to use web resources and web based services for research and academic purposes. Majority of them agree that information is easily available on internet, but. it needs to be evaluated before use. A model curriculum is proposed to impart digital literacy skills to the students of Master of Business Administration. They have adopted information and communication technologies (ICT) to impart digital literacy skills to their students. An understanding of the use of ICT by the students helps in framing curriculum for the digital literacy course. A study of the use of various ICT tools and web based services by 220 students, registered for II Year of Master of Business Administration course in six institutions of higher education in Chennai. Tamil Nadu State was undertaken during the year 2014. Questionnaire was used as the data collection tool.

Keywords : ICT knowledge, Digital literacy, Information literacy, ICT tools, Student community, Business administration

1. INTRODUCTION

This exploratory study examined attitudes and usage of ICT among PG Management students in Chennai, Tamil Nadu, India. Of the sample of 220 students, the majority indicated they had access to a computer, and had access and regularly used the Internet. In addition, more females than males had access to a computer off campus. In today's globalized economy, possessing knowledge and having the ability to use that knowledge is critical to personal and professional advancement of individuals. Likewise, having a well-informed, skilled and globally focused workforce is very essential for the success of any organization. In this situation, institutions of higher education have two central responsibilities, (i) preparing their students for the challenges and opportunities brought on by globalization, and (ii) to be the major supplier of the well trained intellectual capital (knowledge workers). Higher educational institutions in advanced countries have adopted information and communication technology as a means to impart upon the students the Information and communication technology (ICT) is defined as a 'diverse set of technological tools and resources used to create, store and disseminate information. In this context, an attempt is made to understand the status of ICT awareness among student community of Master of Business Administration course and propose a model curriculum to impart basic and cognitive digital literacy skills to them.

1.1. What is Information Communication Technology (ICT)

Information and communications technology (ICT) refers to all the technology used to handle telecommunications, broadcast media, intelligent building management systems, audiovisual processing and transmission systems, and network-based control and monitoring functions. Although ICT is often considered an extended synonym for information technology (IT), its scope is broader. ICT has more recently been used to describe the convergence of several technologies and the use of common transmission lines carrying very diverse data and communication types and formats. Techopedia explains Information and Communications Technology (ICT); Converging technologies that exemplify ICT include the merging of audiovisual, telephone and computer networks through a common cabling system. Internet service providers (ISP) commonly provide Internet, phone and television services to homes and businesses through a single optical cable. The elimination of the telephone networks has provided huge economic incentives to implement this convergence, which eliminates many of the costs associated with cabling, signal distribution, user installation, servicing and maintenance costs.

1.2. Digital Literacy/Knowledge

They are used in one to one Communication, Banking, Businesses, medical science, education, media, sports, weather prediction and in our daily lives activities like entertainment. Computers have provided an entirely new medium for literacy. Information and communication Technology have introduced a new society where people can share information freely, anywhere, at any time, across the World. Internet has become clear the skills required are not merely how to use computers or how to get information, but rather how to solve problems and how to create values with the help of other through information networks. Digital literacy/knowledge is the Combination of the two terms - Digital and Literacy. Digital Information is a symbolic representation of data, and literacy refers to the ability to ready for knowledge, write coherently, and think critically about the written world. Digital literacy researchers explore a wide variety of topics, digital technologies. Research also encompasses a variety of hardware platforms, such as computer hardware, cell phones and other mobile devices and software or applications, including web search or Internet applications more broadly. Literacy means the ability to read and write. The term "Information Literacy" is to refer to set of skills required to identify information sources, access information, evaluate it, and use it effectively, efficiently, and ethically.

Digital Information is becoming essential to almost every aspect of modern life which means that there is a need as never before, for learners and teachers who are information literate in a digital context. User community require digital information literacy, and a skill to use computers and the Internet for many aspects of academic and research which resulting them with digital information capability in a knowledge based society. So called digital literacy is nothing but the information literacy. Digital literacy/knowledge is the ability to locate, organize, understand, evaluate, and analyze information using digital technology. It involves a working knowledge of current high technology, and an understanding of how it can be used. Digitally literate people can communicate and work more efficiently, especially with those who possess the same knowledge and skills. Research around digital literacy is concerned with wider aspects associated with learning how to effectively find. use. summarize, evaluate, create, and communicate information while using digital technologies, not just being literate at using a computer.

1.3. Importance of Digital Literacy/Knowledge

The Information Communication Technology is an emerging field widely used by user community in academic institutions for improving their skills in their area of interest and to acquire information effectively. The aim of this study is to ascertain how digital resources are effectively utilized and the influence of internet in their academic efficiency. Digital Literacy is as important a right for children today as reading and writing skills were at the inception of the Education Act in 1850. Whereas writing and reading have been the cornerstones of literacy since modern education began, increasingly, digital technologies are superseding the manual process of writing, and reading is increasingly an activity carried out using digital facilities rather than paper resources.

At the current time it seems inevitable that the usage and reliance on digital technologies will continue to grow. While reading books and paper resources and manual writing remain fundamentally important, this current period in time may well represent a pivotal point in the march towards digital domination. Digital literacy/ knowledge is a key to teaching in order to provide the skills, knowledge and understanding for young people to enter the workplace, further education and higher education. Increasingly, digital literacy is becoming the primary form of information transfer and communication, taking over from letters, phone calls and even face to face interaction. Business transactions without face to face contact would have been rare twenty years ago. Digital literacy involves using emerging Technologies to communicate meaningfully across technology, language social, cultural and intellectual barriers.

A variety of devices, platforms and web standards need to be incorporated into the educational experience to ensure pupils are fully literate in digital technology. Digital literacy covers: (1) Understanding the impact of new technologies on society, (2) Understanding and being able to manage digital identities appropriately and (3) Being able to locate, organize, understand, evaluate, analyze and present digital information. Digital Literacy/ knowledge encompasses computer hardware, software, the internet, cell phone. PDAs and other digital devices. Digital literacy is so closely connected to the traditional association of literacy and democratic rights as well as to more specific notions of e-government.

2. REVIEW OF LITERATURE

In India, importance of information literacy programs in digital era has been discussed in these studies confirmed that they most frequently use e-journals, followed by electronic theses and dissertation and e-books. E-archives, ICT awareness and online databases are the least used e-resources. Search engine is the most frequently used Internet tool and e-mail is the most widely used web based service. Internet is mainly used to update their knowledge, to support their research and to prepare for teaching. E-books and online reference sources such as Wikipedia are extensively used by them. Internet use is more among teachers and students of science and commerce faculty compared to faculty of arts. Ninety percent of the students use e-mail and search engines extensively.

The National ICT Literacy Panel was formed by the National Forum on Information Literacy and the council conducted numerous studies on information and communication technology literacy skills. The ETS iSkills assessment arose from these studies. The ETS iSkills Assessment was studied and a recommended minimum score was determined in a study conducted by Tannenbaum and Katz in 2008. The tool evaluated knowledge of technology and critical thinking skills used in a technological manner. The iSkills assessment determines proficiency in the following areas:

1. **Define :** Formulate a research statement to facilitate the search for information.
2. **Access :** Find and retrieve information from a variety of sources.
3. **Evaluate :** Judge the usefulness and sufficiency of information for a specific purpose.
4. **Manage :** Organize information for later retrieval.
5. **Integrate :** Summarize or otherwise synthesize information from a variety of sources.

Use of e-resources and Internet by the students of business management course was studied. Results reveal that majority of the students have been using e-resources and internet two to four years prior to the conduct of these studies. They use internet at least once in a week and they spend at least one hour during each session. E-mail is the most frequently used web based service. E-books and e-journals are occasionally used to support their studies, while electronic theses and dissertation were never used. It is clear from the above review that all the studies have concentrated on the use of internet and e-resources, which is part of digital literacy. A study of the use of ICT tools, web based services and digital literacy among students of semester of Master of Business Administration (M.B.A.) course, enrolled during August 2012 in six institutions of higher education in Chennai, Tamil Nadu State, India was conducted and the result of the study is presented in this paper.

3. OBJECTIVES OF THE STUDY

The study was conducted with the following objectives:

- To access the amount and familiarity in the use of digital resources
- To find the purpose and utilization of digital resources

- To identity the difficulties encountered by the user while using digital resources
- To access how the internet influenced their academic efficiency
- To identify the specific problems militating against using digital resources by the students
- To identify ICT tools used by student community and purpose of using them;
- To know the digital competence of Arts and Science college Students.
- To identify the importance of digital literacy

4. METHODOLOGY

Many business schools in India are offering Master of Business Administration (M.B.A.) course, spread over four semesters (two years), and accredited by All India Council for Technical Education (AICTE) or University Grants Commission (UGC). New Delhi. The minimum qualification required for admission to M.B.A. course is a bachelor's degree in any discipline. The course is designed to introduce students to various areas of business such as accounting, finance, marketing, operations management etc. Chennai, Tamil Nadu is located in the south part of India and the city of Chennai, Tamil Nadu is the headquarter town of the district. The district is well known for its higher educational institutions, including Chennai, Tamil Nadu. There are five institutes of higher education offering M.B.A course.

5. DATA ANALYSIS

The total number of candidates admitted to the course in each institution and the number of students responded to the questionnaire is given in Table 1. Questionnaires were distributed to all the 250 students admitted to Semester M.B.A. course during the year 2014 and 220 students responded. The response rate is 88%.

Students of semester were selected for the study with the assumption that they have good exposure to essential information and communication technology tools web resources and services.

Table 1. Details of Questionnaires Distribute and collected from Respond

S. No.	*Name of the Institution*	*Distributed Question aires*	*Responded Questionn-aires*	*Not Responded*
1	Natesan Institute of Cooperative Management, Chennai	50(100%)	46 (92%)	04 (8%)
2	MEASI Institute of Management, Chennai	50(100%)	45 (90%)	05(10%)
3	Gojan School of Business And Technology, Chennai	50(100%)	42 (84%)	08(16%)
4	Indira Institute of Management and Research, Chennai	50 (100%)	44 (88%)	06 (12%)
5	Mohammed Sathak College - Management Studes, Chennai	50(100%)	43 (86%)	07(14%)
		250(100%)	220 (88%)	30(12%)

Table 2. Level ICT Tools using for research/Project works

Sl. No	*Technology*	*Highly used*	*Frequently used*	*Occasionally used*	*Rarely used*
1	Internet	142(64.55%)	78(35.45%)	-	-
2	E – Mail	55(25%)	75(34.09%)	65(29.54%)	25(11.36%)
3	Phone	165(75%)	30(13.63%)	-	25(11.36%)
4	Video conferencing	-	52(23.64%)	90(40.90%)	78(35.46%)
5	CD server	30(13.63%)	35(15.90%)	75(34.09%)	80(36.36%)
6	FAX	-	-	47(21.36%)	173(78.63%)
7	DVD	66(30%)	24(10.91%)	75(34.09%)	55(25%)
8	Mass media	110(50%)	63(28.64%)	47(21.36%)	-

In this Table 2, Level of ICT tools using for research and Project works using the MBA Students, the Majority of the Students Using ICT Tool of PHONE 75% is Highly Used, then next is INTERNET 64.55% of the Students Used. At the same time Very Rarely used ICT Tool is FAX.

Table 3. Level of satisfaction regarding the following ICT sources available in Institution

S. No	*Technology*	*Highly satisfied*	*Partially satisfied*	*Normally satisfied*	*Dissatisfied*
1	Internet	-	85(38.64%)	110(50%)	25(11.36%)
2	E – Mail	27(12.27%)	33(15%)	122(55.45%)	38(17.27%)
3	Phone	85(38.64%)	95(43.18%)	25(11.36%)	15(6.82%)
4	Video conferencing	-	74(33.64%)	66(30%)	80(36.36%)
5	CD server	-	52(23.64%)	80(36.36%)	88(40%)
6	FAX	23(10.45%)	32(14.55%)	55(25%)	110(50%)
7	DVD	-	56(25.45%)	122(55.45%)	42(19.09%)
8	Mass media	76(34.55%)	54(24.55%)	52(23.64%)	38(17.27%)

The Table 3, is level of satisfactory of the above MBA students ICT sources using in the Institution. Most of the Students Accessing the Information thorough E-mail and DVD facility is normally satisfied this is 55.45%, at the same time the Fax Facility 50% of the students is dissatisfied.

5.1. Web 2.0 Services

Over the last few years, Web 2.0 based services such as blogs, wikis, photo- and video sharing sites and online social networking sites have gained unprecedented popularity, especially, among younger generation. These networks are described as social, because they allow communication with friends and colleagues, and strengthen the ties between members of these networks on the web. It is observed that web 2.0 based services are used mainly for personal purpose and for networking with friends E-mail is the most widely used web-based service, which is in agreement with the earlier studies. Among social networking sites, Face book is widely used mainly for personal work and networking with friends, while Google+ is used for class work, study and for personal work. YouTube and Slide share are the preferred means for sharing audio and video data on Internet. It is clear that the students are conversant with the web 2.0 based services, but they are using these services mainly for personal use and for networking with friends. There is need to create awareness among them about the possibility of using these services for market research. Also, there is need to impart skills required for evaluating the information available on these websites for quality and authenticity before using it.

5.2. Opinions on merits and demerits of ICT tools

Opinion of the students was sought regarding the merits and demerits of ICT tools and Internet, Majority of the respondents agree for both the merits and demerits listed in the table. They agree that the information available online is current and faster access is possible, but, quality of information available is not evaluated and copyright violations are more in case of web resources.

Table 4. To Feel the services offered in above mentioned Institution Library

S. No.	*ICT Technology Services*	*Excellent*	*Good*	*Satisfactory*
1	Computer / Servers	34(15.45%)	38(17.27%)	148(67.27%)
2	Telecommunication & Its Facilities	-	93(42.27%)	127(57.73%)
3	Photocopying	17(7.73%)	58(26.36%)	145(65.91%)
4	Microfilm / Microfiche	15(6.82%)	43(19.55%)	162(73.64%)
5	Internet / Intranet	42(19.09%)	55(25%)	123(55.91%)
6	Online Database / E-archive / Journals	-	74(33.64%)	146(66.36%)
7	Digitization	27(12.27%)	43(19.55%)	150(68.18%)
8	Satellite / Modem	33(15%)	26(11.82%)	161(73.18)
9	Video Conferencing	51(23.18%)	47(21.36%)	122(55.45%)

The table 4, explained to us, what level MBA Students feel the ICT Services in the following institution Only Video Conferencing 23.18% is mentioned his Excellent, the next 42.27% is mentioned good for telecommunication, and Most of the students mention Satisfactory for Microfilm and Satellite/Modem is 73.64%.

5.3. Model curriculum for imparting digital literacy skills to student community

It is clear from the findings that majority of students are conversant with ICT tools, internet resources and web 2.0 based services such as e-mail. Face book, YouTube and Slide Share. In this regard, Littlejohn has observed that there is no correlation between the ability to use technologies in social settings and competence in using technologies for formal higher learning. To harness the use of above mentioned technologies in an academic setting among student community, a model curriculum is proposed. The curriculum progresses from introduction of basic ICT skills to imparting cognitive skills such as formulation of search strategy, and criteria for the evaluation of web resources.

- *Unit I* : Basic computer skills, operating system; Internet: tools such as www, FTP, search engines, TCP/IP, web browsers; Local library resources: OPAC/Web OPAC, Online databases (Bibliographic and full text); E-books, e- journals, electronic thesis and dissertation, Open access initiatives; web-based services: e-mail; social networking sites; RSS Feeds etc.
- *Unit 2* : Domain specific online information resources: Web-portals, Online databases available in Business and Management; Institutional Repositories; Digital Libraries; formulation of search strategy; criteria for the evaluation of online resources.

- *Unit 3* : Introduction to Web authoring tools – Definition; types; HTML, Microsoft FrontPage, Macromedia Dreamweaver; Web authoring software; E-commerce.
- *Unit 4* : Application of Digital competence to problem solving: current and retrospective online literature search; designing a web portal ; use of web 2.0 based services for market research; use of SPSS or other relevant software for tabulation and presentation of results of market research, Report writing, and citation style manuals

6. CONCLUSION

The present study includes the Professional students of different Management Studies colleges studying in Chennai. The data were collected from those students who actively use library and make use of information communication technology for collecting required library resources for their study as well as research purposes. The users who are using information communication technology with maximum extent are considered for the present study. The data collection period of study is the year of 2014. Information needs have high effect on education, communication, and student's future life. Any student who goes to college, see environment and culture different from her/his life and in this new environment, for doing assignment, research, studying, and scientific communication with others, applies to learn Information seeking behavior suitable methods and has to increase his/her Information Literacy level, otherwise not only student would not be successful, but also he/she would have problem in his/her academic life specially postgraduate education. While students are competent in using latest ICT tools, and web based services such as e-mail and Face book for personal use, their ability to use them for learning and market research is found to be minimal. Hence, there is need to train them in basic and cognitive digital literacy skills outlined in the model curriculum, so that they can use online information resources such as online databases, digital libraries, open access e-books, e-journals and electronic theses and dissertation, institutional repositories, and web portals more efficiently in their higher learning and research.

REFERENCES

1. Parvathamma, N. & Danappa, P. (2013). Digital literacy among student community in management institutes in Chennai, Tamil Nadu State, India. *Annals of Library and Information Studies,* 6 0, 159-166.
2. Coleridge, S. T. (2007). *The rime of the ancient Marinere. in words worth and Coleridge.* Lyrical Ballads 1798. London: The Echo Library.
3. Karisiddappa, C. R. (2008). Guest editorial. *DESISOC Journal of Library & Information Technology.* 28(2).
4. Gowda, V. & Shivalingaiah, D. (2009). Attitude of Research Scholars towards Usage of Electronic Information Resources: A Survey of University Libraries in Karnataka. *Annals of Library and Information Studies,* 56(3). 184-191..
5. Katherene Ray & Joan Ray (1998). Students Attitude towards Electronic Information Resources. *Information Research.* 4(2).
6. Mahesh, G. & Mittal, R. (2009). Digital content creation and copyright issues. *The Electronic Library.* 27(4), 676-683.
7. Sivasubramanian. G. & Sadik, Batcha M. (2012). Provision of infrastructure facility to access e-resources/ on Line resources to the faculty members of Pondicherry University and affiliated colleges a case study. *Asian Academic Research Journal of Social Science & Humanities,* 1(3), 200-12.
8. Sudha, S. T. & Hari Narayanan. N. S. (2009). Use of E-Resources in Academic Environment by College Students: A Study. In *International Conference on Knowledge Networking in ICT Era.* pp 598-605.
9. Thanuskodi, S. (2011). Use of Internet and electronic resources for medical science information: A case study. *Journal of Communication,* 1, 27-44.
10. Association of College and Research Libraries - *ALA Presidential Committee on Information Literacy:* Final report.

1989. Retrieved Oct. 11, 2009 from http://www.ala.org/ala/acrlpubs/whitepapers/presidental.htm.

11. Shabana T., & et.al (2014). Digital Literacy Awareness among arts and Science College Students in Thiruvallur District: A Study. In *National Conference International Journal of Managerial Studies and Research (IJMSR).* 2(4), pp 61 -67.

12. Sanjay J. Shenmare (n.d.). In *National Conference in LIS in collaborate with library and information science study circle,* Amravati.

13. American Library Association. (1989). *Final report of Presidential committee on intimation literacy.* Washington, DC.

14. Techopedia - *https://www, techopedia.com/definition/24152/information-and-communications-technologv-ict*

Abstracts

Library 3.0: Dynamic Web 3.0 Applications for Libraries

Mohd Tasvirul Islam
Librarian, Kendriya Vidhyalya Sangthan, New Delhi,
Jai Prakash Singh
Assistant Librarian,Dr. B.R.A. University, Agra (U.P.)
Dr. Krishna Kumar Kesharwani
Assistant Librarian, Dr. B.R.A. University, Agra (U.P.)

ABSTRACT

The paper explains the concept of web 3.0 since its evolution from web 1.0. The traditional version of web i.e. Web 1.0 started as a Read only medium; the next version Web 2.0 established itself as Read/Write medium. Now the currently evolving version of web, viz., Web 3.0 is said to be a technologically advanced medium which allows the users to Read/Write/Execute and also allows the machines to carry out some of the thinking so far expected only from the human beings. In a short time, Web 2.0 and now Web 3.0 have created new tools and technologies for facilitating web based education & learning. To begin with, this paper discusses some definitions of the Web 3.0, its evolution and characteristics. Next, we have discussed about the possible future Web 3.0 technologies, trends, tools and services that will assist in the areas of knowledge construction powered by the Semantic Web.

Keywords : Web 3.0, Semantic web, Library 3.0, Trends, Features

From Library User Education to Information Literacy

Jitendra Ahirwar
Librarian, Smt B M Ruia Mahila Mahavidyalaya,
Grant Road, Mumbai-400 007

ABSTRACT

This paper focuses on the position of the students after the information literacy sessions were conducted for them, this questionnaire was given to them post IL session for audit of information literacy of BMRMM students, The problem areas considered are explained further in this paper. The students visiting BMRMM Library were asked to answer this questionnaire online, a total of 73 students answered the questionnaire from all the classes, the results of which are presented below, and the benefits aimed & achieved.

Impact of Electronic Resource Management System in Academic Libraries

Krishna Kumar Kesharwani
Assistant Librarian, Central Library, Dr. Bhim Rao Ambedkar University, Agra (U.P.) 282 002

Pradeep Kumar Trivedi
Librarian Govt. P.G. College, Barghat, Seoni (M.P.)

Prabhat Singh Thakur
Librarian BTIRT Sagar (M.P.) 470 004

ABSTRACT

The growth of reliance on electronic resources in academic libraries has led to the recognition of electronic resource management as a new problem area and specialty within librarianship and to the development of a variety of electronic resource management systems and services that have been widely adopted by academic libraries. This paper looks at the origin of the ERMS (E-resource Management Systems) and the available ERMS in the library digital landscape.

Keywords : ERM, ERMS, Digital Libraries, Integrated Library Systems, Collection Management

Preservation, Conservation and Restoration of Library Material

Gurdev Singh
Librarian, Sri Guru Gobind Singh College of Commerce, University of Delhi, Pitampura Delhi-35, India

Monika Sharma
Research Scholar, NIMS University, Rajasthan

ABSTRACT

The present paper describes the methods, importance and need for conservation and preservation of library reading materials. The paper describes various methods of preservation and conservation of various types of documents in the library. It also describes the preventive measures to protect the library material from destruction and measures to safeguard the library material from further decay. The method of digitization is being used as a preservation technique in modern libraries. This paper discusses the techniques and process of digitization briefly.

Tools and Techniques of E-learning

P. Suresh Kumar
Librarian, Chaitanya Engineering College, Visakhaptnam

ABSTRACT

Discussed the concept, objectives and types of e-learning. The tools of e-learning, techniques of e-learning and advantages and disadvantages of e-learning are stated.

Keywords : e-learning, information and communication technology, teaching, tools, techniques.

Knowledge Management in the Academic Libraries

Mallikarjun Vaddenkeri
Librarian, PDA College of Engineering, Gulbarga, Karnataka

ABSTRACT

This paper highlights the significance as to what knowledge is and how it relates to or differs from the information. It further explains types of knowledge and role of librarians to manage explicit and tacit knowledge. Concludes that how important is Knowledge management for librarians to update their knowledge and skills in the changing arena.

Keywords : Knowledge Management, Library and Information Science (LIS), Explicit Knowledge and Tacit Knowledge

The Role of Licensing in Electronic Resource Management (ERM): An Overview

Suchismita Dash
National Institute of Science Education and Research (NISER), BBSR

ABSTRACTS

As libraries build ever larger collection of Electronic resources, finding ways to manage them efficiently become a major challenge. The number of electronic journals, e-books, citation databases and full-text aggregations held by most libraries has grown rapidly. Managing these electronic resources involves providing library users with convenient ways to find and access them and providing library patron the most reliable scholarly resources published in electronic media. Libraries need to implement an ERM system to manage the information flow better and to administer their electronic resources in a better way. The terms and conditions for using these resources are set out in electronic resource licensing agreement between publisher and libraries. Several issues relating to licensing agreement between the publisher and libraries are briefly discussed in this paper.

Keywords : Electronic Resource Management (ERM), Licensing, LOCKSS, COUNTER, SERU

Library Consortia : Need and Importance

Sambhaji G Patil
Librarian, MET's Institute of Engineering, Bhujbal Knowledge City, Adgaon, Nashik-3, Maharashtra

Sachin Jayawantrao Gadekar
Jr. Library Assistant, Dr. Babasaheb Ambedkar Marathwada University, Aurangabad

ABSTRACT

This research paper describes the concept of "E-Journal Consortia" highlighting the advantage and disadvantages. Consortium is increasing in the developing countries and in the future more and more consortia would emerge to serve their members. The Consortia should take a lead role in the development of a national strategy for information provision for research in higher education. The growth of information technology, proliferation of information, increased demand of users, financial constraints, inflammation in Indian currency etc, makes the library impossible to acquire all the information resources. It fulfils the needs of information seekers self-sufficiently. The use of E- Consortia in 21st century Libraries and Information Centre's in India is discussed.

Digital Marketing Services of Academic Library Challenges faced by Librarians: A Study

Prasanna Kumar H. E.
Research Scholar & Librarian Sri. JCBM College, Sringeri 577139

F. G. Patil
S G Librarian, STJ College Chikamagalore, Dist 577101

Karunakaran N.
Research Scholar & Librarian, Govt. First Grade College, Hunasur, Mysore

Prabhakar S.
Research Scholar & Librarian Subbaiah Medical College Shimoga

ABSTRACT

This paper deals with the marketing of library and information services in the digital era. It discusses about the marketing concept of today's library and information centres covering various topics such as management of libraries and commitment to customer's satisfaction. It also defines the marketing and its current approach to library and information services in the global era. The services should be the value added according to the current requirement of the users. It is concluded that the modern libraries are information markets and the library users are consumers of information. The objective of the marketing of library and information services should be the dissemination of the right information to the right customer at the right time.

Keywords : Marketing, Digital library services, Marketing strategies.

Open Access Journals and Scholarly Communications of Digital Contents in Indian Perspective

Subarna K. Das
Associate Professor, Dept. of Library and Information Science, Jadavpur University, Kolkata-700032
Narendra Bhattacharya
Research Scholar Department of Library and Information Science, Jadavpur University

ABSTRACT

Open Access aims at providing free, immediate and unrestricted availability to digital content without any hindrance. This paper examines the types, merits and demerits, benefits of open access journals and its importance to the system of scholarly communications. The present study mainly discusses the role of major open access journal providers in India and the future trends of publication.

Keywords : Open Access, Digital content, scholarly communications

Electronic Resource Services in Libraries: An overview

Basanta Kumar Das
IGNOU Regional Centre, Ranchi
R. K. Mahapatra
Principal & Head, Dept. Of Library and Inf. Science, SMIT, Berhampur.

ABSTRACT

Due to the information explosion, the information is growing rapidly. Information technology has brought unprecedented changes and transformation to academic library and information services. Conventional library information services such as OPAC, user's services, reference services, bibliographic services, current awareness services, document delivery, interlibrary loan, audio, video services and customer relations can be provided more efficiently and effectively using information technology through Electronic resources. The advent of Information Technology has made a clear and pervasive impact in almost every area of library services. Moreover, as the popularity of e-resources increases, the librarians and staff are also concerned about e-resources, their methods of accessing, evaluation, selection, organization etc. The present paper gives know-how about encouraging the use of e-resources in the academic context.

Keywords : Information Technology, OPAC, E-Resource, Electronic Library

Library Services through Mobile Technologies : Some Issues and Challenges

Shiba Bhue
Librarian, KendriyaVidyala INS Chilka, Odisha, India
Nabakumar Bhoi
Asst. Librarian, Rajiv Gandhi University of Knowledge Technologies-Nuzvid, AP, India

ABSTRACTS

The development of mobile technologies has generated a considerable amount to change in shifting the academic environment from traditional settings to mobile learning settings. Cellular phone access rates are much higher than broadband internet access via computers. Mobile technology has been more widely and quickly adopted than any other technology ever. New applications are being developed and introduced on a daily basis. This article will discuss a few of the new and exciting services libraries are offering on mobile devices.

Keywords : mobile technology, library services, Optimized website

Electronic Resources : Scope and Challenges in Academic Libraries

Archana Saxena
Research Scholar, Shri Venkateshwara University, Gajraula, Uttar Pradesh, India

T. N. Dubey
Research Supervisor, Shri Venkateshwara University, Gajraula, Uttar Pradesh, India

ABSTRACT

The chapter addresses the concept of electronic resources, scope, and challenges of electronic resource in academic libraries. It defines electronic resources as sources of information that are available and accessible electronically through the use of computers. Digital technology has fundamentally changed academic library collections. Forever gone is the era when an academic library's physical collection determined its repute. In the modern networked technological era the emphasis has shifted from ownership of physical resources to access the electronic resources that are globally accessible. Digital technology is busy transforming the nature of academic libraries. A variety of terms such as hybrid, digital and virtual library are used to refer to the academic library.

Keywords : Digital Resources, Electronic Resources, E-resources, Digital Information Resources

Collection Development and Services of Private Engineering College Libraries of Howrah District, West Bengal

Madhuparna Mukherjee
Former Student of MLISC in Digital Library
Jadavpur University, Kolkata-700032

Subarna Kumar Das
Associate Professor & Former HOD, Dept. of Library & Information Science Jadavpur University, Kolkata-700032

ABSTRACT

This study intended to carry out a survey of collection development and services of private engineering college libraries of Howrah district. The present study demonstrates and elaborates the various aspects of use of collections and services, purpose to visit the library; adequacy of library hours, infrastructure facilities, use and collection of documents that is, internet information resources. The paper also identifies the levels of use of various services provided, access of online databases services, database search techniques, and users' awareness about different types of library network. Highlights satisfaction with overall functions of the library. Suggestions have been given to make the collections and services more beneficial for the academic community of the mentioned engineering college libraries.

Keywords : Collection development, information resources, users' awareness, engineering college libraries.

Changing Role of Librarians In Digital Environments and Digital Libraries

Chandrakant, Chavan
Librarian, Deputy Manager Kalyani Center for Technology & Innovation Bharat Forge Ltd Pune

Vishwas, Hase
Asst. Librarian, Kalyani Centre for Technology & Innovation Bharat Forge Ltd Pune

ABSTRACT

In Digital Environment of digital information, e-technology, W3 growing popularity, Rom Products, and digital libraries offer a huge range of Information. It is well accepted that libraries all over the world are undertaking revolution, particularly owing to the development in information and communication technologies. Conventional libraries are moving towards digital libraries and the 21st century libraries are being set up progressively of the digital kind. As a result, there is general interest and subsequently, a lot of R&D activities being carried out in this area world over. In India a number of organizations are also in the process of setting up digital libraries and many researchers and experts are conducting study on digital libraries. Mittal (2008) describes that India published nearby many High scholarly periodicals in the field of LIS. Articles on digital libraries in India have been published in National and International papers.

Keyword : Digital Library; Electronic Library; Virtual Library; Library Portal; DL

Electronic Resource Management Systems for Libraries

C. Krishnamurthy
Associate Professor, Department of Library & Information Science, Karnatak University, Dharwad-580003

Manjunath Angadi
Research Scholar, Department of Library & Information Science, Karnatak University, Dharwad-580003

ABSTRACT

Electronic information resources are becoming evitable for the academic communities and are considered as inseparable part of libraries. In the present context where the electronic resources are increasingly getting popular and constitute a major portion of library holdings, institutions require tools to properly manage their electronic collections. Management of e-resources is a difficult task, due to their digital nature and ever changing attributes. This paper highlights on Electronic Resources Management (ERM) systems in administering the issues and activities related with electronic resources.

Keywords : ICT, Electronic Resource Management, E-Resource Management System,

Best Practices with NAAC in University College of Science Library of Tumkur University, Karnataka: An Overview

Rajalaxmi A. Govanakoppa
Assistant Librarian, University College of Science,
Tumkur University, Tumkur, Karnataka.

Kumara B.
Assistant Librarian, University Library,
Tumkur University, Tumkur, Karnataka.

ABSTRACT

Best Practice may be innovative and be a philosophy, policy, strategy, program, process or practice that solves a problem or create new opportunities and positively impact on organizations. Institutional excellence is the aggregate of the best practices followed in different areas of institutional activities. The Library and Information Center of University College of Science was established along with the College and the library has adopted an open access approach to promote the use of information resources. In this paper as per NAAC guidelines best practices of the library of University College of Science, Tumkur are discussed.

Keywords : NAAC, Best practice, University, Libraries.

E-Resources in Special Libraries of South Assam: Awareness and User's Satisfaction

Sudip Bhattacharjee
Guest Faculty, DLISc, Assam University,
Silchar- 788011, Assam

ABSTRACT

The value of libraries for the individual and for society has long been seen as self-evident. However, in times when users are becoming increasingly independent in their information seeking, when information seems to be free on the web. The electronic resources available in a library play prominent role in facilitating access to the required information to the user are an expediency manner. Further one need not go to the library to make use of print formats as the electronic resources can be made use of by any user through online access. The familiarity and use of electronic resources in special libraries for rapid development is very important and necessary. In view of this, here it is tried to highlight the present position of the special libraries as well as the thinking and satisfaction of the different categories of users. On the basis of the findings after the data analysis, the paper provides some suggestion for the implement of the present scenario of e-journal services at those libraries.

Keywords : E-Resource, Special Library, E-journals, User service, South Assam.

Best Practices in Central Library, Central University of Karnataka, Kalaburagi : A Study

P. S. Kattimani
Deputy Librarian, Central University of Karnataka, Kalaburagi, Karnataka

Suman Muddapur
Librarian, SRFGCC, Belgaum, Karnataka

ABSTRACT

The library and information services of higher education institutions play vital role in enhancing the quality of academic and research environment. The several factors are forcing academic libraries to change. Some of the highlighted practices here are well accepted practices experimented in different environments in optimizing the use of library and information services. The paper covers the use of technology in designing and delivering the information products and services. Institutional repository content management, open source and internal requirement customizing as per the user requirements with remote access is one of the globally adopted best practices in large libraries. The paper includes reference services, text services, book bank services, SDI, CAS, reprographic service, professional training, UGC-Infonet, Touch screen facility and database search service etc. There are such bodies like NAAC, UGC, NBA etc, in India. The best practices mean, the services provided by the library is standard one. One can trust the services rendered by the library.

Keywords : Education, Best practices, professional training, information and services .

Usage of Electronic Information Resources in Institute of Science Poona's Institute of Business Management & Research, Pune, Maharashtra

Santosh V.Dagade

Librarian, Institute of Business Management & Research Survey No. 130.Pune- BangloreExpress Highway Wakad, Pune-411057

ABSTRACT

I.B.M.R Wakad, Pune is the one of the well-known institute in Pune since 1984 This paper is investigates the electronic information use pattern and trend of accessing electronic resources by the students and faculty,. Academic libraries must understand the information needs. This study analyze the kinds of academic information needed by students and faculty, which information resources they require, methods for locating information and level of satisfaction of library collection, services and facilities. The descriptive survey method was used and data was gathered via questionnaires from 180 respondents. The paper provides information for understanding use of electronic resources in institute.

E-Resource Management in Central Library of NIT Rourkela: A Case Study

Dibya Kishor Pradhan
Asst. Librarian, Biju Patnaik Central Library, National Institute of Technology Rourkel

Bhojaraju Gunjal
Dy. Librarian & Head, Biju Patnaik Central Library National Institute of Technology Rourkela

ABSTRACT

Electronic Resources are important components of the collection building process of the library. E-resources refer to those materials those are accessed through computer or mobile device which are accessed either remotely or locally. Some of the frequently used e-resources in the libraries are e-journals, e-books, e-database such as full text, citation & abstracting, reference, images, audio-video materials, etc. This study reflects the practice and management of e-resources in the central Library of National Institute of Technology Rourkela (NITR). The Library is committed to preserve its e-resources to ensure permanent access to its collections along with other formats. The example of e-resources include, but not limited to website, online database, e-journals, e-books, whether free or fee-based required to support research and academic activities of NITR fraternity. The present study streamline the tool & techniques used by central Library NITR to manage all its e-resources.

Keywords : Electronic Resources Management, e-journals, e-books, e-database, tools and techniques

Mobile Technology: A Vital Information Dissemination Tools in Academic Libraries

Srikanta Sahu
Technical Assistant, National Institute of Technology, Rourkela, Odisha

Premananda Bhoi
Librarian, Kendriya Vidyalaya Sangathan, Belgaum, Karnataka.

Ghazala Firdous
Technical Assistant, NSHM Knowledge Campus, Kolkata

ABSTRACT

With the advancement of the information age and development of technology, library has always tried to use various ICT tools to improve its services. Though libraries are perceived to be the sanctum sanctorum of man's quest for Information, where humanity has traditionally journeyed to quench their thirst for knowledge, today's information society seems to beliving in a world where the library is engulfed in their own mobile phones right intheir very own pockets. This paper looks at the overall impact of mobile services, their application in libraries and looks at the specific area of reference services in the libraries where the potential, demand and opportunities are more for mobile applications.

Index

AUTHOR INDEX

SUBJECT INDEX